# BLACK
## SATURDAY

# BLACK
## SATURDAY

**Stories of love, loss and courage
from the Victorian bushfires**

Edited by John McGourty

HarperCollins*Publishers*

**HarperCollins***Publishers*

First published in Australia in 2009
by HarperCollins*Publishers* Australia Pty Limited
ABN 36 009 913 517
www.harpercollins.com.au

Compilation and arrangement copyright © News Limited 2009

**HarperCollins***Publishers*
25 Ryde Road, Pymble, Sydney, NSW 2073, Australia
31 View Road, Glenfield, Auckland 0627, New Zealand
1–A, Hamilton House, Connaught Place, New Delhi – 110 001, India
77–85 Fulham Palace Road, London W6 8JB, United Kingdom
2 Bloor Street East, 20th floor, Toronto, Ontario M4W 1A8, Canada
10 East 53rd Street, New York NY 10022, USA

ISBN 978 0 7322 9010 8

FRONT COVER: Design by Vinnie Taylor. Photo by Alex Coppel, *Sunday Herald Sun*: smoke
from Black Saturday fires turns day into night as CFA volunteers race towards a new firefront at
Labertouche

INSIDE COVER: Photo by Mark Smith, *Herald Sun*: trees like burnt-out matchsticks show
the fury of Black Saturday's fires

BACK COVER: Design by Natalie Winter. Photo by Trevor Pinder, *Herald Sun*: belladonna lilies
spring out of the ash and blackened earth in the days after Black Saturday at Steels Creek

Internal design and typesetting by News Limited
Printed and bound in Australia by Griffin Press
70gsm Bulky Book Ivory used by HarperCollins*Publishers* is a natural, recyclable product
made from wood grown in sustainable forests. The manufacturing processes conform to the
environmental regulations in the country of origin, New Zealand.

9 8 7 6 5 4 3 2 1    09 10

# Helping The Salvation Army
# to help others

"My wife and I were among the first to arrive at Whittlesea on the night of Saturday, February 7. We were involved in the Ash Wednesday fires years ago but it was impossible to prepare for what was to unfold that evening. There were people badly burnt, others searching for lost loved ones, families who had lost everything. We were able to provide support and promise financial aid, but the most important thing we had to offer was a listening ear and a supportive shoulder to lean on."

**Major Rodney Barnard**
**Divisional Commander, Melbourne Central Division**

The Salvation Army is a worldwide Christian movement. In Australia we are known as one of the nation's largest welfare providers. We are dedicated to helping Australians in crisis. Raised up by God our mission is to transform lives, care for people, make disciples and reform society.

Each year The Salvation Army assists more than one million people, our core areas of work include assisting families facing crisis, family and domestic violence, homelessness and addiction services.

The Salvation Army has been providing support to Victorians affected by the bushfires since they began on Black Saturday, February 7 2009. The Salvos were on the ground providing aid to communities that suffered great loss, as well as supporting the emergency service teams battling the fires that raged for weeks. During the critical response phase of operations, The Salvation Army served more then 40,000 meals, provided immediate financial assistance to more than 10,000 people and provided personal and emotional support to thousands involved in the Victorian bushfires.

The Salvation Army is committed to supporting devastated communities as they rebuild. Long after the debris is cleared and visitors return to the towns that were evacuated, The Salvation Army will be there. The Salvation Army is dedicated to assisting local communities in a way that is best suited to the needs of that specific community.

Your support of The Salvation Army's Victorian Bushfire Appeal means that together we can ensure that the communities affected by the worst bushfires in Australian history are supported for the weeks, months and years to come. Thank you for contributing to The Salvation Army's Victorian Bushfire Appeal.

**Heavy toll: A man reacts to news from his father and a friend**   Picture: Norm Oorloff

# contents

# Preface

**John Hartigan**

No event in recent history has overwhelmed us with such unprecedented scale or unimaginable devastation as the Victorian bushfires of 2009. No natural disaster or act of terrorism has affected us as profoundly as a nation. This book is a lasting tribute to the victims of Victoria's bushfires, to the people who lost their lives and their grieving families and friends.

It recognises the incredible bravery of our firefighters and other emergency services workers and the generosity of so many volunteers.

It won't bring anyone back. Nor can it convey the full, relentless, inconceivable brutality of the fires. Instead, it is a humble testimonial to the courage and compassion, the spirit and the tenacity of ordinary Australians who lost control of their lives during the extraordinary events of February 7 and the days before and after Black Saturday.

It acknowledges the many stories of sacrifice and generosity. Those who have given so much to help their fellow Australians survive, cope with the immediate aftermath and start, however tentatively, to rebuild their lives.

The words and images on the following pages are a record of what has been endured. They include first-person accounts of loss and survival contributed by our readers. They are heartbreakingly poignant. In these stories we find testimonials to our fundamental humanity and determination to confront and triumph.

Most of the contributions are the work of our reporters and photographers. Many risked their personal safety to bring our readers first-hand accounts and frightening pictures from the firefronts. Others kept working even though they or people they loved had suffered tremendous loss.

Journalism is about more than reporting the news. It acknowledges those who are suffering, unites people in their grief and allows the victims to understand they are not alone.

Journalism is also a public service and there is no better example in our nation's history of the media's capacity to mobilise community action to help those most in need.

The people who work for our company live in the communities they serve. Like so many others in Victoria, our colleagues lost family members and friends. People we know well lost their homes and livelihoods.

News Limited, HarperCollins Publishers, and the retailers who are selling this book, are donating the proceeds to The Salvation Army Victorian Bushfire Appeal. In some small measure this will add to the staggering amount that has already poured into relief funds.

It is therefore appropriate that this book reminds us not only of what we have lost but what we should celebrate; the spirit and generosity of ordinary Australians in the hour of our country's greatest need.

**John Hartigan**
Chairman and Chief Executive, News Limited

**Trauma: Kevin Rudd comforts Black Saturday firefighters**       Picture: Craig Borrow

# Foreword

**Hon. Kevin Rudd MP**

The firestorm that swept through Victorian forests, fields and towns on February 7, 2009 caused unspeakable sadness and loss for thousands of Australians. The scale of the destruction was catastrophic. More than 200 people lost their lives. More than 800 presented to hospital with injuries, some with horrific burns. More than 1800 homes were destroyed and more than 500,000ha were burnt. More than 15,000 people registered as affected by the fires at relief centres and other official areas.

Many people lost family, friends, neighbours, homes and everything they owned. For many, the 2009 fires will be forever in their memory and generations to come will long hear the stories of that day – the raging fires, the fear, the narrow escapes, the heroism of the firefighters and the stories of the family and friends who were lost. This book will help us to remember. It tells stories of the communities that were forever changed by Black Saturday, when the fire took on a fury that even the most experienced firefighters had never seen before.

Dorothea Mackellar wrote of our land's beauty and its terror but on Saturday, February 7, it was all terror. In its power, its speed, its capricious shifts in course and its want of mercy, fire revealed its full catastrophic force.

The scene in the fire towns in the days that followed barely even resembled planet earth – the scorched ground, the smouldering embers and the burnt-out shells of cars, houses and buildings.

In the days I spent on the ground in and near the fire towns – in places such as Yea, Whittlesea and Alexandra – I saw more tragedy and trauma than anyone would want to see in a lifetime. But I also saw and heard a matter-of-fact determination among survivors to get on with the job, to stitch their towns and lives back together.

Amid these terrible scenes we witnessed extraordinary bravery and resilience from our firefighters, volunteers and emergency service workers. We saw an army of courage called the CFA. As the fires stormed towards towns the CFA fireys raced to warn residents of the danger, plucking many from its path. As the fires burned, they fought around the clock to save lives, homes and communities. And as the fires finally retreated, they kept working as the hard-going, heart-breaking work of recovery began.

In the days that followed, we learnt of their remarkable acts of heroism, courage and self-sacrifice as they risked their lives to save people they had never met. Many had experienced tragic losses of their own but they battled on in service to others.

Those events introduced us to a band of true Australian heroes who, in a typically Australian way, seemed surprised by all the fuss. Barry Mapley was just one of them. A CFA captain who saved the lives of a man and woman who were fleeing the Mudgegonga fire near Beechworth, with the woman's hair alight. When people started calling him a hero for putting his own life on the line, he responded: "I'm not a bloody hero. It's just the Aussie way."

Another was Peter Thorneycroft, a 43-year-old paver and tiler who spent an hour on the roof of the Kinglake National Park Hotel, dousing hot ash and wetting vents and drains while the fire roared around the pub, threatening the lives of the 20 women and children sheltering inside. "There's no one who's heroic," Mr Thorneycroft said later. "Everyone's forgotten about their own lives, they just did what they did."

In these days of great sorrow that have followed the fires we have drawn inspiration from the unbreakable spirit of the firefighters and volunteers. The catastrophic loss of life and property would have been far, far greater without their extraordinary efforts.

More than 1000 firefighters came from other states. More than 120 firefighters and other emergency workers came from the United States, New Zealand, Canada and Indonesia. Expressions of sorrow and offers of assistance flooded in from around the world.

Nor should we forget the tireless work of the Australian Defence Force personnel, the Australian Federal Police, the Red Cross, the Salvos, the churches and hundreds of volunteers who worked on the relief and recovery operation.

The response of the wider community, too, has been remarkable. When we see the storehouses of donated goods being loaded on to trucks and we hear of the millions of dollars donated from communities across Australia and others across the world, we should remember this is not something that just happens spontaneously. It happens because hundreds of thousands of ordinary Australians in their homes and offices, in their factories and on their farms, have stopped and said to themselves: "How can I help? What can I do?"

Less than a week after it had been established, the Victorian Bushfire Appeal Fund, set up by the Victorian Premier in partnership with the Commonwealth Government and the Red Cross, had raised $130 million. It is, for so many people, just a natural impulse – if my neighbour is in distress, I must help.

So they dig deep. They volunteer, they pray, they organise their community to raise funds. They reach out and they make a difference.

It is the cumulative effect of these efforts that is so extraordinary. The grandmother selling her chutney at the street stall, the secretary taking up a collection in her office, the primary school students organising a walk-a-thon and the youth group doing a car wash at the local service station.

There was the Campbelltown garbage collector in Sydney's west who, moved to tears by television footage of the fires, organised to donate goods to families in Victoria with the help of local storage and transport firms whose drivers were prepared to make as many trips to Victoria as it took.

In the ACT, farmers sent 150 tonnes of fodder to bushfire-hit farmers in Victoria. They remembered the kindness of those same Victorians when their own paddocks were ablaze during the 2003 Canberra fires. There was the Brisbane football club that donated sporting equipment to those who needed it.

Others have simply left the office and taken time away from family and work to offer their services – doctors, lawyers, wildlife carers, counsellors, carpenters, drivers, and so the list goes on.

The staff of government agencies such as Centrelink and emergency authorities also worked together around the clock to bring relief and begin recovery and reconstruction. There was immediate co-operation and co-ordination between Commonwealth and state agencies on a level seen all too rarely.

The Australian Government, together with the Victorian Government, has made clear its commitment to stand by these communities. Within days of the fires we had agreed to establish the Victorian Bushfire Reconstruction Authority, with the funding and authority to cut through normal bureaucratic processes and start rebuilding the shattered communities right away.

We will study with great care the findings of the royal commission when they come. As Victorian Premier John Brumby has said, everything is on the table. We must prevent a tragedy of this kind from ever happening again.

The road to recovery will not be easy, or fast. We must rebuild infrastructure, like power lines, phone towers and water supply. Homes must be built, farms must be made viable again, small businesses must be able to open their doors once more. It will take months and years to rebuild lives and communities. At times it will be frustrating. But we will be there for the long haul. Brick by brick, school by school, community by community, we will rebuild.

And thanks to books such as this one, we will remember.

**Hon. Kevin Rudd MP**
Prime Minister of Australia

**All that's left: Pat and Lindi Leddin stand amid the ruins**    Picture: Ian Currie

# Chapter 1

# Kilmore East & Wandong

Paul Kent met survivors of the flames as they shared tales of courage and heroism. Here, for the first time, Paul tells the full story of that day — how a small bushfire turned into Black Saturday

- **Origin**
  At 11.48am the Country Fire Authority logs a fire at Kilmore East. By 1pm the blaze sweeps through Wandong, growing in size and speed
- **Destruction**
  Fire burns through more than 1000ha before changing direction and heading southeast
- **Toll**
  Six firefighters lose their homes in Wandong. In total, 41 houses are destroyed in the small township

The fires went through two days ago now, which makes this a Monday. By now we are familiar with what has happened. The fires started on Saturday and most of us, if we have caught the news at all, go to bed believing it to be no different than many other bushfires emergencies. Even when the late news comes through that there have been 14 deaths it seems simply another Australian tragedy. But that was our mistake. We are familiar, but we do not know.

Sunday comes and we get updates. Kinglake is virtually gone and little is left of Strathewen and St Andrews. And nobody has even been able to get into other towns such as Marysville and Flowerdale to determine what happened there. As the day continues the enormity begins to emerge. More details are emerging and every one seems to be worse than the one before.

The bushfires begin leading every news bulletin. More, they begin taking up the whole bulletin. Newspapers are clearing out their first 15 pages, their first 20, to cover the story.

By Monday, much of Australia's focus is on Whittlesea, the designated relief centre. Emergency crews are filling the Whittlesea Showground, which is filling up with tankers, other emergency vehicles, firetrucks. Every few hours a crew rolls out while another rolls in, its men black and exhausted.

Survivors are at the Whittlesea Community Centre, many ignoring the food and drink and comforts offered, to continue searching for family, friends, neighbours. All around, mothers and teenage children are crying or softly weeping to themselves, but what you notice is the men.

Nobody has ever seen so many grown men crying. Some literally shake. Others cannot stop their noses running. Others get halfway through a sentence and dissolve into tears, gather themselves and start again.

And among all these people stands a man in a grey T-shirt. He is not crying, just sort of standing there with his hands in his pockets and his head down. His eyes keep flicking around but fail to make contact with anyone, as if they might see the truth. While he is surrounded by friends, he is all alone.

His name is Ross Buchanan. His 15-year-old boy Mackenzie and nine-year-old daughter Neeve are already confirmed dead. The men gathering closely around him are protecting him. A man in the bright orange overalls of the Country Fire Authority grabs him roughly around the neck, pulling him in.

"You right, mate?" Ross buries his head in his mate's neck and he stays there for seconds that become long minutes. He wraps his arms around him.

Around this, other survivors seem to know what is happening. They keep their own suffering down, as if almost in respect. At one point, Ross is asked if he will say a few words to the media. Nobody is much comfortable, but Ross nods. He looks at the ground a long, long time when he tries to speak. Too brave to cry, he is too much a father not to.

"No," he says, shaking his head. "My wife said try and stay away from this. I don't want to upset her."

Often, the kind of devastation that is seen here comes in strife-torn places, in cities of conflict. As such, the people are, in their own way, prepared for what might be worst case. But these people, they are totally unprepared for what happens.

Some sit down to watch Gregory Peck on TV, some are babysitting, others want nothing but a cold beer. The measure of their shock is the depth of their grief. It will take days before they even begin to get themselves together and some will never be the same again.

Days later the figures will soon start coming out: the fire takes out 1823 houses and buildings. Town halls and community centres. Golf clubs, farmhouses, hay sheds, machinery sheds, police stations, primary schools, factories and dairies. Even beehives, as this fire shows no prejudice.

On top of that: more than 320,000ha burn out, much of it pasture. Gone is 4500km of fencing. Stock dead or missing run to 6668. Gone are cows, horses, pigs, crops and orchards and hundreds of small businesses. But all the time it is not about the houses. It is not about the golf clubs or hay sheds or factories or dairies.

It is about the people. Always the people. This is their story.

**Scorched: Rosaleen Dove contemplates her ruined garden**

# Old men do not normally shed tears in public. Yet after the fires, grown men could be found, head in hands, wandering the streets

John Ferguson of the *Herald Sun* was one of the first journalists to walk through the charred remnants of the towns destroyed by Black Saturday's fire.

They were the fires that made the old men cry. The worst of them ignited in dead dry Kelly country just 60km north of Melbourne.

Sadly weather-beaten, Kilmore East's creeks and valleys are torn and twisted by years of drought and erosion. Its balding hills are, nonetheless, steeped in history. Ned Kelly's clan were frequent visitors to the district and those who live along Saunders Rd cling to the eastern edge of the Great Dividing Range like babies to their mothers.

It was in these hills above, below and all around the Saunders Rd community that the Kinglake disaster began. The fires blackened thousands of hectares and razed several houses in the immediate area but most importantly left a haunting legacy further down the road.

Noel Baker, a farmer who was among the first firefighters on the scene, summed it up in three words: "A total disaster." Noel fought bravely when fire broke out in the late morning on a ridge near his house, helping organise the rescue of 15 children from humanitarian Moira Kelly's refuge for the sick and injured.

Fuelled by a galloping northerly and century heat, the Kilmore East fire had a life of its own, spotting frenetically. It moved so quickly that at one point it literally jumped Noel's truck before spearing southeast in the early afternoon towards the names of towns we now know so well. Wandong, Kinglake, Strathewen, St Andrews, Flowerdale. There they died in their scores.

How to live in the knowledge that the worst of Black Saturday began across the valley? Liz Jackson is doing just that. When the gully winds intensified, she had cause for concern. With the temperature already rising into the high 30s – and soon to hit the high 40s – Liz had a near-perfect view of the action. She ran to the phone and dialled for help. It was 11.20am and no one could have imagined the hell that was about to be unleashed.

"Liz is devastated," a friend said later, battling survivor guilt. It's an emotion felt by hundreds of people who had only bit parts in the fiery horror show. Soon after Liz's call, the flaming penny dropped throughout the district. Farmer after farmer, tree-changer after tree-changer was stunned when smoke billowed into the air.

The exact cause of the fire is not known and may not be known for years, if ever. Legal action has, however, been launched against the Victorian Government and a private electricity company.

A pleasant, nervous woman in late middle-age, Liz is uncomfortable with her status as the woman who saw the smoke and flames first. When people speak of disasters or try to piece together how the fire marched from Kilmore East to Kinglake and beyond, they are hungry for facts. Yet the fires were almost beyond our conventional understanding of the truth. For every victim had their story, every firefighter their answer. Every blaze its own path.

Such were the conditions – record heat, roaring winds and a big fuel load – it has been rare to get the same story repeated with the same facts. Fire has that effect.

The key to a calm life, it could be said, is the perception of control. The Black Saturday fires could not – absolutely could not – have been controlled. Which is why the fires were so physically and emotionally devastating. These fires were, for me, the natural disaster that made old men cry. Old men do not normally shed tears or sob in public. Yet after the fires struck, grown men could be found in a wide band from Kilmore to Marysville, head in hands, wandering the streets and their yards in disbelief.

At nearby Wandong, Prime Minister Kevin Rudd was brought to the brink of tears at a prayer service for the victims. His emotions were genuine but the tears I am talking about are borne of the sorrow of losing everything.

We flew into Marysville early on Sunday morning, among the first to see the devastation. It was unbelievable. Marysville was a flattened, devastated mess. Part fire, part cyclone.

The helicopter landed on the local golf course, where a logging truck was still smouldering. A convoy of dazed locals could be seen heading out to Alexandra. Giant native trees were ripped from the ground, roots and all. Parrots, their feathers barely ruffled, had expired on the 18th green.

We hitched a ride with locals heading back to town to assess the damage. On arrival, Marysville was a ghost town and Daryl Hull was trying to make sense of it all. Like Liz Jackson, he was middle-aged. All his life he had had a family connection with that town. He had lost his house; his past gutted by fire. Daryl wept as he told how, just hours before, he had jumped into a small lake near the football oval to save his skin. The fire, he said, seemed to single him out, flames burning all around him. "It was pandemonium," he said. "I thought, 'Jesus, this is it'."

Further up the road, an elderly man went from house to house turning off dripping taps. Why? All around were flattened houses, gas bottles flaring in the morning chaos. The skeletons of homes still ablaze. No one was bothering to put them out. "Where are they?"

the old man grumbled. He, too, was in tears, wanting to know why the water authority wasn't around to do their job. Precious water was being wasted, he said. Too traumatised, the old man couldn't see that it was game over.

Not far away and by the side of the road, a body lay in a clump under a blanket. It was too gruesome to consider looking. A local farmer emerged roughly 10 minutes later, peered pragmatically under the blanket to confirm that, yes, this was what we feared. How could it be that a body could be left lying on the road for the world to see?

It was the same story across the ranges in Flowerdale, where a friend – probably at the same time as we were wandering, stunned, through Marysville – saw multiple bodies on the roadside. This, too, was many hours after the fire had swept through. This was not meant to happen in Australia, a country that paddles in a sea of perfectionism. The dead are always to be respected. And yet these discarded bodies point to the extent of the chaos that unfolded on Saturday afternoon and into the evening.

The flames were out when we walked down Coombs Rd, Kinglake West, on the Monday after the fires. It was a smouldering wreck. House after house gone. Many were dead, including former Channel 9 great Brian Naylor and his wife Moiree. As we walked the length of Coombs Rd, yet another ageing chap pulled up in his battered 4WD. He was shaking violently. You'd better get to a doctor, I told him, and with that, this poor mental wreck roared off down that blackened road to hell.

Further along, a charming man called Joe Ropar could be seen feeding hay to his sheep and cattle. Joe knew Brian well. "I loved him," he said. A retiree who estimated he lost 20 friends, Joe had built a new house with multi-million dollar views that gave him an eyewitness account of the fire roaring towards him. By the time the

Kilmore express hit Kinglake West, it was unstoppable. Joe, aged in his 60s, cried as well, overwhelmed by what he had seen.

Further down the road was the Naylor house and all the anger and the suspicion that comes with grief. A friend of the Naylors lashed out when he saw the former newsreader's ruined home being photographed. Brian, he said, didn't like this sort of thing. The venom was understandable. But if ever there was somebody who would understand, it would be the man who was for so long the face of TV news in Victoria. Brian was fire ready, as the authorities say. It didn't matter. Nothing was going stop that fire.

A few kilometres away is Pine Ridge Rd. The name may or may not ring a bell. In just 510m of dirt track, 31 houses were razed. Bang, bang, bang, bang, bang. One after the other. At least 10 died, including five children, in the first 220m of the road. Oh for the benefit of hindsight.

Tina Wilson returned to her home at No.7 Pine Ridge Rd and perished next door, along with her children Crystal, 15, Nathan, 13, and Teagan, 6. Tina's partner, Sam Gents, could be seen from a distance on February 12 returning to the house to see what had happened. Imagine his horror. Little left. His house had exploded. The neighbour's home, which was meant to save his family, was a little better off with a brick wall at the front masking the devastation behind. Crime scene tape suggested the four died before they even got inside No.9.

The police chaplain, Reverend Peter Owen, has seen a lot in his life but he describes Pine Ridge and the fires around it as the worst of the worst. Everywhere they went, the firefighters, most of whom were volunteers, had a horrid task.

So did the victim identification teams, who spent days and weeks sifting through the ashes of Black Saturday. In many cases the fires burnt so hot there was nothing left. It sounds like a tautology but some fires are hotter than others. This fire literally blew houses apart. It melted metal and glass. Many houses looked like a bomb had been detonated.

Evidence of the mayhem was everywhere. Further down Pine Ridge Rd a pair of jeans lay discarded in the front yard of a flattened house as if ripped off in a roaring hurry. That house also had a long piece of blue and white police tape outside it. The short piece of tape meant that police had checked the site and there were no bodies. The long piece of tape suggested a crime scene. This looked like bad news for those who lived in the house with the denim jeans.

The Sunday morning after the firestorm produced all the evidence of the physical damage. The full extent of the psychological damage will never be known. On a grand scale, those who, self-evidently, deserve most sympathy are the families of the dead, the injured and those who lost property.

What about those tasked with retrieving the bodies, the police who shepherded the grieving and the emergency workers forced to tread through the haunting ashes? Superstition is unnecessary. But some areas razed by the fires felt utterly weird. Marysville for one, Pine Ridge Rd another. Flowerdale, definitely.

There were two ways to witness the fires. On the ground, the devastation unavoidable. The sweet-smelling smoke, the blackened timber, the gutted houses and cars.

The view from the air added another perspective. On the morning after the fires, our helicopter was circling low over Kinglake in miserable conditions, trying to spot another two helicopters operating in the same, smoke-filled air space. They were nervous times for everyone.

What was clear from the air was the utterly arbitrary nature of the flames. Many houses gone down a street, one left standing. Then many houses standing, one razed down another street. Sheds spared, houses torched. Houses spared, sheds torched. One car melted, another unmarked. Victims dead in cars, victims dead in streets. Elsewhere, survivors walking their dogs like any other Sunday morning. Marysville utterly flattened, except for a small number of houses still standing. Whittlesea still standing. Forty-two houses flattened in Flowerdale in one patch. Against the odds, five still standing.

What you couldn't see from the air or even on foot was the threat from beneath the surface. One elderly Flowerdale local had heard of a house that survived on Black Saturday only to burn a few days later. A burning tree root, he said, had acted like a long fuse under the house. If it wasn't so serious it could have been a scene from the Road Runner. Eventually, he said, the house went up. Surely enough to make an old man cry.

# I thought I'd lost her. I didn't know if she was alive or dead

## Norm and Annie Beaman, Mt Disappointment

Norm Beaman has seen plenty of fires but none affected him as much as his experience on Black Saturday when, for 25 agonising minutes, he thought his wife, Annie, had become one of the first victims of the blaze. Norm's last telephone contact with Annie ended with her screaming that their sheds were on fire.

"She [Annie] told me she was going to jump in the dam with a fire blanket over her. That's where I thought she'd be, but instead she drove through smoke and flames on both sides of the road to a neighbour's property about a kilometre away. She helped them as they battled to save their house but lost, then they took refuge in a partially blackened paddock, which had been burnt just minutes before, and covered themselves with a fire blanket and doonas.

"There were five of them, including one who's been a CFA volunteer, huddling together while the flames roared all around them. They thought they were probably goners, but that was the best they could do – and it worked. Annie said the wind was blowing in three directions at once and the fire was moving incredibly fast.

"I've never felt so useless not being able to get up there and help her. The police were just doing their job, and they have to protect people from themselves, but Annie was taking risks I had to take and I couldn't get there.

"I thought I'd lost her. For 25 minutes I didn't know if she was alive or dead. I was stopped several times at roadblocks, but eventually I ran into a local copper, Peter Gough, who said he'd go and find her and drove through burning bush to the farm.

"I didn't know him then, but I've found out since that Annie taught his kids at Wandong school. He's a CFA volunteer and had fireproof gloves in the police car and used them to clear burning timber off the road to get through. He got to our place and was looking for her in the dam when she appeared and asked him what he was doing. I've never been more relieved in my life than when I finally made contact with her and she said she was OK.

"We were incredibly lucky. A sand tennis court that acted as a sort of fire break is probably what saved our place, along with Annie's efforts in wetting the house and garden down before she had to go.

"We'll be staying. It is God's country the bulk of the time, but we'll be installing bigger and better fire protection systems and next time we won't be so dependent on power to get water under pressure."

**As told to Geoff Wilkinson, *Herald Sun***

# I was frightened I would catch fire

## Steve and Carmen Spiteri, Wandong

Steve and Carmen lived with their children Shayla, 11, Tyler, 10, and Michael, 7, in a modest fibro and weatherboard home in bushland off Mountain Rd. They had just about finished an extension to their house. That Saturday they stored their most precious possessions in the shed. At lunchtime, Steve noticed smoke through a window.

"Funny, we couldn't get insurance on the extension, but she's still standing," Carmen said. "We bought this block five years ago. It used to be a nudist camp, and such a pretty place in the bush. We bought it off the nudists because we thought this was just the right place to bring up the kids. I was petrified, never been so scared. And I was wearing a dress, not even jeans. I was so frightened I would catch on fire, too."

**As told to John Hamilton,** *Herald Sun*

# It travelled like a bullet in the bush

## Ian Marstaeller, Wandong

Ian is a volunteer member of the Wandong CFA. So is his wife Sue, who is also a Mitchell Shire councillor.

"She started about 15km away to the north. That's where the fire started, to the north. But then the wind suddenly changed and drove it east and it came through here so fast … for 15km it travelled like a bullet through the bush."

**As told to John Hamilton,** *Herald Sun*

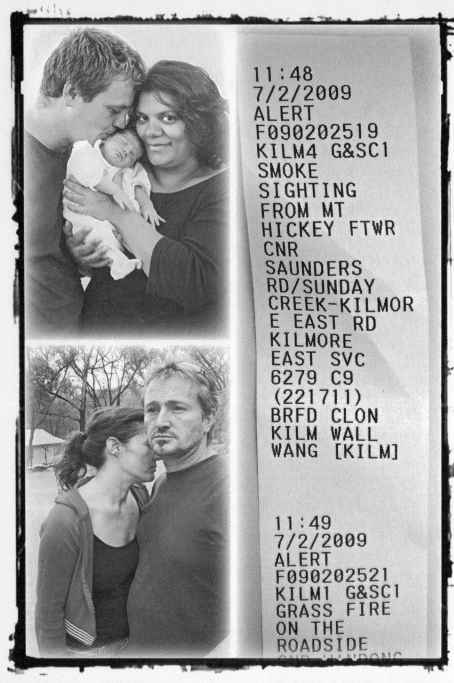

11:48
7/2/2009
ALERT
F090202519
KILM4 G&SC1
SMOKE
SIGHTING
FROM MT
HICKEY FTWR
CNR
SAUNDERS
RD/SUNDAY
CREEK-KILMOR
E EAST RD
KILMORE
EAST SVC
6279 C9
(221711)
BRFD CLON
KILM WALL
WANG [KILM]

11:49
7/2/2009
ALERT
F090202521
KILM1 G&SC1
GRASS FIRE
ON THE
ROADSIDE

**Hope and loss: (clockwise from top) Jillian Buckland, with husband Travis, gave birth to Gypsy just hours after their home was destroyed; the first fire alert, timed at 11.48am, which was sent to Kilmore fire station; and Carmen and Steve Spiteri return to the ruins** Pictures: Aaron Francis and David Caird

# At Kilmore CFA there is a small piece of paper which carries the first alert of the nation's most devastating natural disaster.

In the days following Black Saturday, Piers Akerman spoke with the firefighters from Kilmore CFA. It was at this station that the volunteers got the first call of a small bushfire burning out of control. Hours later that fire would become part of a 100km front that would devastate the countryside.

At 11.48am on February 7, 2009, seconds after a phone call was made to the emergency triple-0 number, pagers issued to Country Fire Authority members began beeping and a printer lit up in the command office of the Kilmore CFA station.

The print-out recorded the report of a fire between Saunders Rd and Sunday Creek Rd and the identical message flashed on the pager screens. That message was the first official notification that the fire storm of Victoria's Black Saturday had began.

At Kilmore the message was read by David Williams, a first lieutenant in the CFA, Russell Court, a second lieutenant, and firemen Graham Robinson and Anthony Archer. Normally, one of these men would have walked through the command office and torn off the print-out, too, as print-outs are easier to read than messages on pager LCD screens. But on that Saturday morning no one needed to take the hard copy as each of them was familiar with the geography of the area and knew they were just minutes from the area where the fire was reported to be.

A minute or so after leaving the Kilmore CFA station house, they could see the smoke rising to the east. Graham, a 74-year-old former electrician, former policeman and former undertaker, and 45-year veteran of the CFA, said: "As soon as I saw the smoke, I thought it looked like it had been burning for about 20 minutes."

David, in the Kilmore CFA's ute, a twin-cabbed Toyota used as the command vehicle, radioed directions to Anthony, who was in the No.1 tanker driving Russell, and Graham, who was driving John Scicluna in the station's No.2 tanker, which has the legend "Graham's Wheelchair" on the driver's door.

His urgent message to the tanker crews was blunt and direct: "For Christ's sake stop it crossing Saunders Rd." Anthony went to the point of origin and Robinson sped to flank it but the blistering 60km/h northwesterly wind had already driven the fire across Saunders Rd and was speeding it across the lightly grassed, moderately hilly country as the noon temperature climbed to a furnace-like 47C.

Graham, who was at Woodend on Mt Macedon, in the middle of the 1983 Ash Wednesday fires, and had sat with three others in the cab of a tanker while the fire front roared over them, said he had never experienced conditions like those on Black Saturday. The fire sped from the point of origin, over the open-grassed area and into a gully where it split into two fronts.

The CFA crews trying to outflank it had no chance as it leapt into a plantation of five-year-old, oil-saturated blue gum saplings which exploded into a towering cloud of black smoke which Graham said "looked like sump oil burning".

Backing on to the blue gum plantation was a fairly mature pine plantation. Anthony estimated that the flames soared 300m to 400m into the air as the pines blazed below.

The men from the three vehicles could do little as the fire swallowed hectares of forest in minutes, gaining in intensity, pushing out greater heat and expanding its front. "It was predicted and we were as prepared as anyone could possibly be," said Graham.

"Crews had been allocated in advance and we were out the door and down the road in a minute and a half after the report from the spotting tower but the conditions were such that within five minutes it looked as if it had been going half an hour."

Anthony said the nine days of intense temperatures between 35C and 43C before the blaze had effectively pre-heated the bush, adding: "The smell of oil coming from the eucalypts was like gas." Fire area maps drawn up by the Victorian Department of Sustainability and Environment show the fire zone fanning out from that first fire at Kilmore, over to Flowerdale and down to Wandong, where the first victim of Black Saturday was claimed.

The broad band moves down before the wind to Glenburn in the north and Christmas Hills in the south. Kinglake was caught in the middle. A second fire which began near Kilmore East and the former Murrindindi Mill then linked in, pushing further to the southeast and wiping out Marysville as it ran down towards the Upper Yarra Valley.

David said that despite all the warnings there were still people who had no understanding of the ferocity of the bushfires. "There was a week's warning," he said. "The forecast was worse than for Ash Wednesday. Many of those who stayed didn't have a fire strategy. Many of those who were caught as they tried to leave left their decision to go too late."

As the crews returned to the station on Black Saturday and subsequent days, they found hot meals prepared at the local pub and served by 50 or 60 members of the community who had prepared their own roster to provide some back-up to the exhausted firefighters before they were rested and returned to the front.

The spotless station house and its team is a source of pride for the town and the people of the region. It is now, tragically, also part of Victoria's history.

The messages which heralded Black Saturday have been erased from the flashing pagers but on file at the Kilmore CFA is a small torn-off piece of paper, no larger than a supermarket receipt, which carries the first alert of the nation's most devastating natural disaster. The time it was received – 11.48am – will be forever remembered by those who were there.

# They gave me the fighting spirit

## Rosaleen Dove, 65, Wandong

Rosaleen had lived in Wandong, with husband Brian, for 28 years. A relative, Aden Ryan, had just arrived from Ireland to spend a holiday with them. Instead, he found himself alongside the Doves as they fought for seven hours to save their house and neighbours' properties. When the wind changed they nearly lost the fight altogether as fire roared up a hill to within 10m of the back veranda.

"This is the 50th anniversary of my arriving in Australia from Ireland. My parents always told me to face things head-on and never give up. They gave me the fighting spirit. The nicest thing was hearing my three grandchildren on the phone today, hearing them say, 'Are you all right Grandma. Are you all right?'

"And I said 'Yes' – and I knew then that we had won and that we were alive."

**As told to John Hamilton, *Herald Sun***

# The house was starting to burn and I couldn't do a damn thing

## Pat Leddin, 62, Wandong

Pat spent 25 years helping save lives and houses as a CFA and SES volunteer. Nothing changed on Black Saturday. But one home was simply beyond saving – his own. Pat and his wife, Lindi, 56, live on Ryans Rise Rd, 14km into the mountainous forests above Wandong. The home they had spent almost three decades building was reduced to scrap in just minutes. To the amazement of their neighbour, Terry Swaniick, the Leddins immediately went to the aid of other neighbours after being forced to abandon their own property.

"We've had fires in the area before. I joined the CFA and SES after Ash Wednesday. Initially we tried to fight the fire, but there is a point when you just have to pull out. I was wearing a full fire outfit and I could tell by the heat on my back that it wasn't safe. The house was starting to burn and I realised I couldn't do a damn thing. It was the force of the wind – it was well over 100kmh – that was the killer.

"We could have had a strike team up here of five trucks and we would have lost five trucks and 15 men. They would not have had a chance. [The conditions] were simply exceptional. Lindi and I had been building our house for 28 years. I actually came very close to finally finishing it the week before the fires. We made the mud bricks from the earth on our property, and we want to make them part of our next home. We want to rebuild here, but I won't be spending 28 years building the next one, I can tell you. The support we've had from the community since the fires has just been phenomenal."

**As told to Evonne Barry, *Sunday Herald Sun***

# I was surviving and getting my family out

## Jillian and Gypsy Buckland, Upper Plenty

Just hours before Jillian delivered her fourth child, Gypsy, her home was engulfed by flames. As Jillian drove out of her driveway, followed by husband Travis, flames began licking at their property. By the time they reached Whittlesea the whole mountain was on fire. Suddenly homeless, but elated to have escaped with their lives and to have welcomed a new child, the couple marked the moment by naming their daughter Gypsy. Ironically, Jillian and Travis had considered naming their unborn daughter Blaze.

Jillian knew she was starting labour but ignored the pains. "I just stopped it. I was too busy doing other things. I was surviving and getting my family out." As she drove away, Jillian knew some of her neighbours had not managed to escape. Not one property now stands on her side of the street.

"It was a very emotional birth. In the last 25 minutes, I just thought, 'Oh my god, we have no home to take her to'. And, after it was all over it hit me: the realisation we'd gotten out alive, and knowing we were seconds from potential death.

"Blaze was a bit too ironic really, so I said to Travis: 'She's going to start her life off as a gypsy. Let's call her that', and then we just looked at each other and laughed. It was perfect. We had to acknowledge and roll with everything that had happened."

**As told to Lauren Wilson, *The Daily Telegraph***

# Often it's a smell or a sound that they can't get out of their head

## Lisa Goldrick, on-call nurse, Bushfire Health and Counselling Service

"The calls are changing a little bit now. At the start a lot of the callers were confused and not coping. A lot of them wanted reassurance. They wanted to know whether they were normal. I kept telling them that in an extraordinary circumstance like this one, there is a big window of normal.

"Now we are getting a lot of … people who might be related or know victims, and we are also getting calls from staff involved on the front line, the ambos and fireys. They call sometimes because they don't want to unburden in the workplace, but in private they want someone to talk to. Often it's a smell or a sound that they can't get out of their head, like the sound of the bushfire.

"Early on there's usually confusion but, later, sometimes they're fed up and angry. Really, the deep-seated stuff doesn't come out until much later, but each call is separate, different. We had a mum who didn't know whether she was coping – her 18-year-old son had been caught in the fires and was burnt down his entire left side and she couldn't stand him in pain … so we are dealing with people once or twice removed, [what we call] the ripple effect."

**As told to Ross Brundett, *Herald Sun***

**No chance: Joe Ropar was stunned by the speed of the fire**   Picture: Gary Richardson

# Chapter 2

# Strathewen & Kinglake West

- **Origin**
  Strong northerly winds push a fire towards the small
  community of Strathewen, population about 200, at 4.20pm

- **Destruction**
  Fire reduces Kinglake West to ash. By 5pm every house
  along the 510m Pine Ridge Rd is razed – a total of 31 properties

- **Toll**
  In Strathewen, 42 people are killed. On Pine Ridge Rd,
  Kinglake West, 21 residents are claimed by the fire

Keith Chasemore is thinking about his fire plan. It is three in the afternoon, February 7, 2009, and the Black Saturday fires are burning through Kilmore and Wandong. If the news reports are correct they will sweep along the ranges, right past his two-storey home. The big beautiful home he has in Pine Ridge Rd, Kinglake West, with the chimney he hates. If the news reports are correct Keith will be safe. If they are correct.

Still, Victorian Premier John Brumby and Country Fire Authority boss Russell Rees warn residents across the state to have their fire plan ready. Keith, 66, is looking at the sky and thinking about his fire plan. His partner Sigrid Roewer asks: "What's our fire plan?" "Evacuate," Keith says. Simple as that.

He sees his neighbours to the left, Paul and Karen Roland. They look like they are staying. Across the road it looks like little Jack's family might stay, too. Kevin and Jackie Hainsworth are his mum and dad. Jack is about five and that's him often holding the hose while Keith washes his truck, the one with the questions that never stop.

The sky is filled with smoke and the light is going and Keith is wondering when might be the right time to evacuate, when the power in his house goes off. Without power, there is no water.

"Let's go," he says to Sigrid. They drive no more than a kilometre to Pheasant Creek convenience store. Already half a dozen people are there. Across the road from the store is a large paddock of strawberries and tilled soil. "If worse comes to worst," Keith tells Sigrid, "we can go and lay in the strawberry patch".

They are hopelessly behind. For much of Victoria, worse has already come to worst. Keith does not know it yet, but his time is about to come. The fire, by now, is already raging through Strathewen. Hundreds are in panic, 42 will die.

The great problem is that in Strathewen's tiny township, a perfect little valley town of just 200 people, there is only one way out. Already cars are colliding with each other. And if not that, trees are coming down and the cars are crashing into them. Those trying to escape the fires realise they are trapped.

CFA captain Dave McGahy, a local farmer, fights the fire with his team of three firetrucks and a tanker. Dave and his men are fighting a front behind town, on Eagles Nest Rd, when Dave picks up his eyes and looks yonder. A great, rolling ball of flame is approaching the town from the northeast. Dave immediately decides to withdraw.

"Even if I had 20 strike teams," he says, "all that would have happened is that we would have had 50 dead firefighters as well."

It is the start of what is a recurring theme of the Black Saturday fires: when the power of the fire is realised, it is too often all too late.

Still, the battle has to be won. Faye and Malcolm Park are huddling under a wet blanket, their home having just exploded. Steve, Alison and Jessica Pascoe have climbed into their above-ground pool. It collapses under the heat.

Joe Shepherd is running towards the fire, armed with nothing but a hessian sack and a hero's courage. His son Danny has driven in from Ocean Grove, more than two hours away, to help fight the fire. How do you record what is happening at this time? It is chaos, cruel and dark and terrifying.

Peter Avola and his wife Mary take their cars to the town oval. Peter finds the gates locked so runs into a paddock. He tells his wife to drive on to a neighbour's house. When the fires eventually pass, she will arrange his funeral. Life and death.

Down the road is Jack Powell, 94. He has lived in Strathewen all his life. His father was the first settler in the area, back in the 1800s, and right now he has burns to his arms and no running water to wet bandages that would soothe his injuries.

It doesn't matter anyway as the bridge at the end of his road is damaged by fire. Nobody can reach him. Many try to flee and many, like Jack, seem beyond help.

When their home explodes Faye and Malcolm Park run until they find a patch of gravel dirt. Their blanket soaked in water, they lay down and pull the blanket over them to keep hell outside. For two hours they lay under that blanket. "It didn't go," Faye says. "It stayed and stayed."

All around them, though, beauty is being destroyed. The Pascoes lay in the mud heap created by the collapse of their pool, and it is enough. The luck, quite clearly, is random.

Behind the school is a fire refuge, a safe haven for the children to escape to should fire ever come while they are in class. Thank heavens this is a Saturday. The fire refuge is alight and will soon be destroyed. The school, built in 1917, is also going quickly. It is one of just two buildings the whole town cares about. The other is the community hall and right now it is not looking so flash either. Opposite the community hall is a sign written in chalk: "Join us for a family day at Strathewen Hall. Craft, Devonshire tea and cakes, children's activities, spinning wheel, BBQ, light music and more."

The family day is to raise money for Marilyn Langmead, something of a matriarch in town. She is fighting cancer and is currently in hospital. Underneath the sign, almost unnoticed, is another sign. A Country Fire Authority sign, warning "fire danger period". Right now, though, Marilyn's twin sister Rosemary is running across the earth and diving into Craig Young's dam. There, the Langmeads and the McKimmies are huddling in the water.

There come other stories of survival. Jack, all 94 years of him, is not alone, but being saved by his great nephew, Steve. As the fire takes over Jack's house and his windows explode they run for it. In the confusion, they have no idea where to go.

"We didn't know which way to run and the road was all alight," Jack says later. Steve grabs his coat and on a patch of burnt earth he climbs over the top of his great uncle, shielding him from the fire.

Two neighbours drive past in their car and they get in. The car does not travel far, stopped by fallen trees. All in all, it has hardly improved the situation. It forces them to spend the night in the car, fires burning on both sides. Knowing the car can't move anywhere because of the fallen trees. Yet Jack manages to survive.

"If it wasn't for him," Jack says of his great-nephew Steve, "I wouldn't be saved."

The fire overwhelms, and the fire kills. Joe Shepherd, last seen running into the fire with a doused hessian bag, is later found collapsed and on fire at the side of the road. He is saved, though, and will live. In the back of their car, his son Danny is found dead. In his early 30s, Danny has been married only three months. There is no reasonable explanation for any of what happens.

How can there be, when one man so easily dies and another survives. It is a question that will be asked over and over again in the weeks and months to come. Nobody will ever be closer to an answer.

Why, for example, do 19 residents find their way into the house of Barrie Tully, another CFA member, and get to walk out after it is over, to see the township flattened? There is no explanation.

As Steve Hayley, who did the electrics when the residents built the community hall, says: "Everyone was getting prepared to fight this fire not knowing that it wasn't a fire but a fireball."

Like the rest of us, Keith Chasemore has no idea any of this is going on. As the people of Strathewen battle to save their lives, the firefront leaving no more than seven houses standing, Keith is convinced the fire is going to come straight through Kinglake West.

The experts are wrong. He can feel it.

Kinglake West sits on the crest of a ridge above Strathewen. The wind is starting to pick up. The forecast southerly is beginning to blow and that, with the steep rise up the range, will see the firefront double in speed.

But Keith, sitting outside the Pheasant Creek convenience store, knows none of this at the time. All he knows is that everything he owns is at home and the fire is coming. So about 5pm he leaves the store. He heads back to Pine Ridge Rd. He is going to get his truck and trailer.

When he arrives home the fire is coming through the pine trees behind his land, the Macedonian temple on fire.

The fire is at his back fence. Next door, where the Rolands live, both cars are still in the driveway. It worries Keith. He does not know the fate of his neighbours. "They were private people," he says, but the Rolands, dad Paul and mum Karen, daughters Caitlin, 15, and Nicola, 12, are fatally miscalculating. Just the day before, Karen says they are evacuating. That is their plan. Yet as the fire comes up the range one of the girls is on the phone to a family member when Karen grabs the phone: "It's too late," she says. "We're trapped." The Rolands' smiling faces, a family snapshot, is one of the first images of the fires we all see. Faces to the tragedy.

It does not look like Jack's family is leaving either. The thought of this will come back to him in a few days, finally making real the horror of what is happening.

Keith climbs behind his Mack and steers it around the corner to where his trailer is parked, reversing to hitch it up. What he sees in the rear vision mirror terrifies him.

"A wall of red," he says. The fire, which isn't there when he turns into the street, is moving that quickly. A truckie all his life, he knows that if the trailer's hydraulics fail or its brakes lock he will be hitched to the world's largest anchor. Escape will be impossible.

He shifts the Mack into first gear and the engine growls, a puff of smoke shoots from the exhaust and he leaves the trailer behind.

By now, many people have begun gathering at the Kinglake West fire station. Some 50 men, women and children have just been led to the fire station from nearby Pheasant Creek. They are taking protection inside the local supermarket when local policeman Roger Wood peeks inside. The fire is coming and they have chosen their best place to hide.

Roger leaves to check the road ahead then returns to tell them to follow him. He takes them to the Kinglake West CFA. These people, remember, are the people Keith finds there when he returns to the station after leaving his trailer behind.

They get to the fire station just before the fire rolls over. Inside, they are safe now and they survive. They do not know it at the time but, shortly after, the supermarket they were cowering in burns to the ground. Keith drives the truck straight up and parks next to the Kinglake West fire station, joining the others.

Nowhere to be seen is another Kinglake West resident, former Channel 9 newsreader Brian Naylor. Brian not only led the news broadcasts of the Ash Wednesday fires in 1983, he survived them, living in this very same home. It appears as if he believes he can survive this fire. As the fire rips along Coombs Rd, Brian, 78, and his wife Moiree climb into their bathtub. When they are eventually found they are still in the bath, fused together in an embrace. All around there is tragedy. The fire reduces Pine Ridge Rd to ash. Not a house stands and 21 people in the street are dead.

Including the Roland family. Days later, Paul's mum Dianne reveals the ache of a mother. "I just keep ringing Paul's mobile so I can hear his voice on the message machine," she says.

Kinglake West is burning, the fire station one of the few places where people survive. Keith and Sigrid make it off the mountain and for a good while Keith deals with his distress through jokes and wisecracks. For an old truckie, that is his way. Until he gets to thinking one morning about Jack, the little boy with all the questions when he used to hold the hose.

The poor little boy is only five years old and with no word of the family Keith weeps for him. "A terrible morning," he says.

Then, it's funny how things happen, later that morning a call comes from a journalist. He happens to be tracking what happens in Pine Ridge Rd. No, Keith is told, Jack is alive. He made it.

Well, for a moment, at least, the world is a beautiful place. For a moment there is hope.

**Paul Kent**

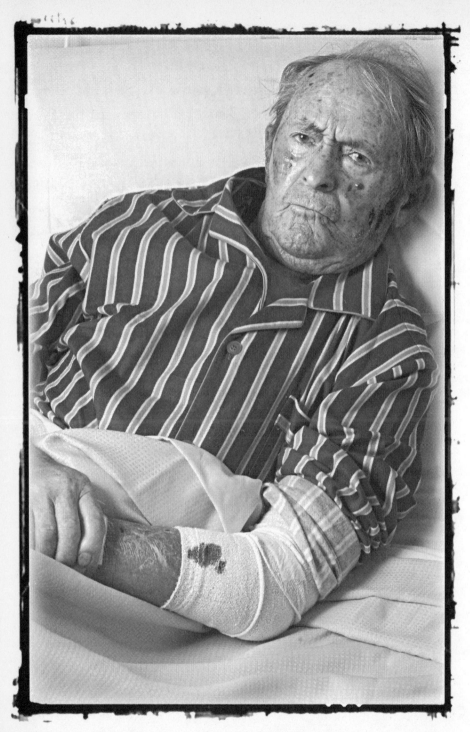

**Recovery: Jack Powell was saved by his great-nephew Steve** Picture: Chris Scott

# Embers blasted against the walls like machine gun fire

## Warwick Tozer, Strathewen

Leaving his home in Brighton, Warwick drove to Strathewen to help his son Cam defend his bushland home. They were prepared for the worst but the flames that roared up the valley towards them were bigger than they had imagined.

"It is impossible to describe what was coming. Like a monster, an apocalypse in the form of a huge black mass filling the whole southern horizon and with an enormous nucleus of black orange. This was the source of the noise which kept increasing until it was a thundering scream. We ran for the house, Cam went underneath to start the pump, I waited halfway to the front door urging him to hurry. Thank God the pump started first pull, the sprinklers were on and we ran for the door with about 30 seconds to spare.

"We had planned to shelter from any radiant heat in the bathroom which had windows to the west, south and east. Within 30 seconds the sky was as black as the darkest night and a huge curtain of fire came from nowhere, suddenly appearing the full length along the western ridge. It was a solid wall of iridescent yellow flames probably 10m high. After about 30 seconds the flames crowned and began to recede. I shouted to Cam that this looked good as the fire appeared to be slowing and I thought [it] might burn more slowly downhill towards us. It was spotting in the snow grass but looked almost manageable. I had forgotten the monster to the south!

"Through the forest came flames, about twice the height of the 10m trees, at enormous speed, the brightest neon orange against the blackest of black. We moved into the centre of the house and looked out and up through the mezzanine windows at a firestorm beyond my capacity to describe or comprehend.

"The window glass began to splinter with loud cracking sounds, but held. The fire roared over us from the south then up out of the valley from the east then back down from the north. It created a fire tornado which hurtled around the house in all directions. The embers being blasted against the corrugated walls sounded like machine gun fire. Showers of tiny sparks were forcing their way under the eaves and floating down inside but fortunately were too small to ignite. The house filled with smoke. The inferno continued for about 30 minutes, all we could do was watch in awe of this amazing spectacle and hope the sprinklers would not fail.

"We had heavy woollen clothes wetted down, woollen beanies, heavy boots and proper breathing masks. After about 30 minutes we attempted to go outside but the heat was massive. The flames had finished in the tree tops and were now incinerating everything on the ground. It was a further 15 minutes before the life-saving sprinklers allowed us out into what was now a forest of glowing tree trunks, the bark of every tree was radiating heat with bright red embers from top to bottom.

"Everything else was black. In choking smoke we worked our way around the house. Cam found a substantial fire in the highest gable. With the fire hose, an extension ladder and exceptional teamwork we somehow got it out but then found many small outbreaks around and under the house. Up the hill his car was on fire for a long time, burning black acrid smoke and finally the petrol tank exploded with a thump. Later we found that the engine block had melted and run down the hill in a silver river.

"My eyes felt like they were full of sand and I had difficulty seeing.

Although the wind had dropped, the background noise of the fire was still amazing. Trees were falling constantly. We worked solidly for about an hour dealing with spot fires, including one inside the house that Cam found downstairs. We had saved the house and the house had saved our lives.

"Before the fire, the bush was green and you could see maybe 100m to 200m through the trees. Now you could see for miles. In many areas all that was left on the ground was pale grey ash, not a leaf, not a stick, not a log, nothing. Everything had been vaporised. The trees were stripped of all their leaves and many of their branches. Thousands of them stood like blackened toothpicks as far as the eye could see."

**Via email**

# Peter was my hero to the end

## Mary Avola, 67, Strathewen

She built a life in Strathewen but it was taken away in one terrible night. Mary survived 40m-high flames, but her husband, Peter, didn't. The community she once called home lost 42 residents and was the hardest hit area on Black Saturday. A loved mother of two and grandmother of four, she is now a widow.

"It was like World War III, I have never seen anything like it. The fireball came down the mountain on three fronts. The fire front was everywhere; our house was burnt to the ground. There's a couple of tree plantations in our area so it went up like a tinderbox. Some of the flames were twice the size of the trees – at least 40m high.

"When the house went up we ran to our cars, which were parked at the front of our property, ready for us to escape. Peter told me to drive the Ford Fairlane while he jumped in the Falcon. I think he knew, it was his plan to go in separate cars. I think he knew how bad it was and he wanted one of us to survive.

"Peter was my hero to the end – he put my life ahead of his own – his car was fitted with an LPG gas tank. He told me to head to the oval. It would be safe there away from the flaming trees. He was behind me in another car. We realised the oval gates were locked. He just told me to go and that's the last time I saw him.

"I drove through the flames and then found a safe house and managed to survive. He jumped out of his car because he was worried that the gas tank would explode. My Peter was found lying face down in a paddock about two hours later. I stayed overnight in what was left of Strathewen. I drove out at 6am on Sunday to my son Andrew's house in Whittlesea. He was devastated; he had lost his best mate. They really loved each other. Peter and Andrew rebuilt an EH Holden together. It was in the sheds which were destroyed at our place.

"Andrew's children Braydon, 10, and Corey, 3, don't have their grandfather now. He always watched them when they played sport – football or cricket, he was there.

"My daughter Suzie, 37, lives in England. She had to fly over here when she heard the news. She was inconsolable. Her husband Ray and their children Gracie, 10, and Taylor, 8, came with them. I can't imagine what that flight would have been like.

"All I can remember now is meeting Peter – the shy man who asked me to dance at Leggett's Dance Hall in Prahran almost 50 years ago. I was wearing a red dress and he had pointy black shoes, with tight black pants and a skinny black tie, a long curl over his forehead, he looked a little bit like Elvis, but not as tall.

"We were together five years before we were married on October

30, 1965. We had a great life together. Peter was a proud and passionate Richmond supporter; he was really looking forward to see Ben Cousins play. I survived but we lost a kind, gentle man."

**As told to Stephen Drill, *Sunday Herald Sun***

# We didn't have any warning. It just all happened

## Craig Young, Strathewen

Craig was one of the last to leave as fires circled Strathewen. He and his wife, Jean, had been in nearby St Andrews, but returned home to get their dog when they heard the fire was near.

"A lot of those people were our friends.  We were very lucky, we got out, but a lot of people didn't. It is very hard for us to comprehend."

Over a CB radio scanner, Craig could hear farmer and fire captain Dave McGahy saying firefighters were unable to control a blaze that was building and swirling behind the town on Eagles Nest Rd.

"He was saying over and over again, 'This is out of control, I need more assistance, this is completely out of control'. There was no way anyone could survive that. It was something you could never dream of. We didn't have any warning. It just all happened. We thought we would have time. Everyone thinks they've got enough time, but by the time we were driving out everything was on fire.

"Most of our friends wouldn't have chosen to stay. They couldn't get out this way and they couldn't get out via Kinglake and they had no warning at all, they were just trapped there. We tried to ring a couple of them, but, you know …"

**As told to Stuart Rintoul, *The Australian***

# We didn't know which way to run

## Jack Powell, 94, Strathewen

Jack's family started Strathewen more than 100 years ago. Now he is one of the last ones left. He is still alive thanks to an act of incredible bravery by his great-nephew Steve, who protected him with his body and a coat.

"We didn't have time to get out. We didn't know which way to run and the road was all alight. We had to get out of the house. It was all [prepared] nicely for the fire but the fire didn't take any notice. It was such a small place and, just whoosh, it all happened, all gone. If it wasn't for [Steve] I wouldn't have been saved."

**As told to Michelle Pountney, *Herald Sun***

# The sky was like someone had dropped a bomb

## Greg Annand, 72, Kinglake West

Police had named Greg as missing after fire swept over his house.

"A big fireball went right over the top of us and just burnt the place. We were lucky to get away. It burnt all around us. In five minutes, our house was gone. The police couldn't believe we were still alive because they had us down as deceased. They couldn't find us.

"We had no warning. All of a sudden it sounded like two jets coming over. I thought that must be thunder or something, but it wasn't. The sky was like someone had dropped a bomb. I'll never forget. We had a little Shetland pony on fire. He was running but we couldn't do anything about that. Fire went around us but the fireball came over and burnt the garage. It sort of missed us where we were. There must be someone up top looking after us."

**As told to Ewin Hannan, *The Australian***

# It was like watching a war movie

## Jason Webb, Kinglake West

Jason and his neighbours fought for four hours to save their homes. When the wind changed he hid behind a water tank, dousing the flames lapping at his porch before he was rescued by firemen.

"It was like watching a war movie. Behind us was a mechanic's shop with gas tanks blowing up. It was horrible. It didn't seem that bad and then the smoke just blacked out the sky and it had a real ominous feel about it."

**As told to *The Advertiser***

# We only had minutes to get out

## Keith Chasemore, 66, Kinglake West

Keith towed his caravan to the Whittlesea the week before the fires. His street, Pine Ridge Rd, was ripped apart by the inferno.

"We just stood there and watched the smoke," he said. "It was just black. We only had minutes to get out. It used to be so lush and green here. I came here and I knew I was home."

His house was gone, but he heard his truck was OK and he wanted to get back up and check his trailer. The 66-year-old is a truckie by trade. "Dad," his daughter Melissa said. "It won't have any tyres left."

"That's all right," he said, "It's got two spares."

"They'll be gone, too!"

"Well, I'll bring it down on its rims," he said, "I don't care."

**Paul Kent, *The Daily Telegraph***

# The car knew it had to get there, it was on empty all the way

## Carl Agius, Kinglake West

Carl was at home when he saw the fires coming. He escaped in his Ford Mustang rescuing Helen Fischer and her three children. But no matter how fast he drove, the fires kept up with him.

"F... this," Carl said. He climbed into his Mustang, the tank on empty, and drove to Helen's place. "Get in."

"I'm staying," she said. "Get in," he repeated. When he got Helen's children, their two dogs and a cat in the car, he turned the Mustang towards Yarra Glen. "The car was doing 70 miles an hour and the flames on the side of the road were keeping up with us," Carl said. Eventually the fire caught them. The car was engulfed in flames.

He turned it towards Yea and drove back through the flames, breaking clear when the firefront rolled over them. All the while, the needle nudged E on the fuel gauge.

"The car knew it had to get there, it was on empty all the f...... way. We're the luckiest in the world. We only have the clothes on our back but there's hundreds of people dead up there. Hundreds."

**Paul Kent, *The Daily Telegraph***

# You thought you were going to die

## Peter Thorp, Kinglake West

Peter fled his property in a car to pick up a friend before police turned him back, telling him fire was racing up the valley. He drove back to his house to pick up a coat and then raced towards town where he took refuge on a burnt-out piece of land, thinking it couldn't burn twice. He was right.

"By the time we drove back to the top of the hill, the whole valley was on fire. But by the time we turned around and came back, the whole place got so dark it was unbelievable. [The fire] sounded like a 707 taking off at Tullamarine. It was so fast. It was like electricity, mate. It was unbelievable. You thought you were going to die. I thought, 'OK, I've lost everything – everything that I own and possess', and to cap it off, I'm uninsured. I forgot to pay the premiums. I thought, 'Well, I'm alive, but these poor other people are all gone, they've perished, burnt', and stuff like this."

**As told to Ewin Hannan,** *The Australian*

# Gone in minutes

Brian Naylor was not just a TV legend, he was a good neighbour and a friend to many in the community of Kinglake West. He and his wife, Moiree, had survived the Ash Wednesday fires in their home, but sadly Black Saturday was just too intense for the loving couple.

TV legend Brian Naylor and his wife, Moiree, were never going to make it. Such was the lie of their land, they couldn't even see the fireballs coming. The signs among the ruins of their idyllic retreat suggest they fought until the end. Coombs Rd bore the brunt of the Kinglake West fire disaster. Bang, bang, bang, the houses went down. Within minutes many people were dead along the ridgetop road.

The Naylors may have seen the smoke and embers coming, but not the flames. Their immaculate brick home was about 80m below the ridge line and facing away from the firestorm. It gave terrific views of the city that the former newsreader loved so much. Come that Saturday, it was facing the wrong way.

Joe Ropar lives on the other side of the road, just up the hill. Unlike the Naylors, he saw the fire coming. He said it was like a horror show in IMAX that cost him 20 friends. Sobbing at times, Joe said it took just two minutes for the flames to travel 20km, roar up the Sherwin Ranges and explode over the top. "The fire was jumping like a big-foot giant. Giant steps," Joe said.

Brian was immaculate on the screen and immaculate at home. The property was so fire ready that it looked dressed and poised to star in a CFA brochure. There were bulldozers and other earth-moving equipment. Unlike most other properties, the Naylors were not surrounded by bush. They had created a significant firebreak. But, as Joe said, he was up against it: "There was no hope. No hope."

Testament to that was a Mercedes 4WD backed up to the ruins – unmarked by the fire, but for blistering at the back; teddy bears in the boot; firefighting equipment attached to a trailer.

Brian was loved on the TV screen and loved at Kinglake. Neighbour after neighbour lamented his death. Joe loved Brian from the moment that they met eight years ago when the Ropars bought into the Toorak Rd of Kinglake. The TV star wandered up Coombs Rd with a carton of beer and a bottle of scotch and, with all the sincerity he showed on the screen, welcomed him to the community. "I loved him," Joe said.

All that remains of a dream home are a filing cabinet here, a wheelbarrow there. A mangled mower; a melted treadmill; an outdoor table, probably made of stone, still stands with some iron chairs, as if waiting for guests.

One neighbour said that journalists were ghouls; then again, Brian would have been the first to have presented this fire story and to have done it in a manner that made his station great. It's an hour's drive to Melbourne from Kinglake West, but Brian loved the freedom.

At 77, he was still healthy enough to enjoy the view, spot the occasional deer, dodge wombats and enjoy the solitude – so tantalisingly close to the city, but far enough away to guarantee his privacy. He knew Kinglake was one of the most beautiful places in Australia. This is why it will be rebuilt. It's what Brian would have wanted.

**John Ferguson,** *Herald Sun*

# I didn't believe it was so quick

## Joe Ropar, 60, Kinglake West

Joe retired to Coombs Rd, Kinglake West, eight years ago. The late Channel 9 newsreader Brian Naylor befriended Joe as soon as he arrived. Joe fought the blaze and saved his house. Brian – for decades the face of Nine – and his wife Moiree perished.

"I loved him [Naylor, but] there was no hope. No hope. The fire was jumping like a big-foot giant. Giant steps. We see it, but I didn't believe it was so quick. I feel sorry for everybody but I can't do a thing. I lost maybe 20 neighbours."

**As told to John Ferguson,** *Herald Sun*

# It is nothing short of a miracle, but my house was still standing

## Juliet Moore, 35, Kinglake West

With its sweeping views and bush setting, Juliet's hilltop home was an idyllic refuge from her city workplace. She shared the house with kelpie-rottweiler cross Poncho. Her devotion to Poncho almost led to disaster just as she was being rescued from the fires. Poncho was in her arms but wriggled free. Juliet unfastened her harness and fell back into the inferno. Priscilla Wakefield had moved in with Juliet shortly before Black Saturday. In an incredible feat of bravery — and helped by sheer luck — the women saved themselves and their animals. Guided through the inferno by a policeman in radio contact with the helicopter above, the pair drove themselves to safety.

"There was no way I was going to leave Poncho behind. She's my best friend. The fires started in Kilmore at midday and I could see them from my house. I watched the smoke get bigger and began to worry.

"Priscilla arrived at 3pm. By the time she got out of the car the wind turned to gale force. Trees started to fall around us and leaves were flying up into the air. It was at this point we heard the fire. We couldn't see the flames but the noise of the fire was haunting, we realised it was too late to try and leave. It was a matter of minutes before the power cut and as my water supply is pump driven, the hoses stopped. We were left to rely on the sprinklers on the roof.

"We were extremely fortunate that a helicopter monitoring the fire front flew over the house and saw us. It hovered over the house and a policeman was lowered to the ground on the winch. He put the winch strap around my waist and with Poncho in my arms they started to lift me up. But Poncho wriggled and I dropped her. I undid the winch and ran after her. The policeman on the ground was in radio contact with the helicopter and he said, 'Get in the cars and drive'. The helicopter hovered above us and they guided us through it by radio to make sure we didn't drive into the flames. With the horse galloping next to the car and the float with the other horses behind, we drove into the fire.

"The helicopter was keeping us informed of which directions to take in the thick smoke. The sound of the chopper overhead was the eeriest soundtrack. When we got to the bottom of the hill we found a clearing near the golf course and we stopped. We could see my house up the mountain surrounded by flames and, although we could see the fire sprinklers on the roof still working, it was like throwing a teaspoon of water on to a bonfire. The flames were 200 feet [60m] high. As it went dark I watched the flames pass over my house, I retreated to the safety of town thinking everything I owned was gone. When I managed to fall asleep I dreamt of flames. When it was light we ventured out again to try and get back to the house. The roads were closed and the fire still burning. I ignored the road blocks, took the back road and drove through a fence.

"It is nothing short of a miracle, but my house was still standing, the fire seemingly tracing a path around it. Every house in my street had been burned to the ground and a number of my neighbours never made it out alive, including Brian Naylor and his wife. This was apocalyptic. It was like the films of the Hiroshima bomb going off and annihilating everything. Nearly every house on Coombs Rd is just ash."

**As told to Norrie Ross, *Herald Sun***

# Get in the car. Grab all your stuff. Let's get out of here

## Shaun Robertson, 12, Kinglake West

His Saturday started like any other. But as the skies began to darken and the rumble of the fire came close, Shaun escaped with his family to the sanctuary of the Kinglake West fire station.

"After brekkie I stayed on the computer for a while until my sister Tara got up, went outside and hopped on her bike. I joined her. We did the usual and daily course. Round the backyard's fireplace, through the veranda, across the stones round the car and up the steep hill at the same time and extra fast down through the stones past the veranda and the course starts again. After about an hour or two, I realised that the sky was red with smoke. I told Mum and Dad, Dad was awake before all of us. I saw the smoke and glow of the fire and for some reason I thought of Pompeii and volcanoes. The whole sky was red.

"Soon the phone rang and it was my friend saying that they were coming to our place for the fire had reached their place and that they had just escaped. They got out of the car teary. Murray sobbed: 'We're going to lose our house'. I kept riding my bike until I heard this rumbling roar. I thought it was a jumbo jet but just to be sure I asked Murray, he said: 'That's the fire!'

"Suddenly the lights and power turned on and off, on and off until it eventually turned off completely. My mum gasped: 'What is that noise?' Aunt replied: 'That's the fire'.

"Dad went to check, and then straight away he ran back down and yelled: 'Get in the car! Grab all your stuff! Let's get out of here!'

"I ran to my room and grabbed the thing that I wanted the most

– all my deceased nanna's stuff. I ran outside and chucked it in the car. I ran back to the house and saw my St Basil's Cathedral model that had won second prize in the Whittlesea show. I chucked that in the car and ran back to my bedroom with my heart beating 1000 times a minute and my mind panicking like mad. I grabbed my phone, PSP and the games for it. I ran but just before I reached the door I grabbed my memory cards for the PlayStation 2 and ran outside leaving my tears all over the carpet. I went to run inside but Dad yelled, 'No more time for stuff! Let's go!' Tara, Dad and I jumped in our 4WD and Mum jumped in her new Holden Commodore. Everyone started up their cars and zoomed up the driveway.

" 'Is that the fire?' I asked. 'Yes', Dad replied. 'OMG', I said to myself. We eventually got to where we were heading to – Kinglake West Oval. Next to it was the Kinglake West fire station. A firewoman said that there was going to be a change and that it would bring the fire to where we were. Tara and I were put in Mum's car and then we drove off. Eventually the air started to get thicker and thicker with smoke until it was hard to breathe. We pulled over and decided we were going to go back to the fire station. On the way at an intersection it turned black as night.

"Fire was on the side of the road coming closer and closer to the cars on the road. My mum pulled over and it felt as if all the happiness was taken from the world. We all said 'I love you' to each other. My mum was trying to ring [my] aunt and eventually got on to her. She said that they were going to the Kinglake West fire station. My Mum did a U-turn and was on course. Eventually we got there. It was real smoky and hard to breathe. You couldn't see 10m in front of you. It was a long and sad night. I only got two hours of sleep. Now we are living in a motel with heaps of stuff that people have kindly offered.

**Via email**

**Staying put: Warren Rees is living in a temporary shed after his property was razed**
Picture: Craig Borrow

**Best friend: Juliet Moore risked her own life to rescue her pet dog Poncho**
Picture: Rebecca Michael

# Bodies were still lying everywhere. It looked like an atomic bomb had hit

## Warren Rees, CFA volunteer, Strathewen

Warren came home to find his home razed and his two horses and many of his neighbours dead. He has since set up a temporary shed amid the ashes.

"We were down the road at Eagles Nest Rd during the fires. I believe we saved at least one house. It's actually still a little bit blurry, there was so much happening. I got back and everything on the street was still burning. Bodies were still lying everywhere. It looked like an atomic bomb had hit. It was just fireballs.

"I kept working because I had nothing to worry about at home. It's a lot easier for me because I'm by myself. If I had a missus I don't think I would be here.

"It's really just helping the general community with whatever – whether it's fencing, helping with the stock, or just moral support. I think it's easy now. The amount of support we have been getting, not just from the area but from Australia, has cushioned what we have gone through. It's going to get hard in a month or two. That's what I'm worried about for a few people.

"Some people call it [my temporary home], the Strathewen Hilton. [Swimming in a dam] doesn't bother me. I have been living in the bush my whole life. The water's a bit cold but it's not too bad. I still love this place. It was burnt down in the '39 bushfires and they rebuilt it in 1942 and it had been standing there since. I had it completely finished and renovated on the Wednesday before the fire, I had the curtains fitted then. I was actually looking forward to enjoying the place.

"I want to build it back up and get some more stock when the grass grows again this year and re-do the garden. It will be different this time, though. I may never see another bushfire here, it may take at least 10 years just until it grows back to be a threat again."

**As told to Matt Johnston, *Herald Sun***

# We've put too much into this, we're not giving up to a fire

## Tony and Barbara Barbeta, Strathewen

As fires raced towards them, the couple hosed down their house and surrounding areas, filled the gutters and downpipes that had melted from the heat, then pulled the doors shut and rode it out. At one point, the force of the fire blew an airconditioner off the roof and across the house. They went from room to room, checking for smoke and breaks in windows. They even punched a hole in the ceiling to check for embers under the eaves.

"This was just a maelstrom. Roaring. You hear them say it comes like a locomotive, but about 10 minutes before the fire hit, maybe more, there was this roaring. There was no smoke and there was no fire, but there was this roaring. That roaring went on for probably 10 minutes and then it came over the hill: a ball of flame. It must have been 50 feet in the air." Asked why they didn't leave, Barbara said: "We've put too much into this. We're not giving up to a fire. Simple."

**As told to Stuart Rintoul, *The Australian***

# It doesn't even resemble
# the place we knew

Among the ashes of the devastated town of Strathewen, nature's
devastating fury also offers up some tiny surprises.

Faye Park suddenly gives a little squeal of delight. She has spotted a
pink flower poking its head through the ash and then another. It is
amaryllis belladonna, known as "naked ladies". Amaryllis is from the
Greek "to sparkle".

"Nothing kills the naked lady," Faye says, her face glowing at this
first sign of life and colour and beauty in a town that has been so
devastated. Faye and her husband, Malcolm, went back to Strathewen
to look at their destroyed home, to bury their dogs and to stare at the
patch of dirt where they lay huddled together under a wet blanket
after their home exploded in flames. Around them, the fire roared and
circled, a tunnel of fire and wind, for two terrifying hours.

Shane Pugh, son of the famous artist Clifton Pugh, also returned
to his home at Strathewen, to recover a collection of his father's
paintings that survived in a concrete safe room. "The fact that the
paintings survived is nothing less than a miracle," he says. Little
miracles in the ashes.

At their home above Strathewen, Mandy and Steve Hayley talk
about friends who lived and friends who died and friends who are
missing. About a community, too, faced with pulling itself together
after its darkest hour. They talk about Rosemary, the twin sister of the
town's matriarch Marilyn Langmead, who survived with four people
in Craig Young's dam: Langmeads and McKimmies, old Strathewen
families, huddled in the water as the fire roared around them.

Survivors speak of seeing them coming up the hill from the dam after the fire, black from ash, like something out of a movie, four people coming up through the smoke. The town had planned to hold a family day fundraiser for Marilyn Langmead, who has cancer. A sign opposite the destroyed hall where it was to be held is still there. "Join us for a family day at Strathewen Hall," it says. "Craft, Devonshire tea and cakes, children's activities, spinning wheel, BBQ, light music and more." All that changed on Black Saturday.

Instead, Marilyn is fundraising for the town, from her hospital bed. Steve Hayley smiles. "We were rallying for her," he says. "But now she's rallying for everyone else. She's not a lay-down sort of lass. That's Marilyn for you."

The days have been long and full of emotional turbulence: tears, rage, gratitude for outpourings of help, the need to stay close to Strathewen, the desire to run away, the strangeness of seeing people alive when you had been told they were dead.

Mandy says: "Life has ceased as we knew it. It's like we're living in limbo. Everyone knew someone. We all knew lots of people. No one has been left untouched." She talks about the pain of not knowing. She talks about those who survived against the odds, such as Lynne and Dave Andrews, who found enough water in their duck pond to stay alive; and Steve, Alison and Jessica Pascoe who clambered into an above-ground swimming pool that was being used for water storage. It collapsed around them but they survived in the mud. And Peter Jenkinson, who fought the fire while his wife, Debbie, and son Brett took refuge in their dam. "Muddy and smelly, but they stayed there and it saved them," Mandy says.

For Steve Hayley, the scene was apocalyptic. "It doesn't even resemble the place we knew," he says.

"Before the fire, every day was green."

**Stuart Rintoul, *The Australian***

# I thought they were all gone

## Jay Russell, 13, Humevale

Two days after flames ravaged their town, the Russell family heard faint chirping noises while putting out spot fires. Jay lost about 60 pet birds on Black Saturday. But the noise led Jay and his family – parents Jamie and Joanne, and 18-year-old brother Luke, to a baby budgerigar, which had been trapped under the ashes for 48 hours.

"I don't know why I like birds, I just like them. I started looking after birds with my uncle about four years ago. Before the fire I had about 60 of them. I used to go out and feed them every day. I thought they were all gone [after the fire]. But then Dad heard noises in the nest. I couldn't believe it. We found him in the nest and I decided to call him Lucky. He is starting to eat seeds and I feed him water with a dropper. He's OK. I'd like to have a lot of birds again."

**As told to Evonne Barry, *Sunday Herald Sun***

# I didn't give water to a koala but I did give narcotics to a marsupial

## David Kervin, paramedic, Kinglake West

When wildlife carers couldn't find a vet to treat a badly burnt wallaby joey in Kinglake West, ambulance officer David came to the rescue. He named the four-month-old Cathy, after Cathy Freeman.

"It was nice to be able to do a nice deed for her. I have always loved animals but I have never treated one before. We normally wouldn't treat animals, we would refer them to a vet but these were extreme circumstances. I went home that night and I said, 'I didn't give water to a koala but I did give narcotics to a marsupial'. She seemed to perk up as soon as I gave her the pain-relief treatment."

**As told to Megan McNaught, *Herald Sun***

# Sometimes I want to cry and sometimes I do

Stuart McEvoy, a photographer for *The Australian*, tells how it felt to be first at the firefront as Black Saturday attacked.

**Sunday, February 8, 6.30am:** The morning after Australia's worst ever natural disaster. I'd just woken from the spot I lay down, a gravel driveway, no more than an hour before. The sun is rising and I can already hear stories of survival filtering through the otherwise silent air. It had taken me more than five hours, on foot, during the night, to get here – but now I was in Kinglake West.

**Saturday, February 7, 2.30pm:** Melbourne's hottest day on record, 46C with a strong northerly wind gusting over bone-dry countryside. The tarp covering our house extension in suburban Melbourne had blown off and I was on the roof trying to tie it down. I could see and smell smoke and although I knew there was a fire in Kilmore, this seemed much closer. I checked the web, still the reports say Kilmore. I check the map for possible scenarios. The fire is going but still doesn't seem to be moving very fast. I decide then that I need to be in a position in case it does start to break out. The next decision I made may just have saved my life. I look at the possible impact areas. Given the conditions, Wandong is directly in the path of the oncoming fire, followed by Whittlesea and across to Kinglake, which seems highly unlikely, given the slow progression to date. The easiest path from my house would be to head to Kinglake, driving along the top of the mountain to be in position for a fire threatening Whittlesea.

**4pm:** To go via Kinglake now seems ludicrous and so I head directly for Wandong via Whittlesea but it is too late. By the time it takes me to get there, the fire is streaking across the hills above Whittlesea and impacting on Kinglake West. I try to cut back in front of it but it is too fast, all roads into Kinglake from the West are cut by fire. There is nothing I can do now but wait.

**7.30pm:** I'm sitting at a police checkpoint just outside Wandong as the giant plume rises over Kinglake, a police officer inquires, "Is that a storm cloud?" "No," I replied. I had seen it once before (back then, an entire mountain range had disappeared before my eyes). "That's smoke." As we watched the jet airliners making a mad dash to avoid the ever-increasing column, I knew that if anyone had survived such a horrific event, I needed to be there to document it.

**8.15pm:** I leave Heathcote Junction, heading southeast to find a way in. The Kinglake district is for most parts a single strip of bitumen running east-west along the length of a ridgeline that forms part of the Great Dividing Range.

**10pm:** I arrive at the base of the mountain. The road is blocked with emergency services. I look for another way in and find one but I am not alone. People are desperate to get in. They have had calls from people on top of the mountain: "Send help, we need help." We're driving through the burnt-out area together for safety, trying to get through, but fallen trees block the road at every turn. Some can be moved but as we get higher, the trees get bigger. We can go no further, it's too dangerous. I return to the bottom of the mountain. Weighing up the situation I decide the safest way to access the area is on foot. I leave my car at a house; the owner tells me the woman next door did not make it out. She was on the edge of the fire. It's a sobering message.

**Midnight:** Following the road all the way up, carrying everything I can, a deer passes in front of me. Desperate to get off the mountain, it careers down the steep slope without stopping. The forest is glowing all around me and as I gain altitude I can see through the trees to the surrounding hills, all of which are burnt out. The air is silent. Nothing stirs, except the occasional crash of a falling tree. I am well aware that this is my biggest danger and I am constantly alert. The moon is rising; it is full and allows me to see some of the surrounding devastation. I pass what remains of houses. They smoulder in the moonlight. I don't linger. Finally I reach the main road. A convoy of ambulances races off the mountain, escorted by emergency services. I push on.

**Sunday, February 8, 5.30am:** I have come to a junction. The smoke is still thick but I can see a sign pointing to Kinglake and I can hear voices. It is the first sign of life I've come across. I head towards it. Several residents have taken refuge in the centre of town waiting for daylight. They had survived and I had made it to Kinglake West, the first town on the mountain to be hit by the fire. Exhausted, I lay down on the gravel drive and waited for the sun to come up.

**6.30am:** The sun was rising and people were starting to emerge in the small town that is not much more than a general store. They began to compare stories to try and piece together what had happened. There was no warning – a sentiment that would be echoed again and again, wherever I went, in the following days. "The first we knew of it was when everything was on fire," they said. It was estimated that at its peak the fire was travelling at 80-100km/h. You can't outrun something like that although many tried. The roads were littered with burnt-out cars travelling in every direction. As one man said: "You couldn't see a thing [in the thick smoke], but you couldn't slow down either." He shrugged his shoulders: "What choice did they have?"

To stay or go did not apply on this day. People reviewing this policy must understand that it is only relevant when you're given the opportunity to do so. Without warning, there is no choice. You always have this impression that a fire front is a single entity. A line, a wall, let it pass and you'll be OK. Ask anyone who has been through it and this is far from the case. Fire is cunning and deceitful; it will try to sneak up on you when your back is turned, take whatever it can, again and again. There is no reasoning why it takes one house and not the other, one life and not another and that is in its mildest form. What Victoria faced on that day was nothing short of a firestorm. I've heard it many times over, from the mouths of the people who were there. You feel their pain, you see their disbelief.

You have a job to do but it doesn't make it any easier, often harder. Sometimes you want to cry, sometimes you do. Sometimes you put the camera up to protect yourself, pretending it's just a picture. Exposure, focus, framing, keeps you occupied until the office rings: "Call your family. Let them know you're alive."

I haven't spoken to them for 24 hours and at last contact I was heading for Kinglake. My four-year-old says: "Don't cry Mummy, Daddy will be all right, he has a woollen fire blanket in the car."

You want to hold them tight and never let them go. You hope that they or anyone else will never have to face that day again, but deep down you know they probably will and that you will probably be there to document it.

**Stuart McEvoy, *The Australian***

**Gruesome: A forensic officer sifts through the devastation**    Picture: Craig Borrow

# Chapter 3

# St Andrews & Steels Creek

- **Origin**
  At 4.30pm a southerly fans flames towards St Andrews, population 1536. The fire moves on to Steels Creek, a town of about 100 people

- **Destruction**
  St Andrews is razed in less than 30 minutes. In neighbouring Steels Creek, every visible hillside property is destroyed

- **Toll**
  A total of 22 people are confirmed dead in St Andrews. Steels Creek's population is reduced by more than a tenth, with 11 dead

B efore we go any further, let's take a breath and ask how we got here. A fire is burning to the southeast of Melbourne, in the Bunyip State Park. It is Saturday morning. It was ignited by a lightning strike earlier in the week. On top of this, as everybody well knows, Victoria is going through a series of heatwaves. So severe, people are dying as each day pushes past 40C.

Hospitals are enacting mini-disaster plans to cope. Then the day before, the Friday, Country Fire Authority chief executive Russell Rees addresses his troops. Two words should stand out here: uncharted territory. That is what Russell tells his people.

"If I said our [weather conditions] were bloody horrible, I am underestimating it. I have never seen figures like this," he tells them.

Every indicator says this will be potentially the most dangerous day in the state's history. The state is deep in drought, "a tinderbox" Victorian Premier John Brumby calls it. The temperature is again expected to be in the mid-40s. There will come a dry, hot wind and conditions will get only worse when a strong southerly blows in late in the afternoon. Brumby adds to the alarm on this Friday. He uses a press conference to say the danger is greater than Ash Wednesday in 1983, when 75 died, and 1939's Black Friday, which killed 71.

So Saturday comes and many residents put their fire plan into action, surrounding their houses with buckets and mops and generators to keep the pumps working when the power inevitably cuts out. Many homes have had sprinklers installed on the roofs for something just like this.

And then it starts, as well as anybody knows, at Kilmore East. At 11.48am there is a report to the Kilmore station of a fire. On a paddock above Saunders Rd, west of the Hume Freeway, a power pole carries power lines across the property. The royal commission will decide once and for all but witnesses living near the property report seeing smoke after a power blackout. Either way there is smoke and then there is fire.

Within the hour the hot northerly wind picks up the fire. It jumps the freeway and is carried southeast, towards Mt Disappointment in the Kinglake National Park. Fire crews are called in to fight. The fire is rapidly spreading and soon other crews from other towns are heading west to add to manpower. This will be one of the problems later.

About 45km east, another fire is about to start in Murrindindi. More than three weeks later, this fire is still the focus of Operation Phoenix, the police investigation into arsonists they believe started about half the fires that broke out across Victoria.

As this fire feeds on the dry winds and tinderbox countryside, many towns in its path will be left exposed because their own CFA crews, manned almost entirely by local volunteers, are out fighting other towns' fires.

By now most of the state is already above 40C and it is not yet midday. The hottest part of the day is still to come. There will be reports of the temperature reaching as high as 48C, while some residents insist their own thermometers climbed even higher.

And the temperature is only part of it. As Russell says later, and often: "It was the only time the wind was hotter than the sun."

In Reedy Creek, Tracey Flowers and her husband Paul take notice. She returns from work at Strathewen Pub and takes their two children, Cheiron, 8, and Rhea, 3, to Broadford, 12km away. This family is used to fighting. Returning to fight the fire with her husband Paul, they are simply shaping up to fight one more round. Little Rhea, whose blonde hair is only just winning its own battle to stay with her, is suffering a form of cancer, her situation so extreme the fires will force her to put off aggressive chemotherapy treatments and put back her operation to have a kidney and part of her liver removed a week later. All these little towns, each with their own story. Tracey and Paul see out their fire as it comes over the range, surprising them by coming from the south instead of the north. They do not know it but their neighbour, local doctor Chris Towie, is lying dead beside his car. He dies, it is believed, trying to save his animals.

With the first front gone Tracey and Paul can only watch when, as they continue mopping up the embers, another front rips through their gully. It passes no more than 100m from their home, yet this fire does not even flirt with the house.

Their house has nothing more than a handful of superficial burns yet all around them the earth is black. One of the kids' plastic gym toys in the backyard, "You know the kind you buy in Kmart," Tracey says, has completely disappeared. It leaves nothing but a pale shadow on the ground where it used to be.

Further south, and knowing his wife Carolyn and 18-year-old son Stuart are at home, Allan O'Gorman ignores the flashing warning lights from his business partner who spots him racing home. "I tried to flash him to stop and he kept going," says Robert Rainey, a partner in Allan's real estate agency.

Already the first signs of what these people are up against are showing through. The O'Gormans are prepared for the fire. They have a fire plan. Yet it is useless in the face of what is coming. Might as well be spitting into the flames. Others also quickly find out.

Humevale, St Andrews, Arthurs Creek, Steels Creek, the fire finds them all. They are small townships populated, mostly, by people that have lived there all their lives. Towns so small city folk never hear about them, let alone ever consider moving there. Which, it might be said, is the way they like it. It's as if they have found their own piece of perfection and don't want the secret out. The fire pays no favours, though. It continues advancing southeast through houses and farms and stores, ripping through some of Victoria's best-known wineries, just to show no prejudice. And just as they begin to deal with this, thinking the worst is done, the wind is about to change. It is the fire's cruel trick.

The southerly is about to roll in and what people are already describing as the perfect fire is about to get worse. It is somewhere near 4pm. There is no let up.

The fire tears into St Andrews, to the home of Jacinta and Garry Bartlett and their daughters, Maddison, 12, and Erryn, 5.

By now, the fire is fully formed. We only hear about it later but there are reports of flames 50m high. When the radiant heat is thrown in, the heat given off by the flames, although not the flames themselves, has the power to kill from 200m away.

As the fires fill their window, Garry and Jacinta cannot find Erryn. They tell Maddison to put on long pants and go. A family friend, known only as Judith, grabs Maddison and runs to the dam. The fire reaches them shortly before they reach the dam. They dive in with superficial burns but they survive. Naturally, all that is behind them is gone.

This is the story of the fire. The loss and false hope and near-saves. Among all this sadness, here is another. A 12-year-old girl, now without family. A mother and father and a little girl, and their final minutes too terrible to speak of. To think about it sends you crazy. Think about it too long and it, well, it paralyses you. It makes no sense. When it is over there will be 22 dead in St Andrews, from a population of 1536 people. Among them is Reg Evans, the *Blue Heelers* actor. He stayed to fight the fires.

By the time St Andrews is gone it is still only 4.30pm. Yet around the state it is only about now the full horror is becoming evident. On ABC radio, in their bright, cheery radio voices, they are still calling on residents to call in and tell how the fire is affecting them. The people are fighting for their lives, that's how.

Inside Melbourne's Integrated Emergency Co-ordination Centre, a place colloquially known as the "war room", Russell Rees and other emergency services are co-ordinating the fire plans. They are a mile from the truth. Throughout the morning and into the early afternoon there is a hope the day is panning out OK.

Now, as St Andrews burns, they are starting to believe only some property might be lost. The truth is, lives have already been lost. The dreadful truth, that all the fire predictions are coming true, is being understood only out in the towns.

The people of Steels Creek know this. It is a remote place. A hilltop township of about 100 people. It does not know it is about to bear the brunt of the fire. As we know, the fire gathers speed, gathers muscle, when it rolls uphill. And so after the fire has spread east from its origin at Kilmore East it reaches the foothills at the southern tip of the Great Dividing Range and looks up, whereupon the little township of Steels Creek rests. Nothing survives at Steels Creek. Every visible property, hilltop and hillside, burns to the ground. Seven will die. Again the people try to escape.

John Barnett, an associate professor at Melbourne University, and his wife Jenny, a researcher with the Victorian National Parks Association, are found dead in their car. Their story is like so many others: they tried to flee too late.

Such is the panic, Dorothy Barber's daughter Nicole, living just 500m away from her mum, bundles her two small children into her car and flees. Dorothy, 63, is trapped at home.

Later, darkness begins to fall and her son Tim is stopped at a police roadblock. He wants to go up and find his mum. He knows he is looking for a corpse. Still, police say no. But with Dorothy's son-in-law, grandson and two family friends alongside him, they get out of their car and walk. The police can stop their car going through, they figure, but they cannot stop them walking through.

What they speak about nobody knows. The smell of the bushfire is strong and trees are down across the road. It stings every time you blink. They walk for four hours and after finding the charred remains of his mum's car still parked in her driveway Tim and his crew begin the solemn search for her body.

For 15 minutes they look and why they do can never be explained. Sometimes, people need completion. Then Tim hears a scream – of delight. There, in a crawl space about a metre square under her home, they find Tim's mum.

"When the boys came they were a bit cross I didn't sing out," says Dorothy. "But there was just a wall of noise. My hearing had been affected so I couldn't hear."

Forgive your mum, Tim. And hug her.

It is worth remembering that most fighting these fires, and the thousands more that survive them, are simple people. Normal people. They are tradesmen and they are hopelessly outmatched. Plumbers and electricians. Builders and shopkeepers. Simple men and women fighting to protect what's theirs because that is what we do in life. We do our best and hope our best is good enough. Alan Mitchell is one of those men.

He stays behind to save his home at Steels Creek, fighting the fire and doing OK until he runs out of water.

Now, when fighting a fire, running out of water can best be described as worst-case scenario. Alan quickly searches for alternatives when it becomes clear he has a decision to make and it is some dilemma: the only liquid he has left is his beer.

"It was breaking my heart," he says the next day. "I didn't know whether to throw it on the fire or drink it and kiss my arse goodbye." In no small sacrifice, the last of Alan's beer goes on the fire.

**Paul Kent**

**Gone: Reporter Gary Hughes comforts his family**     Picture: Stuart McEvoy

# A plastic key ring saved our lives

**A reporter for *The Australian*, Gary Hughes, tells of his family's Black Saturday miracle survival on the Monday after the fire.**

They warn you it comes fast. But the word "fast" doesn't come anywhere near describing it. It comes at you like a runaway train. One minute you are preparing. The next you are fighting for your home. Then you are fighting for your life. But it is not minutes that come between. It's more like seconds. The firestorm moves faster than you can think, let alone react. For 25 years, we had lived on our hilltop in St Andrews. You prepare like they tell you every summer. You clear. You slash. You prime your fire pump. For 25 years, fires were something that you watched in the distance. Until Saturday.

We had been watching the massive plume of smoke near Kilmore all afternoon; secure in the knowledge it was too far away to pose a danger. Then suddenly there is smoke and flames across the valley, about a kilometre to the northwest, being driven towards you by the wind. Not too bad, you think. I rush around the side of the house to start the petrol-powered fire pump to begin spraying the house, just in case. When I get there, I suddenly see flames rushing towards the house from the west. The tongues of flame are in our front paddock, racing up the hill towards us across grass stubble I thought safe because it had been slashed.

In the seconds it takes me to register the flames, they are into a small stand of trees 50m from the house. Heat and embers drive at me like an open blast furnace. I run to shelter inside, like they tell you, until the fire front passes. Inside are my wife, a 13-year-old girl we care for, and a menagerie of animals "rescued" over the year by our veterinary-student daughter. They call it "ember attack". Those words don't do it justice. It is a fiery hailstorm from hell driving relentlessly at you. The wind and driving embers explore, like claws of a predator, every tiny gap in the house. Embers are blowing through the cracks around the closed doors and windows. We frantically wipe at them with wet towels. We are fighting for all we own. We still have hope.

The house begins to fill with smoke. The smoke alarms start to scream. The smoke gets thicker. I go outside to see if the fire front has passed. One of our two cars under a carport is burning. I rush inside to get keys for the second and reverse it out into an open area in front of the house to save it.

That simple act will save our lives. I rush back around the side of the house, where plastic plant pots are in flames. I turn on a garden hose. Nothing comes out.

I look back along its length and see where the flames have melted it. I try to pick up one of the carefully positioned plastic buckets of water I've left around the house. Its metal handle pulls away from the melted sides.

I rush back inside the house. The smoke is much thicker. I see flames behind the louvres of a door into a storage room, off the kitchen. I open the door and there is a fire burning fiercely. I realise the house is gone. We are now fighting for our lives.

We retreat to the last room in the house, at the end of the building furthest from where the firestorm hit. We slam the door, shutting the room off from the rest of the house. The room is quickly filling with smoke. It's black, toxic smoke, different from the superheated smoke outside. We start coughing and gasping for air. Life is rapidly beginning to narrow to a grim, but inevitable choice. Die from the toxic smoke inside. Die from the firestorm outside. The room we are in has french doors opening on to the front veranda. Somewhere out of the chaos of thoughts surfaces recent media bushfire training I had done with the CFA. When there's nothing else, a car might save you.

I run the 30 or 40 steps to the car through the blast furnace. I wrench open the door to start the engine and turn on the airconditioning, as the CFA tells you, before going back for the others. The key isn't in the ignition. Where in hell did I put it? I rush back to the house. By now the black, toxic smoke is so thick I can barely see the others. Everyone is coughing. Gasping. Choking. My wife is calling for one of our two small dogs, the gentle, loyal Gizmo, who has fled in terror.

I grope in my wife's handbag for her set of car keys. The smoke is so thick I can't see far enough to look into the bag. I find them by touch, thanks to a plastic spider keychain our daughter gave her as a joke. Our lives are saved by a plastic spider. I tell my wife time has run out. We have to get to the car. The choices have narrowed to just one option, just one slim chance to live.

Clutching the second of our two small dogs, we run to the car. I feel the radiant heat burning the back of my hand. The CFA training comes back again. Radiant heat kills. The three of us are inside the car. I turn the key. It starts. We turn on the airconditioning and I reverse a little further away from the burning building. The flames are wrapped around the full fuel tank of the other car and I worry about it exploding.

We watch our home – our lives, everything we own – blazing fiercely just metres away. The heat builds. We try to drive down our driveway, but fallen branches block the way. I reverse back towards the house, but my wife warns me about sheets of red-hot roofing metal blowing towards us. I drive back down, pushing the car through the branches. Further down the 400m drive, the flames have passed. But at the bottom, trees are burning. We sit in the open, motor running and airconditioner turned on full. Behind us our home is aflame. We calmly watch from our hilltop, trapped in the sanctuary of our car, as first the house of one neighbour, then another, then another goes up in flames. One takes an agonisingly slow time to go, as the flames take a tenuous grip at one end and work their way slowly along the roof. Another at the bottom of our hill, more than 100 years old and made of imported North American timber, explodes quickly in a plume of dark smoke.

All the while the car is being buffeted and battered by gale-force winds and bombarded by a hail of blackened material. It sounds like rocks hitting the car. The house of our nearest neighbour, David, who owns a vineyard, has so far escaped. But a portable office attached to one wall is billowing smoke.

I leave the safety of the car and cross the fence. Where is the CFA, he frantically asks. With the CFA's help, perhaps he can save his house. What's their number, he asks me. I tell him we had already rung 000, before our own house burnt. Too many fires. Too few tankers. I leave him to his torment. I walk back towards our own house in a forlorn hope that by some miracle our missing dog may have survived in some unburned corner of the building.

Our home, everything we were, is a burning, twisted, blackened jumble. Our missing dog, Gizmo, Bobby our grumpy cockatoo, Zena the rescued galah that spoke Greek and imitated my whistle to call the dogs, our free-flying budgie nicknamed Lucky because he escaped a previous bushfire, are all gone, killed in the inferno that almost claimed us as well.

I return to the car and spot the flashing lights of a CFA tanker through the blackened trees across the road. We drive down the freeway, I pull clear more fallen branches and we reach the main road. I walk across the road to the tanker and tell them if they are quick they might help David save his house. I still don't know if they did. We stop at a police checkpoint down the hill. They ask us where we've come from and what's happening up the road. I tell them there's no longer anything up the road.

We stop at the local CFA station in St Andrews. Two figures sit hunched in chairs, covered by wet towels for their serious burns. More neighbours. We hear that an old friend, two properties from us, is missing. A nurse wraps wet towels around superficial burns on my wife's leg and my hand.

We drive to my brother's house, which fate had spared, on the other side of St Andrews. The thought occurs to me, where do you start when you've lost everything, even a way to identify yourself. Then I realise, of course, it doesn't matter. We escaped with our lives. Just. So many others didn't.

# Get out and tell the neighbours

## Jeff Purchase, St Andrews

As a CFA volunteer, Jeff could only do his best as his own town caught fire. He saved lives and houses but it came at a cost.

"The pager went off just after 3pm: Smoke sighting at Everard Track. I grabbed my turnout gear and headed straight for tanker 2. On the way to Everard we had another pager message: Turnout to grass and scrub Eagles Nest.

"As the wind was blowing from that direction and could impact on our town, we diverted away from Everard. On the way to Eagles Nest we stopped on a ridge and looked back to Everard – no smoke, we felt relaxed. On arrival at Eagles Nest everything seemed under control. That's when we turned towards St Andrews and saw what would become Armageddon. We raced back to where we had just

**Gamble: Tracey Flowers plays with Rhea, 3, in the garden of the home she saved**
Picture: John Grainger

**Hero: Levi dragged his owner Val Cross into a dam as flames engulfed her home**
Picture: Mark Smith

been. Twenty minutes earlier it was peaceful, now it had erupted into a seething angry dragon that, helped by insanely strong winds, reaped its vengeance on all around it. The crew swung into action fighting the blaze from the tanker. And then the horror hit me. It was heading right for the township where my wife and children were.

"I grabbed my mobile and frantically rang my wife. 'Get out and tell the neighbours to get out,' I yelled down the phone. From St Andrews we spent the rest of the night in Kinglake and surrounds responding to pager calls, all crew members of St Andews tanker 2 did the best they could under dangerous situations – driving past burning houses of people you know, not knowing if they were alive or dead."

**Via email**

# We did not expect it, and then it was all around us

## Ian McLeish, St Andrews

Between St Andrews and Strathewen, Ian and his daughter Jane endured swirling winds, cars exploding and fire alarms screaming when the fire hit the edges of their property on Black Saturday. Like many people in the area, they were not initially worried.

"It arrived in spot fires. First one, then another half a kilometre away. The wind picked up and it just took off. Within five minutes, it was in the front yard, tearing at the sheds. It was all around us."

Ian's mother, Lee, weeps and says she feared they would die in the blaze. As she looks at the sweep of the fire, she says: "I didn't realise the range of it."

**Stuart Rintoul, *The Australian***

# Spot fires became infernos

## Kerryn and John Edmonds, St Andrews

> The Edmonds – Kerryn, John and their children, Orianna, 9, Tahlia, 4, and Micah, 2 – lived in Olives Lane, a meandering back road in St Andrews with five houses. By Saturday afternoon, none was left standing after fire swept over the hill.

Kerryn: "The whole mountain was ablaze. So we literally had to drive through the flames. The conditions were appalling. Spot fires would become infernos within minutes. Just massive fire fronts of their own. We got out with each other, and that's the most important thing. We're better off than those who lost their loved ones. Our neighbour didn't make it. And another neighbour, very dear to us, died in the shed. There are so many who didn't make it. That's the hardest thing, it's the people we don't know about. It's the waiting and the not knowing."

**As told to Russell Robinson, *Herald Sun***

# It climbed the hill in five seconds

## Alf Gonnella, 76, St Andrews

> Alf watched the fire skirt the edge of his home on Saturday. For a while, Alf fought the fire with just a knapsack filled with water.

"They [his neighbours] left their houses to save my house. Flames went left, right and centre. In five seconds, it went right down the creek and up and over the houses there, I said to myself, 'If I stay here, there is no way known I can survive'."

**As told to Stuart Rintoul, *The Australian***

# Someone came running down the street swearing at the kids to get the hell out

## Darren Wilson, 40, Chum Creek

Darren should have been celebrating his 40th birthday on Black Saturday. But a family occasion turned into a fight for survival.

"From what we could tell, the fires were down towards Yarra Glen and a friend of ours that had left said there was a lot of smoke near the highway so my wife didn't want to leave. We had a plan and had everything ready but things just kept getting worse, things were dropping from the sky and turning to ash."

With the house surrounded by dense bush, the father of three quickly enacted the family's fire plan, still unsure about the severity of the blaze. "I told the kids to fill up buckets, I filled up the bathtub and got the fire pumps out and started watering everything down."

About 6pm Darren rang friend Bart Young who, in the midst of fighting off ember attacks further down the road, told the family to get out. "That was like, 'Go, go, go' after that," Darren said. "We didn't want to go in three cars, so we threw everything back in the house and got everyone and the dogs in my car."

In the last few moments the family spent at their house, the fire they had spent all day anticipating had set their street ablaze.

"Someone came running down the street swearing at the kids to get the hell out," Darren said. "The kids started yelling for me. I came back around to the front, kicked the boat off the car as quick as I could and we left. We had to drive through the flames. There was a caravan off the road and when I got down to Chum Creek there was one fire truck. I wound down the window and thought I would be telling him yesterday's news but his jaw just dropped, he had no idea of how bad things had got."

On returning to his home after the fire, the only thing Darren could do was find small consolations in the face of enormous devastation.

"It's a bit of a sob story but my dad died three years ago from a sudden heart attack and the only thing he really liked was his boat, fishing and stuff like that," Darren said. "The boat was still standing, with 80 litres of fuel in it and embers in it. I knew roughly where my wife's jewellery box was so I put my hand in and pulled it out. I pulled out her wedding ring and my dad's ring." Darren said community support had helped his family cope. "It's just amazing. We live up here to keep to ourselves, and it's a pity it's taken something like this but it makes you realise how lucky we are."

**Shaun Turton,** *Lilydale And Yarra Valley Leader*

# We didn't think we were going to live through this

## Paul and Christine Simmons and son Aiden, 12 months, St Andrews

Paul, Christine and Aiden sheltered in their house but as it started to collapse, they frantically began looking for another haven with their neighbours Colin and Sonia, and their two-year-old son Sam.

"It was like orange hail, I've never seen anything like it. There was smoke everywhere and windows smashing around us. I heard a huge crash and I knew the roof was falling in. Colin and Sonia went down to the creek. We walked up the track and got into a car. There were others alight. But I couldn't find the keys and pulled a burning branch out. I rolled the car away from a huge gas tank, which I could hear was hissing and it was going to explode. The steering wheel was locked and I could only get a few metres away. We got him [Aidan] into the car and he went to sleep. We worried he'd stopped breathing. We didn't think we were going to live through this."

**As told to Anthony Dowsley, *Herald Sun***

# There was no time to get out, it just happened so quickly

## Carole Webb, St Andrews

Carole's house had sprinklers on it and she frequently cleared the gutters. But when the fire struck, she found herself separated from husband, Marcel Smits, and unable to rescue him. The 56-year-old rang Carole to tell her he was concerned because he saw smoke. Carole tried in vain to reach her husband at their property.

"I was on my way home but I wasn't allowed into that area. We were at the police barrier trying to find out. It was horrendous. He was dying as he rang me. He was trapped and couldn't get out. It was like a nuclear wasteland. My son and I drove into that fire to try and get him out and found him, very sadly, deceased. We weren't stupid people, it was a double-brick home, we had sprinklers on the roof; we had cleared out the gutters. But people had no warning, no information. There was no time to get out, it just happened so quickly."

**As told to Milanda Rout, *The Australian***

# I sat in the car with my cat and watched everything I own burn

## Carolyn Kelmar, Steels Creek

Carolyn survived the inferno that raged through Steels Creek by cowering in her 4WD with her panic-stricken cat for four hours.

"It doesn't seem fair that I made it out and [my neighbour] didn't, he was such a lovely man. I put the cat in the car and was going to go back into the house to get more when I saw the flames and realised I had to go. When I saw the burning trees across the drive I thought, 'That's it. I'm too late, I've had it'. I rang my friend Glenda and said, 'I think I've had it. I sat in the car for four hours with my screaming cat and watched everything I own burn around me."

**As told to Megan McNaught, *Herald Sun***

# If anyone was going to survive that fire it was Val

## Jo Spears, friend of Val Cross, Steels Creek

Val, 90, was dragged to safety by Levi, a stray terrier no one else wanted. As the house exploded in flames Levi dragged her more than 100m into the farm dam.

Jo Spears: "The house completely caved in. I kept thinking, 'We've lost Val'. We were pretty much in mourning for her. I came in and rang her niece and told her to expect bad news. I asked some passing firefighters to look for her. Later, they came past and stopped at the front gate, I looked in the car and there was Val in the front seat. No one who knows her is surprised. If anyone was going to survive that fire it was Val."

As told to Megan McNaught, Herald Sun

# If you have a plan, stick to it

## Tracey Flowers, Reedy Creek

Tracey drove her children to safety before returning home and found herself, along with husband Paul, cut off from the outside world. As the fire circled their home, the couple fought the embers for seven hours and won.

"Every year, in October, the local CFA leave fliers attached to your gates. We'd been ready for a couple of weeks. We'd had the hottest couple of weeks and we live where we live. I chose to live here and if you do that you know that you're in a high-risk environment."

Two weeks ago the couple put a bag of emergency items next to their door. "Goggles, gloves and face masks, woollen jumpers," Tracey said. The couple put woollen blankets in the bathroom, in case their children Cheiron, 8, and Rhea, 3, were trapped by fire. Then last week they put fuel in the pump at their dam, ready to go, and put out the mops and buckets around the veranda. "We'd been out wetting everything down," she said. It came so quickly the door handles, even in gloves, were too hot to grab, and they had to run to the far side of their house to get cover inside. "If you have a plan, stick to it. Don't wait until the fire gets to your house and then think you might put the kids in the car and get out."

Paul Kent, The Daily Telegraph

**Romance: Firefighters Jim Cox and Lynne Murray are reunited**   Picture: David Caird

**Aloft: Shawn Stavang witnessed the horror from the skies**   Picture: Trevor Pinder

# I'm always nervous until I see him come in on the back of the truck

## Lynne Murray and Jim Cox, Healesville

The Healesville CFA volunteer husband and wife team hardly saw each other after Jim was called to tackle what he thought would be just another scrub fire the day before Black Saturday. For more than a week Jim battled raging blazes on frontlines across the state while wife Lynne co-ordinated communications from the CFA's Healesville headquarters. The couple who live together, work together and fight fires together, found the separation difficult, as well as the demands of caring for a young family of four during the worst natural disaster in our country's history. But after the toughest week of their lives, lady luck delivered the couple a pair of aces when CFA officials demanded they have a day off to spend Valentine's Day together.

"We were absolutely exhausted but you have to do it. Healesville is our home, our community. You can't just let it go. I worry about Jim when he goes out. It's different when we're fighting side by side, but when I'm back at the station I'm always nervous until I see him come in on the back of the truck. And if I don't see him, there's always someone shouting out at me to let me know he's back and safe. It always brings a big smile to my face. Despite everything it's a great lifestyle.

"We were ordered to stand down so we can have a break and spend some time together. We really didn't think we'd be spending Valentine's Day together and we certainly didn't want to take time away from the job. But they are insisting we need to refresh, so the rest will be really good. It's weird — even though we do everything together, we're always separated on these special days.

"We married on Australia Day so we could always do something special on our anniversary, and there has only been one so far that Jim hasn't been fighting fires."

**As told to Shannon Deery, *Herald Sun***

# He couldn't make it. Now I have nothing

## Petra Envers, St Andrews, lost her husband Arthur

# We sat outside and watched the mountains catch fire, one by one

## Edana Oakley, 15, Yarra Glen

Edana sought refuge in the basement of the Yarra Glen racecourse building along with her sister, Kara, and mother. She watched as the skies turned black and orange knowing the full impact of the fires on her neighbourhood would be devastating.

"My mum turned around so fast as if there was no tomorrow. The look she had in her eyes was frightening but yet again I could see bravery. I could see smoke ahead of us in the town. It was hard to breathe but we could bear it.

"As we turned to drive up another road in the distance I could see flames coming off trees and houses. What we could see wasn't just some small bushfire it was a nightmare, a living disaster. Nearly at Grandma's house we turned up her road. I saw a car that was on its back and in flames. People were stopping to see if the people inside were all right, but I guess it was just too late as there was no way they could have been saved. It was chaos outside.

"We drove on from the terrible scene with the car, heading up Steels Creek Rd and we saw this great big trail of fire jump over the mountain so fast you couldn't even blink. We were all so scared because Grandma's house was just five minutes away. We rocked up to her driveway and all we could see was just smoke and flames everywhere. We couldn't tell if her house was on fire or not. All we knew is that we had to get out of there before it would get any worse, with Kara in the back being brave but still very scared and me in the front crying. We had to go evacuate somewhere.

"We had got told to evacuate down the racecourse if there ever was a fire so we did. Me still crying and in shock and Kara getting more scared and Mum panicking but being really brave towards us kids, we went to the Yarra Glen racecourse. I rang my dad as we were on our way there because I needed to tell him what was going on. I couldn't speak clearly to him because of the horrifying shock I was in and me crying so I had to keep repeating it all. We parked the car in a hurry under a big shed, all got out and went to what looked like a basement [under the racecourse clubroom].

"When I got out of the car and started walking towards the door to get inside a massive gust of wind just swept past me, Kara and Mum. We finally got into the clubhouse and people were pretty calm but still feeling scared like us.

"It was very emotional seeing people crying and hugging one another. The conversations you would overhear about houses burning down or people and their pets stuck inside were devastating. Mum was starting to get even more worried as she couldn't reach Grandma or Grandpa. As it got darker we sat outside and just watched all the mountains catch fire, one by one, and the orange shadow where the fire was burning behind the mountain's shadow. It was really sad to even think that the fires that we were watching while we were safe were destroying people's houses – all those memories and photos they would have had – all gone.

"It is a tragedy what happened and I hope we don't have to relive this at all. I pray to God we don't and I am very sorry to those who have lost loved ones and their houses. I can't say to them I understand because I didn't lose my house or loved ones in the fire but I can see how it makes them feel and I feel very bad for that."

**Via email**

# We're just trying to work out where they're at so we don't drop down on them

## Shawn Stavang, Elvis helicopter pilot

Shawn provided hope for those desperately trying to defend their properties, dropping 90,000-litre water bombs. In his 16 years of fighting bushfires, the Californian has never seen devastation on this scale.

"It didn't matter how many aircraft you had. There were just too many fires. I don't know how they all got started, but they're just everywhere." During his two-hour stints in the air, he refilled Elvis's tanker about 30 times from nearby dams and ponds before heading back to the fire front.

"When the fires really kick off there's nothing you can do, plus they're so big you can't stop them. Just go to asset protection. I see people working with buckets trying to save their stuff. We're just trying to work out where they're at so we don't drop down on them."

**Anne Wright, *Herald Sun***

# We expect to find virtually nothing left. We find even less

A few days after Black Saturday, *The Australian*'s Gary Hughes had time to reflect on the horror scenes that ravaged his home.

White ash a few centimetres deep spread surprisingly evenly over a concrete floor slab. That's what your life, everything you and your family owns, everything that makes you what you are, every memory and every treasured possession, becomes after you turn a blast furnace loose on it.

A blast furnace so intense it melts window glass and sheets of roofing iron. A blast furnace so intense it shatters bricks. A blast furnace so intense a household fridge collapses in on itself like a crushed cardboard box.

Yesterday my family and I made the journey we had dreaded. A journey into a past and lost life that was destroyed in a matter of minutes late on Saturday afternoon, when the worst bushfire in Victoria's living memory swept over the hilltop at St Andrews, north of Melbourne, which we called home. My wife, Janice, and I had watched the house burning around us, before fleeing to the safety of our car and seeing it explode in flames.

We expect to find virtually nothing left. We find even less.

With our 24-year-old daughter, Kirsty, who thankfully wasn't home at the time, we drive as far as possible up the driveway of our 8ha property, then climb over the twisted, blackened trunks of fallen trees. What we find is recognisable as once being a house because part of the rear brick wall is still standing. It sways menacingly in the wind. To gain our bearings we look for familiar landmarks in the ash, like navigators plying uncharted waters.

We use the collapsed fridge as an initial compass point. From there we find the kitchen sink lying under debris. Then we pinpoint the loungeroom. Kirsty goes in search of her beloved dog, Gizmo, which on Saturday had run terrified into the boiling black, toxic smoke inside the house looking for sanctuary. On the day, in the split-second decision to escape the firestorm inside the house by running through the firestorm outside to reach our car and save ourselves, we had to abandon him. Only the younger pup, Missy, made it out with us. Gizmo's fate has haunted us since.

Now Kirsty finds his remains, huddled under what was once his favourite chair near a front window. She crouches and gently strokes the charred remains. We decide we will bury him there, on the property, where he so loved to run free. Then we find the collapsed cages that once held our two pet birds, the grumpy cockatoo, Bobby, and Zena the galah. They, too, we had to abandon in our flight for survival.

We start sifting through the ash in the hope of finding anything that might have survived. Within minutes, it becomes clear it is a waste of time. There is simply nothing.

Janice points to a corner of what was once our bedroom. "My engagement ring should be over there somewhere," she says. Then she shrugs. Like other survivors of this nightmare, we are quickly learning the futility of trying to cling to our past.

I walk around the house. The garage is a molten, jumbled mess.

My mountain bike, which I loved to ride though the adjoining bushland now reduced to blackened sticks, has all but disappeared, its alloy frame melted.

The cheeky rabbit that lived in a burrow under the compost heap had tried to make a run for it. He didn't get far. I find what's left of him halfway down the paddock. Even a rabbit in full flight couldn't outrun the fireball that rolled over us and our neighbours.

At the end of our exploration we take stock of what we now own. All that remains intact are the plastic pegs on the clothesline out the back. Maybe bushfires have a sense of humour.

A police team arrives. They ask us who we are and seem surprised when we tell them. They say we are still officially listed as missing, feared lying dead in the ashes under our feet. We assure them we are very much alive. They continue on their grim task, heading towards a nearby property where we know death came on Saturday.

Later we stop at the small St Andrews community centre, now packed with donated goods and relief workers. We find familiar faces, some we feared we might never see again. We share the joy of being alive. We also hear the names of others who didn't make it and those still missing. It is a long list.

**On the tiles: With hose, buckets and a dodgy right arm, Peter Thorneycroft helps fight the fire atop the National Park Hotel at Kinglake** Picture: Tanya Cadman

## Chapter 4

# Kinglake

- **Origin**
  A fire, intensified by mid-40C temperatures and hot winds, thunders into Kinglake, population 1483, at 4.30pm

- **Destruction**
  With some flames reaching 50m high, the radiant heat from the inferno can be felt 200m away

- **Toll**
  Trapped in their cars, at least six die on the roads as they attempt to flee Kinglake. In all, 37 are killed

t is time for a hero. As we know by now, so many fighting the fires are hopelessly outmatched. Ill-equipped and under-manned. Among those, Peter Thorneycroft would have to be example one. He is wearing thongs. He has no shirt, shorts that are suitable only for the job site, which in Peter's case is laying tiles, and a dicky right arm that ain't what it used to be. And against the biggest fires in Australia's history, he is armed with a garden hose.

Peter, 43, loses his home to a fire 11 years ago. He makes a promise to himself after that. He says he is going to rebuild and this time he is going to build a house that the devil himself cannot burn down. Maybe that makes his decision easier. Or maybe he is everything they say he is.

Either way, as the day breaks from stifling heat to full-blown fire emergency, and as the fire turns towards the hills, he leaves his house and goes looking for people. It is not hard to find them. Kinglake, like all these communities, is a small township. It has a population of 1483, a community politely referred to as treechangers. People grown tired of the city, choosing a simpler life. It is not quite accurate. Kinglake more closely resembles an extension of the mortgage-belt in the outer suburbs of most cities. Many live here because they cannot afford to raise a family closer to Melbourne's CBD. Also, whereas the majority of Australian workers in the cities nowadays are white-collar professionals, a majority over tradespeople, Kinglake is the opposite.

Yet they know something the rest of us don't. On weekends it swells as city folk venture out in search of a little peace and sanity, driving to Kinglake for picnics and lazy afternoons. It is the most vulnerable victim of the fires. Part of its beauty is the tall gums that hang over the roads, cathedral-like, which are wonderful, but dangerous fuel for the perfect fire. As well, both Kinglake's tankers have already been deployed to fight the fires in St Andrews. The town is defenceless. "There was nothing on the mountain," says Kinglake CFA chief captain Paul Hendrie, talking firetrucks. That is the code of the CFA. "You fight the fire you've got – you can't predict the predicament that will come."

Like almost every survivor will say in the days afterwards, the fire comes so quickly it gives them almost no time to respond. This explains, better than anything else, why so many fire plans fail to be enacted. Why so many people are killed in their cars. They simply didn't have the time. The fire comes so quickly there is no time for sirens, no fire warnings on radio or the CFA website. No time to get away. Remember, the last these people knew, the fire was going to miss them. Go right by. This also explains the large number of crashed cars seen in the aftermath.

As the fire rolls in and the smoke makes it near impossible to see, many residents realise this fire is something else, a fire that can't be fought, and far too late they try to flee.

Benjamin Banks is one of them. He is in his car when a wall

of flame hits so violently his car almost tips over. The heat melts his window. The liquefied glass drips on to his hand, runs over his car and on to his tyres. His tyres soon burn off, giving Benjamin no choice; he still drives, the car screeching along on steel rims, until in the blackness he smashes head-on into another car.

What do you do in times such as this? Benjamin opens the door and realises his ankle is broken. Limping, struggling to see, he finds his way into a nearby paddock and collapses. He survives.

But the smoke is causing chaos. Those fleeing on the road cannot see cars ahead of them. Inevitably, cars are smashing into each other. Alex and Anna Thomas have their three children bundled in the back and suffer the same fate. They crash and just like that they are out of their car and trying to flag down other cars making it past them. Four cars go past, a fifth. Anna holds no blame.

"Everyone was just doing what they could to survive," she says. She thinks she is going to die. Because she knows this awful truth she cannot look at her kids. Then two strangers, Karl and Jayne Amatnieks, pull over and hustle them into their car.

It really is that close. At least six die on the roads around Kinglake, trapped in their cars. Across town the service station explodes. Most houses and buildings are on fire.

And from this comes Peter, in shorts and thongs. Some 400 locals have gathered at the Kinglake National Park Hotel. They have squeezed the best of 200 cars around the hotel and none of them are safe. Trying their best to safeguard everyone, they gather about 20 women and children and pets and hustle them into the hotel's coolroom. Women and children first, like they say in the classics. They will not realise this until later, but it is one of the great escapes. Under different circumstances, the coolroom could well have become their tomb. Publican Craig Lovick, 28, and partner Sharon McCulloch,

40, have been hosing the pub down to safeguard it against the fires. There is panic everywhere. Before they see the fire they can hear it coming. More, the embers have started rushing in, the air is hot and the combustible gases that rush ahead of the fire front start lighting spot fires. That's when Peter, the tiler with the dodgy arm, climbs to the roof and takes over. People start handing up buckets, drawing water from a semi-trailer parked nearby. Hauling the buckets is killing him. In his right shoulder he has torn the biceps from the bone, an injury so severe it also severed the pectoral muscle from his chest. He is in constant pain. He cannot afford the surgery to have it fixed because he cannot afford the year off work to recuperate.

On the ground others have grabbed the hose and are watering around the hotel, keeping the embers from breaking into full-fledged flames. Up top with his buckets, Peter is dousing embers. He tosses an empty bucket down and drags up another. This is one of the keys to saving property from fires. Keeping the embers from taking hold. By now the fire is all around them. The houses across from the hotel explode. One. Two. Three. They all go. Cars in the car park explode. Thick smoke blocks the sun, prompting a thousand budding Hemingways to describe it as the day when "day turned into night".

Inside the coolroom, the power now lost, all they have for company is the noise from outside and their imaginations. It is a terrifying combination. There inside, Jarrod Drews, 8, is with his mum and his brother and sisters, and is absolutely terrified until someone gives him a torch. A big boy, he knows what to do with it. "I was making sure everyone was seeing," he says.

At some point up on the roof Peter is overwhelmed and calls his wife Jodie. "Everyone's dead. Everyone's dead," he says down the phone. Jodie has escaped the area and remains calm. "Shut up and do what you've got to do," she says. Peter reaches for more buckets. He does not know it in his own panic but he is more than just fighting the fires. The image of him up on the roof, a lone man doing what needs to be done, has a calming effect on those on the ground.

"When I saw him doing that … I felt safer," Tanya Cadman says. For some reason she takes his photo. It becomes an image – a man standing on the hotel's roof with the hellfires around him – that goes right around the world. The ordinary Australian, it seems, is a special man. It is one of many images we will remember. One of the better ones. There are so many faces. And of course, not all of them made it to the hotel.

Melanie Chambers is 22. Her sister Penelope is 21. When the fire hits Kinglake the sisters follow their family's fire plan to make it to a safe house in Kinglake.

They escape the intense heat at Jenny Clark's home. Inside are Jenny's son, Danny, and her grandchildren, Mackenzie "Macca" Buchanan, 15, and his young sister, Neeve, 9. Like the smiling faces of Melanie and Penelope, the image of Macca and Neeve are also among the first we associate with the bushfires.

They are the victims, the face of the tragedy. The lost futures we all mourn. In all, 37 will die in Kinglake. It is massive, incomprehensible. Nowhere is safe. And the thing is it is like this everywhere. For reasons we will never properly grasp, Kinglake, like Marysville, will soon be, and will remain, the face of the Victorian fires. Crippling loss, wonderful survival stories. When the fire has passed, and they all survive, Peter's bravery is there for everyone to see. They call him the angel of Kinglake. Peter has none of it.

"He calls himself a fallen angel, not an angel," Jodie jokes.

Better than that, when Peter goes home he finds his own house is still standing.

**Paul Kent**

**Slightly singed: Bessie McMahon, 83, and pet cockatoo Cocky** Picture: Craig Borrow

# None of us can even work out how we survived. It's a miracle

## Bessie McMahon, 83, Kinglake

Lifelong Kinglake resident Bessie knows a thing or two about fire, which helped save up to 35 people. Bessie fought burning embers with her hands and saved her house as flames licked a pergola. Dozens of neighbours — and Bessie's son Anthony, wife Marie and four children — sheltered on the 80ha farm she shared with husband Jim, 89. They even saved their 40 cows and pet bird, Cocky.

"I've been in Kinglake all my life and I know how to handle fire. When you've lived on a farm all of your life you have your little techniques. It came so rapidly. It came in every way. It sort of came over and it came down on top of us so hard. It was a case of just run.

"The fire did start up the carport. I managed to put the fire out. I'm fit, don't worry. For my age my doctor said I'm remarkably fit. To start with, I did it with my hands and my feet. It went in to flames but I put my hands under the whole burning bit of it. I went down deep enough to save my hands. I was very lucky.

"I did go down the paddock for about 90 minutes. [The cows] came right up here beside the house. People just started coming in. They were coming in from everywhere. I was giving them all water. None of us got hurt. I can't believe it. We had so many people here. They were just running in and out.

"We've got people in the house all the time. If anybody wanted a bed they've never been turned away. Some of those people have been back and thanked us for saving their lives. [One] just broke down and she said, 'Bessie, you saved my boys'. They want to know if they can come up visiting us every now and then to make sure we're all right. None of us can even work out how we survived. It's a miracle."

Casey Butler, of Mill Park, wrote to thank Bessie for saving her partner Cameron Dalloway, 26, and his brother Mitch Robinson, 17.

"To the McMahon family, thank you for keeping Cameron and Mitch safe. Thanks to you and your family we are lucky to have the boys safe and well. You all are true heroes. Thank you so much."

**Cheryl Critchley, *Herald Sun***

# The kids were saying: 'we're going to go to heaven together'

## Rod and Maryanne Mercuri, daughter Allyson, 11, and twin sons Dean and Kirk, 9, Kinglake

Houses on all four sides of the Mercuri home were destroyed. When the blaze hit, their house filled with smoke. They couldn't go inside, so they hid in the garage until that caught alight. They ran to a shed, but that went up too. As homes around them exploded, the Mercuris huddled outside and said goodbye and prepared to die together.

Maryanne: "The sound came before we'd seen it and then it started raining fire, literally raining. We only had a bucket and a shovel. I can't describe it. We were gonna die. We said our goodbyes. The kids were saying: 'We're going to go to heaven together'. Allyson was saying: 'Mum, we're all going to die, but at least we're all together'. I think God was on our side, honestly. That's all that I can say. We heard there are some deaths in that street and up on the corner. We can't complain. We can't complain about anything ever."

**As told to Terry Brown, *Herald Sun***

# No one could have stopped that

## Greg Rogers, 43, Kinglake

Standing in just a pair of rugby shorts and thongs, Greg stopped feeling scared as the fires raced towards his dream home, a 1930s guesthouse. Instead he got angry. And it probably saved his life.

"All of a sudden, the place just went black. From that time, I reckon I got to throw about one bucket of water. There are huge 40m pine trees on the back of my property. They were going up like they were dipped in petrol, and I'm standing there with a little bucket of water. You could see the flames and the embers just starting up little fires around our house. It just seemed like only seconds before there were massive flames all around the house.

"I could have been standing in my backyard with a bloody fire truck and hose ready to go, it wouldn't have been any good. You couldn't have stopped it. No one could have stopped that. For about 10 seconds, I got angry. I'm standing there looking at these massive flames. I got really mad instead of scared and I'm abusing them. Have you ever seen that T-shirt with the big eagle and the little mouse that says, 'Last act of defiance'? That was me."

Eventually, Greg jumped into his car and fled. "When I came down the road, if I had turned right instead of going left, I would have driven straight into it. I would have ended up like those piles of cars on the hill. Another 30 seconds and I was gone. It was just pure luck."

Greg intends to rebuild at Kinglake. "I want to live here more than ever. The community, these people are the best bunch of people you will ever meet on the planet, I am telling you now."

**Ewin Hannan, *The Australian***

# We have got our lives and we managed to get a few memories

## Bernie and Jan Hansell, Kinglake

Facing what they feared was imminent death, the Hansells made two heartbreaking phone calls to say farewell to their two adult children, Danielle and Adam, and then said goodbye to each other.

Recalled daughter Danielle: "Mum and Dad said, 'Listen, kids, we can't get out. Our house is on fire. We are going to die in here. We love you, we love you. Please pray for us'."

But that wasn't to be the end for these grandparents of four, who celebrated their 40th wedding just weeks before Black Saturday. With their roof already ablaze, and bushfires fast approaching on two fronts, Bernie and Jan decided to make another move. They ran outside, jumped into their car and dodged flames as they drove 2km into town. It was a courageous trip that proved life-saving – and allowed them to make another two unforgettable phone calls. "How our parents got out was a freak of nature," son Adam said. "It was unbelievable."

With the Australian flag still flying proudly above the rubble, Bernie and Jan returned to their home. Bernie, a Vietnam War veteran and retired federal police officer, also found his service medals and police badge had survived the inferno.

Bernie said: "We didn't have any water. I put out as much as I could with mops. When I could see we could not do anymore we went inside as you are instructed to do. We made two phone calls, to say goodbye to our children. And then we said goodbye to each other. I said goodbye to my darling wife, Jan. Nothing's worse than that, because my natural instinct is to protect her. We thought that was it.

But then we looked at each other and said, 'We have to take a chance'. So we jumped in the car and drove. We could not see two feet in front of us. We drove over power lines and trees … it was as hairy as anything. But somehow we managed to get into town.

"We have got our lives and we managed to get a few memories. That's all we have – lives and memories. That day was just so horrendous. All of your senses are just overloaded – the smells, the sights, the sounds."

**Evonne Barry, *Sunday Herald Sun***

# We didn't get far: a tree had fallen and vehicles had crashed into it

## Darren Wakelin, Kinglake

Like many people that day, Darren thought his neighbourhood was safe from the fires. Within minutes his home was alight and his attempt to escape the blaze in his car meant he had to risk his life.

"We knew there were fires; Wandong was ablaze, but it was a long way off, and the wind was keeping it away from us. The sky was full of smoke, but there was no mention of any direct threat to Kinglake, and after many phone calls to friends on and off the mountain, we decided it was safe to stay.

"The power went off to our home at about 5pm, nothing unusual, it happens up here all the time, so I decided to take a nap on the floor until it came back on. I was awoken at about 6.15pm by my wife and two children. The neighbours' house was on fire across the road. By the time I checked on him, our house was alight. Huge balls of fire were falling from the sky and the smoke was so thick you couldn't see more than a few feet in front of you. My wife Bronwyn and youngest son Samuel were now in our car; my oldest son Jordan had gathered photos from the house and was waiting for me to return. No more time to waste. Time to go. As we backed out of the driveway, the house and property was exploding around us, the realisation that we were now in serious trouble sent a wave of fear across us all. The road was busy, but many cars had either stopped or crashed due to poor visibility.

"By the time we reached the Kinglake Hotel at the top of our road, we could see we were driving into a wall of fire; to stay was not an option, so we drove towards the top of the ridge to try to outrun the fire. The heat and noise was incredible, the smoke was so thick, flames and burning debris were bouncing off the car – I couldn't see, so we turned around back towards Kinglake. We didn't get far: a tree had fallen across the road blocking it and vehicles had crashed into it.

"No choice now, we turned around again to head back up the ridge, but suddenly someone was banging on the side window of the car! Jordan opened the door and dragged him in – he was severely burned and in shock. I continued on driving back up towards the ridge using the car lights and following the centre white line. Many times I drove off the road, completely disorientated, but somehow managed to find it again. Huge burning trees were across the road; we drove through one big tree, which came up over the car bonnet and over the roof. All around we could see exploding houses, and wrecked burnt-out cars on the side of the road, it was like a bad dream.

"We managed to reach the top of the ridge opposite a large paddock which had just been burnt out and we decided to stop here to sit out the firestorm behind us. Four cars ahead of us had collided and were blocking the road – we couldn't get past them anyway.

"The wind was incredible, the car was moving sideways across the road – trees on the right-hand side of us were exploding. The four cars ahead of us caught on fire. We prayed that no one was inside. The firestorm passed after what seemed like an eternity and it suddenly went quiet – the wind had stopped.

"I cracked open the car window and felt that the air was now cool. We got out and sucked cool air into our lungs. We noticed a LandCruiser had managed to drive into the paddock and park next to a home that was still standing – they waved to us and we drove into the paddock with them. It was now about 7pm, pitch black, the air was still thick with smoke – but it was cooler and we felt that we were now in a safe place. As time passed a few other cars and people arrived from the direction of Kinglake West. We all banded together to protect the empty house, put out surrounding spot fires and ensure that those who were injured were stable and made comfortable. There was an incredible sense of togetherness and caring, something that only those present will ever understand."

**Via email**

# I couldn't leave five people lying there waiting to die

## Karl Amatnieks, 56, Kinglake

With the inferno just minutes from their home, Karl and wife Jayne were driving out of Kinglake when they saw a family standing near a car. They pulled them to safety but, as they went to leave, Karl spotted a man in another car. He knew there was nothing he could do.

"As we got to the bottom of the hill we came across this couple with three kids who were stranded. They were stuck on the side of the road after slamming into the back of another car. It was horrific. It was obvious they had crashed because of the smoke. You couldn't see five steps in front of you. My wife got out of the car and called them to get in with us. I couldn't get out as I was sitting there with my foot on the brake. I wanted to get out of there as quick as possible. But I just couldn't leave five people lying there waiting to die – it's that simple. I'm not a hero. Anyone in the same situation would have done the same thing ... they were in trouble and they needed help."

**As told to Shannon Deery, *Herald Sun***

# How do you thank someone who saved your life?

## Alex and Anna Thomas, Kinglake

Alex and Anna and their three young children slammed into another vehicle, trying to navigate their way to safety while virtually blinded by smoke. Eventually, Karl and Jayne Amatnieks stopped, pulled the family into their car and drove them to a nearby house where others were taking refuge.

"We couldn't see where we were driving. It was pitch black and smoky. All we knew was that we were driving into fire. We couldn't move. We were too terrified of being hit by a tree or walking into fire.

"It was an inferno and we were right in the middle of it. We tried to flag down some cars, and I don't blame the four or five that went past, but they just kept going. Everyone was just doing what they could to survive. We thought we were going to die. We couldn't look at the kids. We just kept thinking of them burning to death and couldn't stand imagining them dying that way.

"There were constant explosions, things blowing up in front of us, people screaming. It was worse than a war zone, it was absolutely horrific. We were convinced we were all going to die. There was fire everywhere we looked. But the Amatnieks were great in helping us stay positive.

"We shouldn't be here and if it wasn't for Karl and Jayne, we wouldn't be. How do you thank someone who saved your life? You can't. If we had $10 million we'd give it to them but we can't, we have nothing. But they are our heroes and we can't say thank you enough."

**As told to Shannon Deery, *Herald Sun***

# I tried to drive but there were no tyres. I could feel steel on steel

## Benjamin Banks, 25, Kinglake

Everything that could go wrong did go wrong when Benjamin tried to escape. It was a head-on car crash with a tree that saved his life.

"I've got a weatherboard house and started to get scared so I said to [my cousin] Dean it was time to go. I've faced fire before but nothing as intense as this. We knew nothing about this fire. It hit so fast we didn't know. I knew I had to save my cousin. I wanted to save him before me. I didn't realise how intense it was and didn't realise how thick the fire had gotten.

"Then this big whirlybird tornado of flame hit us. I remember looking up at it and it was as high as the trees. I tried to drive again but there were no tyres left. I could feel steel on steel and could hear the steel rims grinding on the road and I was stuck on this tree. But I think that [accident] was my saving grace because if it had not hit me we would have burned to death in the car.

**Cheese and kisses:
Survivor Debbie
Bisnella gets a kiss
from boyfriend
Adam Zampelis
at Whittlesea
Community Centre**
Picture: John Grainger

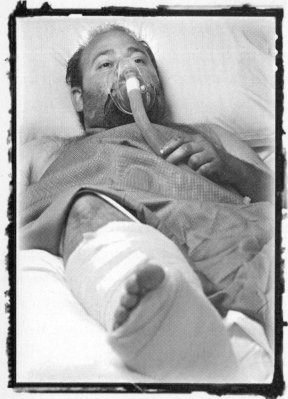

**Lucky break: Even
though he broke his
ankle after crashing
his car, Benjamin
Banks was eventually
dragged to safety**
Picture: Scott Chris

"I pushed Dean out of the car and told him to get in the big paddock. He ran through the nature strip on fire to get to the paddock, which had already been burned. I was stuck in the car. I tried to grab my leg and pull it out from under the pedals but it was stuck.

"I heard a voice come back – the plumber who lives around corner from me. He came back and opened the door and tried to drag me out of the car. Somehow he grabbed the pedals and got me out of the car but I couldn't stand up. I couldn't feel any pain. He had his arm around me and I tried to hobble across the fire. Then we got to a barbed wire fence and I put my right leg over but couldn't put pressure on it. I started falling on the barbed wire and said, "Just drag me over the fence, just get me over the fence'.

"We ran into the centre of the paddock and lay there and held each other trying to talk and cheer each other up. We saw a tractor up in a clearing so he went for the tractor but when he got up to it and tried to start it people came out who had been sheltering in a cool room in their shed. They came down in a car to get us. We went into the cool room but it was hot and smoky so we went into the house.

"I was sitting there and they ran back in to say, 'We've got to get out of the house, the house is on fire'. I was sitting outside on a wheelie bin for ages and the house was on fire in the roof. They managed to put the fire out. I went back inside and lay down on a mattress. I remember thinking how much I appreciate what they are doing for me. I was there for a while and then I remember starting to doze off.

"Then two guys walked up from CFA and said, 'We're here to get you'. They picked me up and saved me. That's when I felt huge relief. In less than 10 minutes the whole of Kinglake was on fire. The whole thing was like a movie that keeps playing over and over."

**As told to Michelle Pountney, *Herald Sun***

# I'm slapping the back of her head, trying to put it out

## Debbie Bisnella, Kinglake

*Debbie was returning to Kinglake with her boyfriend Adam Zampelis when fires started burning on each side of the road. A fireball hit them and sent flames shooting through the open windows of her car.*

"We did a U-turn and came back down the hill. And then another fireball came across the road." It might have been all right had the airconditioning in their car been working. But it wasn't, so Debbie had her window down because she was hot. When the fireball engulfed their car, the flames shot through her window. In a moment, her face was scorched and her hair was on fire. Her entire head bore the full brunt of the flames. "I'm slapping the back of her head, trying to put it out," Adam said. "It was scary." In an instant Debbie had wound her window up as Adam was smothering the flame torching her hair. They flattened the accelerator and punched through the flames until they got to the bottom of their road and safety.

**Paul Kent,** *The Daily Telegraph*

# Even breathing became torture

*Mike Edmonds from the* Herald Sun *(and also a CFA volunteer) was one of the first reporters on the scene in the wake of the Kinglake fires.*

We knew there were bodies in the cars, people who gambled against the odds and lost. Driving past on the back of the CFA's Wattle Glen tanker 2 there was no time to think of Kinglake's dead. We were concerned for the living, to give them some possibility of returning to a scarred but acceptable life. For 18 hours, Wattle Glen tanker 2 drove from fill-point to fire front, each time passing those coffin-cars. Some were hard up against trees, others in ditches, some piled up on top of each other. But all were destroyed, along with the people to whom they briefly offered a chance of escape.

Tanker 2 left the fire station about lunchtime on that Saturday, the crew geared up and rolling minutes after the siren began wailing over the valley. It was almost a local call-out, up the road to Panton Hill, alight in the searing 48C day with strong northerlies.

Tanker 2 was caught on top of a ridge when the wind change came through. While we had warning, we weren't prepared for its intensity. Firefighters in full battle gear were literally blown over. The only thing to do was take shelter behind the truck as a hail of superheated stones, dust and burning bits and pieces was hurled against us. Fire helmets barely hung on by their chin-straps, and our protective yellow jackets were blown open, leaving cotton T-shirts as the only skin protection for a few minutes. Our crew leader had the protective lens of his goggles blown out by the hellish wind. We had no time to begin flash-over precautions, used to keep tanker crews alive when a moving fire "flashes over" them and their truck.

The simple act of breathing became torture because of the temperature of the wind blast, which picked up speed and heat as it raced over paddocks and forests. The shock was quickly put on the backburner as we put out the spot fires around our tanker; our lifeline and the lifeline for the residents who'd also sought shelter in it.

Then came the message to leave, to head for Kinglake. The thought went through the collective mind of the crew that Panton Hill was OK. But Kinglake was taking us a bit far from protecting our own.

At Kinglake we lost a crew member. The heat and smoke took

their toll. Every time tanker 2 returned to Kinglake I was reminded of Ash Wednesday. The Victorian fires of '09 are already the most vicious, hottest and fastest-moving fires I have seen. Kinglake reminded me of Cockatoo on Ash Wednesday, on a more savage scale. I walked into the main street of the Dandenongs village less than half an hour after a fireball had gone through. One side was largely untouched, the other was alight, and houses all around were going up for no reason other than the flames didn't choose their neighbour.

In Kinglake there were three of four businesses intact on one side of the street. The other side of the business centre, and almost every home in the surrounding community had been vaporised. The only reminder this was a thriving community was the LPG pump at what used to be the service station. The gas was cooking off, but nobody felt like putting it out. It couldn't do any damage. And, with no electricity in the town, it acted as a beacon, giving people a sense of place, and an overwhelming sense of powerlessness.

# Hang on, if this pub goes up they're all going to get burned

## Peter and Jodie Thorneycroft, Kinglake

Peter, 43, helped save the Kinglake National Park Hotel after climbing on to the roof in shorts and thongs as 20 women and children sheltered in its cool room. Peter doused deadly embers with a hose and buckets of water for two hours.

Peter: "It was like a cyclone, like a tornado. The ground was constantly shaking. It was absolutely deafening. The whole pub was full of smoke. I said: 'Hang on a minute. If this pub goes up they're all going to get burned'. I'll never forget the shock on their faces. No one knew what to do. I was using my torch to get up on the roof. It was just complete darkness. I couldn't see because it was just black. When I got up there, there were embers above where the cool room is. It was like hell on earth. I never panic at all and I was s.....ing myself. I was just up there to make sure it didn't go.

"I just got to work around the roof putting all the fires out, putting buckets of water through the vents. You just do it. You don't even think about it. You just live on survival mode. Five minutes was like five hours. It was the perfect storm. There's no thanks to be had. There's no one who's heroic, you just do it. No one went out of their way because they wanted to be a hero. Everyone's forgotten about their own lives; they just did what they did. The real heroes are the insurance companies just paying out ... the banks. They're actually keeping us going. I lost really close friends. As bad as it is, the more I do here the less I've got to think about it. I haven't had time to think about anything else. If you just sit there at home ... just thinking about it you're going to go crazy. We just want to get this town back in order. The locals need to be active. We know what has to be done. All we need is obviously funding and some help in different areas. A lot of people are attached to this mountain. They just want to stay, they just want to help."

Jodie: "I kept in constant [phone] contact with him the whole time because he kept losing the plot. Peter reckons there were probably about 200 cars packed like sardines around the pub. Everyone was just in hysterics. He just kept going, 'Everyone's dead, everyone's dead', and I just said, 'Shut up and do what you've got to do'. Everyone kept saying [to him], 'Put a shirt on'. I said, 'Find him one'!"

**As told to Cheryl Critchley, *Herald Sun***

# It was like a massive oxy torch

## Richard Woolley, 39, Yarrambat

> Richard helped save a house with two people inside it before clearing
> the streets of Kinglake in his Bobcat so emergency services could
> enter the area. His home was untouched so the bricklayer spent
> 12-hour days helping the clean-up.

"The fire was travelling at 150km/h, easy. We drove through it, me and Adam [a friend]. Me and Adam got there [Adam's house] and sort of ran in ... and we helped put it out. When we got there the fire brigade didn't know they were in there; they'd actually abandoned the place. Adam's wife was in the fire truck crying. She thought they were dead in the house. They were just amazed that we saved the house. No one could get in there until we [Peter and I] cleaned the road. We went up the day of the fire. First thing in the morning we went back into Strathewen. They've lost about 20 per cent of their population. Right in the heart of Strathewen three blokes for two hours battled the fires by themselves. It's just amazing that they saved their houses. They looked over at each other's houses and they thought they were dead. They all came out of it unscathed. [But] they've all lost many friends.

"Because I haven't got any kids ... I wouldn't understand what it's like to lose all the family. I couldn't imagine what it would be like. When you're up there it's the last thing on your mind. All you're trying to do is help. I really reckon the world's got to see the extent of this fire. It was as big as 10 Hiroshimas. It was like a massive oxy torch. Everyone was a hero. I don't mind helping people. I was more than happy to do it."

**As told to Cheryl Critchley, *Herald Sun***

# I couldn't get to the water so I just grabbed a carton of Pepsi and started spraying the flames

## Peter Crook, 67, Kinglake

Pete helped put out the flames attacking his family home with cans of soft drink. The St Peter's church warden protected his wife from the flames by pulling tops off Pepsi Max cans he had in the house to get through flames to his water supply. It was the second time Peter and wife Wendy have cheated death, after losing their home in the Northern Territory during Cyclone Tracy.

"After the firestorm was over, the house was on fire and the vehicles were burnt. I lost my 4WD and the shed was burning and the generator, too. I thought if I don't get the fire under control, we are going to go up.

"I couldn't get to the water tanks so I just grabbed a carton of Pepsi Max because it's all I had. I pulled the tops off the cans and started spraying them, just throwing the stuff all over the fence. I decided I could do better by putting them upside down on the posts and just letting it come out and go down the posts.

"I think back to when I was in the navy and I thought my career training had helped me out. I used about 30 cans. Then I found some lemonade lying around that we had left over from Christmas. I don't drink so it wasn't a carton of beer. [Pepsi's] my favourite drink. I had a few [sips] as we were going – it was pretty hot! I would usually go through about a carton a week."

**As told to Matt Johnston, *Herald Sun***

# It scorched everything. I had a couple of buckets and just a mop

## Michael Rogers, Kinglake

Armed with two cheap buckets and a mop, he refused to let the fire take his house. As flames licked at his fence and his neighbours' houses disintegrated, Michael fought to save his home.

"[The fire] just hit so fast and so quickly, from two sides where I was. It scorched everything. I had a couple of buckets without handles, they cost 89 cents from Bunnings, and just a mop, and it was like someone had switched on a movie.

"I went out the front and there was a guy standing there naked with just a sheet on him and I stood next to him and I said, 'No way, I'm not going to be like that', and I went back in. I saw the two houses next to me on fire. There was nothing I could do about my neighbours' houses. Half of my wood shed had burned down. I could only stop some of it. The wind hit the place so hard coming up from St Andrews. There's gas bottles lying in paddocks that came from the gas station 150m away.

"I'm an asthmatic. People turned up and my missus went to the main street and got some guys to come back and try to drag me out. I just kept bucketing and bucketing.

"My story's just small compared to some of the people around here. There's no one left around here, it's all rubble. Everyone banded together. There were people doing things streets back from me. We just want to stick together [now]. All I need is some plastic piping to fix my toilet and a generator and I'll feel normal again."

**As told to Matt Johnston, *Herald Sun***

# I got a call to say there was a fire burning down the hill. Ten minutes later, there is this roar

Five families saved from the Kinglake flames by their united front.

How do you save your life, and those of your children, friends and pets, when the whole mountain is burning? You join forces with your neighbours. You stand united. You use your ingenuity. You don't give in. It's because of these things that five families, including nine children, two sets of grandparents and six dogs, are alive today. They had a fire plan that involved getting together in just one house in Kinglake – a timber house – and defending it with all their might.

They ran out of power and, at one stage, had no access to water, but never mind: they had dry ginger ale, and shampoo, and mineral water, and all of that could go into the pump, to be sprayed on the embers. They had a fire hose and a pair of boots. They had mops and buckets.

Their other homes were lost – most of them have, in fact, lost everything. But never mind, they have their lives. The house that survived stands at Robertson Rd, Kinglake. It's a two-storey place owned by Anthony Chrystie, who lives on the ground floor with his son, Brodie. On the top floor lives Lynne Watts, with her four sons, Leigham, 4, Lachlan, 6, Jayden, 8, and Dylan, 13.

Next door, there are the grandparents: Marie and Eric Watts. Down the road, there is a life-long friend of the family, Ron Parsonage. He's got five children; he raised all of them himself, after his wife left when the youngest was two. Ron's son Paul is there, with his girlfriend, Charlene, and their daughter, Chantelle, 18 months. They don't drive, so when it came time to gather at Anthony's house, they had to hoof it through the smoke.

Then there is Jess McDonald and boyfriend Brett Walker. There's Nick Chrystie, who is Anthony's brother, and his girlfriend, Alaina, her three kids – Max, 3, Luke, 6, and Jack, 8 – and her father, Graham. Then there is Ricky Watts, who is Lynette's brother, and his girlfriend, Lauren, who has a newborn baby, Jazmine. Add to that six beloved pets: staffy Bridey, two labs Molly and Gemma, a long-haired thing called Harvey, the neighbour's staffy, Blade, and a Jack Russell, Belle. Add to that one ferocious fire.

Ron says he was working at the King Ross chicken farm until about 5pm on Saturday. His son, Paul, his girlfriend, and their daughter were at home. When he heard that a fire was coming, he went to get them, since none can drive. He packed up a few precious things – his parents' ashes and his father's war medals – opened the front door, and thought: "'I'm going to lose the house.' We didn't have any warning. I got a call to say there was a fire burning down the hill. Ten minutes later, there is this roar." He raced down the hill to the timber house.

Meanwhile, Graham McKee and his daughter, Alaina, were activating their fire plan on Bald Spur Rd. Alaina's mother got her three children off the mountain. Alaina and her father stayed to fight, but when it became clear their house, too, was lost, they ran down to the timber house.

"You have no idea how fast it came," Graham said. "I fell over, I was running so fast. I was just running and stumbling." He now has nothing – "not a thing" – but his own life, and that of his wife, Coral, and their children.

"We'd all made this plan that this house was the safest," Lynne Watts said. "It was pretty chaotic with all the kids and the dogs. People just came as soon as they saw they were losing their own homes. There were eight guys outside at one point, just stamping on embers and hosing things down. It was pitch black and terrifying, but we stuck to the plan."

**Caroline Overington,** *The Australian*

# It was like a snowstorm of red embers. It felt like I was playing hopscotch at one stage to miss them all

## Bill and Sherrill Carta, Kinglake

Bill, 52, and Sherrill, 56, each thought the other might be dead until they met at Melbourne's Alfred Hospital about six hours after the Kinglake fire, each suffering serious burns. Bill arrived by helicopter and Sherrill by road ambulance. Bill tried to escape the fires on his motorbike and Sherrill in the car but they became separated as fire raged through their street. Bill sheltered in strangers' cars and houses while Sherrill made it to the CFA building on foot.

Sherrill: "I wanted to do a U-turn but … a tree had fallen on the road and blocked the road and the tree was burning. You couldn't see anything. I put the car in reverse and it went into a culvert. You've probably seen my car on the telly. It's the green station wagon sitting in the culvert. I didn't know which way to go. I had my two dogs and I didn't know what happened to Bill. I climbed over a tree that was burning and lost my shoes. It was like a snowstorm of red embers. It felt like I was playing hopscotch at one stage to miss them all. The

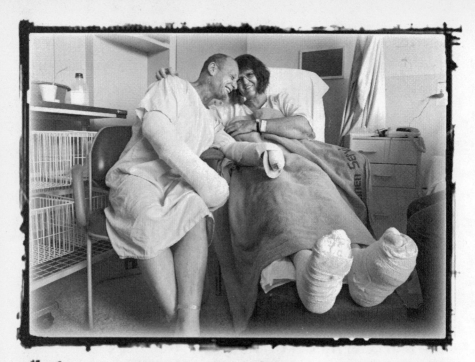

**Together again: Bill and Sherrill Carta were reunited at the Alfred Hospital after becoming separated by the Kinglake blaze**
Picture: David Geraghty

**Baptism of fire: CFA volunteer Kelly Johnson, 17, is back doing Year 12 at Mt Lilydale Mercy College, after fighting the fires at Kinglake**
Picture: Nicole Garmston

wind was really loud and the flames were really hot. I thought I'd lost him [Bill]. I was just really numb … totally shocked. I just couldn't get past the thought that he'd gone and my dogs were gone and the house was gone. I thought at that stage my car was gone as well. Then I just kept walking into Kinglake and somebody finally came and picked me up. Everybody in the CFA shed there … was just brilliant. You realise the value of the people around you. Your house doesn't really matter. [Being reunited with Bill] was great. I could tell him by his big toe, because it looked like the only piece that wasn't burnt at the time."

Bill: "[Once] we left our house and hit the road we realised that our lives were in serious danger. We couldn't get down to the end of the street without seeing fires everywhere. The fire was so thick that you couldn't see 10 feet in front of you. It's just mind-blowing … totally surreal. I was on a motorbike. The tree that Sherrill talked about fell in front of me. We got separated very quickly, very easily, and then just totally disoriented and had to scramble to find our way out of the fire as best we could. Sherrill wound up somewhere else. I wound up diving into somebody else's car and we all wound up just sort of burrowing into the cars … as the fire was going over us. When I found that both her and the dogs were out of the car I realised that she must have been well enough to get out of the car. Then of course my worry was what happened to her after she left the car. These were the streets we'd known for many years and we hadn't seen them in this kind of condition before. It was quite a shock. We didn't realise both of us were still breathing until we got to the hospital. I called out, 'Sherrill!' It was a fantastic moment."

**As told to Cheryl Critchley, _Herald Sun_**

# Normally it comes along the ground but this thing came in the sky and on the trees

## Jason Lynn, 35, Kinglake

With his family sheltering in Yea, Jason stayed behind to protect his western red cedar house. But when he saw the flames crashing through the trees Jason knew he was in for the fight of his life. As the bushfire raged around him, the father of two clung to life on the muddy banks of his dam and used what he thought was his last breath to tell his wife and children that he loved them.

"You do fire guard meetings and they show you what it [fire] is like – it comes along the ground, but this thing just came in the sky and on the trees. When I was in the fire I thought, 'This is just like hell'. I burnt my hands, even with gloves, opening up the door to get in the shed.

"I got a ladder and climbed up [into the shed roof] with buckets of water. The fire was all around and I was trying to put that out but the shed caught on fire from inside. It just exploded. I hung on to the spouting and it fell down and I collapsed on the ground. I just got to that point when you are running and you can't run any more."

Crawling on his hands and knees Jason felt his way to the dam at the back of his property and lay in the mud. He kept his mobile phone pressed against his head as he spoke to local minister Shane Lepp who prayed for him and tried to keep him conscious. "There was just no air. It was like you were breathing vapour. I thought, I don't know how much longer I can breathe. I was sort of delirious. They were trying to tell me stuff [on the phone] and I just said, 'Just listen to me. Tell my wife and my kids that I love them. I can't hang on much longer'. The next thing I heard someone say, 'I found someone down here'. I just remember feeling their glove on my face." The gloved hand belonged to one of the hundreds of firefighters who risked their lives to save residents like Jason.

**Gareth Trickey, *Herald Sun***

# I tried to cope with the rain of embers outside, my head covered in a wet towel

## Robert Deeble, Kinglake

Robert was at a friend's house when fires roared into Kinglake. He helped them find safety in the town before racing back home to his wife and children, who were sheltering under blankets in their home.

"In town there was total mayhem with cars going everywhere and crashing. My wife Lisa was at home alone with our three children and my only thought was to get there as fast as possible and I took the instant decision to drive through the mass of flames, not knowing if the road was actually clear. Fire engulfed the whole road between the township and the turn-off into the bottom of our estate at Thomson Lane. Lisa had the children in the middle of the house covered with wet blankets, a kitchen fire blanket etc., and was attempting to keep the heavy smoke out with wet towels but without success. While trying to care for the children and the house, Lisa kept looking out the window for me and finally saw my car headlights coming at great speed through the smoke and the car screeching to a halt in the front yard. Lisa stayed inside the house with the children while I tried to cope with the rain of embers outside, my head covered in a wet towel. After about an hour when I felt my family and home were relatively safe, I went around other houses in the estate putting out grass fires and disconnecting and removing gas bottles away from houses. My greatest concern now is how our community will come to terms with the terrible loss of life and property and the psychological impact on our young children and ourselves."

**Via email**

# My dad and me are fire rangers and we don't run away

## Jayden Henry, 5, Kinglake

Jayden was playing in his room when the fireball surged towards their home. His dad Paul threw Jayden into the car and they pulled up to another vehicle that had been stopped by a burning tree. Inside was a family, including two children – all dead. One child was Jayden's friend. The Henrys survived after parking their car near a paddock in the centre of Kinglake.

"It was pitch black in the middle of the day and when we got to the top of the street there were all these houses ablaze. There were trees and branches coming down on the road, it was just crazy. Jayden told a counsellor: 'My dad and me are fire rangers and we don't run away from our problems.' I was just gobsmacked. He's my hero at the moment."

**As told to John Masanauskas,** *Herald Sun*

# I actually said to my captain: I don't want to die

## Kelly Johnson, 17, Kinglake

Black Saturday was Kelly's first fire as a CFA volunteer. The Year 12 student helped save several hundred people sheltering in the Kinglake CFA shed. With three other volunteers, including Phil Petschel, she hosed the shed's exterior for about an hour to prevent embers setting it on fire. Nearby, tradie Peter Thorneycroft did the same with buckets on the top of the National Park Hotel.

"I was hoping I was just going to get a little one [fire] to start me off. I joined when I was 16. I've been with them for just over a year. I just thought it would be good to do my bit. When I got up there they made us put on our gear. We were trying to put the fire out because it came towards the pub. I just had a hose. Usually you'd get someone behind you [helping]. I actually said to my captain, 'I don't want to die'. My captain grabbed me and said, 'I promise I won't let anything bad happen to you'.

"Without Phil I don't know what I could have stuffed up. He was just so calm. He was out on the hose with no gear, no gas mask, no helmet or anything, just a shirt and pants, and it was so hot. I actually got paged at nine o'clock saying there was a fire at my home.

"At about four o'clock in the morning we finally got a truck around to my house and my parents had finally got it under control. After that, nothing's ever going to be this bad. I definitely want to keep doing it."

**As told to Cheryl Critchley, *Herald Sun***

# Accelerating down a track in the dark and smoke, our driver's run of miraculous luck ran out

## Dean Leishman, CFA volunteer, North Warrandyte

Trapped in his fire truck as the Black Saturday fires raged outside, Dean had a unique view of the fire's ugly face and the calm heroism of his fellow CFA volunteers.

**9.27am:** Weather observations, temperature 34C.

**9.30am:** My mindset with regard to fires in our area is pretty straightforward. I will probably be on the back of a firetruck, so I'm unlikely to be around if our house was ever under threat so, in reality, our place would be empty and undefended. I start my fire pump, check the sprinklers, put out water buckets around the house, run the garden bed sprinklers and pull out mops.

**11.35am:** Temperature 39C.

**1.02pm:** My pager goes off. Smoke plumes are sighted in the vicinity of Bellbird Lane, which is about 1km from my house. I race up to the station to confirm the situation. It's a false alarm. There is no risk but my danger radar is pinging and I'm really uncomfortable.

**1.16pm:** Smoke reported at Kangaroo Ground from Kilmore. Temp 41C. Humidity still falling, temp still rising, wind picking up. Not good.

**1.40pm:** I'm going to be best served by being at the station, at least there I can keep abreast of the fire radio traffic and be ready to respond locally if needed. A country fire station on a bad fire day is a strange place to be, there is a real camaraderie among the team and there is always a sense of fun but balanced by the seriousness of the situation.

**2pm–3pm:** Big clouds of smoke are coming up from the north. Things are turning more serious in the shed as people start to pay close attention to the radio, their pagers and the northern sky.

**4pm:** 1364 Strike Team dispatched.

**4.15pm:** Huge smoke sightings. Things are obviously getting serious now, radio traffic has stepped up. Reports from Kilmore and Strathewen sound dire but as yet there is no reported loss of life. The fires are still referred to in vague terms like "Grass and scrub fire". Going, not yet under control, spotting activity and while I do know better there wasn't a sense yet of the level of destruction to come.

**5.09pm:** First call to Marshalls Rd. Our pagers go off to a call in Marshalls Rd, St Andrews, we responded along with trucks from Kangaroo Ground, Lilydale and Wonga Park, of these brigades KG and ours are the closest to the fire, Wonga Park and Lilydale a little further out and will take longer to get to St Andrews, we proceed Code 1 [full lights and sirens].

**5.25pm:** Call to Wild Dog Creek. Coming in Panton Hill (before St Andrews) we could see the huge dark clouds of smoke building, while this looked big it still hadn't taken on that "get the f..... out of Dodge" proportion in our minds. We could see the smoke but did not have an understanding of the extreme level of fire activity. The pagers dropped again, this time to Wild Dog Creek Rd where it was reported that a house was surrounded by fire. This ratchets up the stress level considerably because the core purpose of the CFA is to protect the population and private property.

**5.45pm:** Assembly at St Andrews. We have no intelligence beyond the fact that there is a big fire threatening houses and people. Cars come flying down the Kinglake road and drivers are telling us that the fire is in Wild Dog Creek Rd.

**6.03pm:** Another call from Wild Dog Creek: house surrounded. The pagers go off again, another call for the house surrounded by fire and the tension builds because we know there are likely people trapped and we are meant to be helping them. We jump in the truck and move off behind the Panton Hills tanker, our brief instruction is to work up the Kinglake road and see if it is possible to help. Finally we come face to face with the fire, or at least what we thought was the main fire, at this point we were still in relatively clear air, minimal smoke. We could see very high leaping flames up to about 20m and we assumed that this was the front.

6.17pm: Another call from Wild Dog Creek: people trapped. We started into the smoke and fire, driving northeast up the Kinglake road, watching for anyone needing help but light was slowly fading and the smoke was cutting down visibility. Trees were down over the road and the bush along the road was fully involved by the fire. The radiant heat punching through the window was immense. We came upon a house that we could access, the smoke and flame had cleared a little and we could see again. It was partially filled with smoke and we performed a quick primary search and it was obvious that there was nobody home, the occupants had decided to leave. A little further up the road and the smoke was thickening and it was getting harder to see, the flames were very close now and trees along the road were burning. I cannot convey how terrible the conditions were; the howling wind was picking up embers, ash and dirt.

6.23pm: Another call from Wild Dog Creek: people trapped. By this time we knew that we were in serious trouble, the light had faded to a very dark grey. We could not see the sides of the road and the driver had perhaps one or two metres of visibility of the central white line. The pager was going again but at this point we had moved into survival mode and were just trying to get out of danger to allow us to reassess. We had no real understanding that we had driven into a

10km-wide firefront. At first small and then progressively larger trees appeared blocking the road, some intact, some smouldering, some burning, but we ploughed on up the hill smashing through and over any trees that were in our way. At this point it was dark, there was no daylight, despite it being 6.30pm on a summer evening, all we could see were the flames of the fire coming up the side of the hill and across the road. By this point in time we had all the blankets out and were using them to block the radiant heat coming through the windows. Ember attack was constant; flames running up the hill attacked my side of the truck.

7.15pm: Time gets pretty rubbery here. We cleared the ridge line. There is still a huge amount of fire but things are marginally calmer for a couple of seconds. Our driver suggests, "We might just be in a bit of trouble" and that "it could be a good time for a PAN [Possible Assistance Needed]", a radio call to the controlling agency that an appliance is in trouble and may need assistance extricating itself from danger. The fire activity picks up again. We are not through this by any length and it is obvious that we are stuck in the middle of a huge disaster. We have no choice but to keep moving and seek refuge. At one point there is a loud slap across the front of the truck and the sound of something heavy dragging across the cabin. I've looked out my side window and my mind has registered power lines snaking across my window. We drove like that for 100m or so pulling the power cable across the cabin until it finally works free.

Soon after, two cars appeared out of nowhere. I don't exaggerate. It is pitch black with smoke and you cannot see anything except for flames. Visibility is still a metre or two at best.

The first car just missed us and we hit the second car. It moved off and seemed to go around us, looking to drive back down the hill towards St Andrews, the direction we had come from. There was nothing we could do to stop them as they were in full flight. The crash has disoriented us and we picked a patch through tree rubble and smoke that we thought was a straight road. All around us things were burning, trees shooting flame and embers blasting at the truck.

Our road turned into a dirt track and we realised that we had turned off our path. There was nothing for it but to turn around and try to retrace our path to the bitumen. Accelerating down a track in the dark and smoke, our driver's run of miraculous luck ran out and we jumped a ditch and ran off the road into some bushes. We couldn't get out of the cabin because of the fire and the radiant heat. We were stuck in the middle of the fire front. We quickly realised we were stuck and issued the first mayday call. A mayday call boils down to the following: "Clear the channel, I'm in big heaps of trouble and need help NOW". Vicfire received our mayday and tried to confirm a location. We explained that we were stuck and didn't know where we were.

I cannot describe the atmosphere in the cabin of that truck. Five of us stuck, everyone was frightened, hot, sweaty and smoky. Luckily the cabin and all the windows remained in one piece so we were able to keep out the worst of the smoke. We went into full crew protection mode, everyone covered in blankets down as low as possible trying to be below the window line. Outside all we could see was the outline of the flames and hear the roar of the fire. I could make out the shapes of trees and bushes to the front and right of the cabin and could see flames getting closer. Above and behind I could see the fire crowning through the tree tops and it gave me the impression of being at the bottom of a deep gully/valley with fire all around.

Eventually the smoke cleared a bit and we could see that we had crashed near a house which was burning and throwing off huge amounts of heat. We tried another mayday call but there was little more information we could provide. There was the sound of a massive explosion and I could see a huge glow out the front/right of the truck in the distance. I have come to believe that it was the sound of the petrol station exploding but am not 100 per cent sure.

This was the low ebb for all of us in the truck, the point where I started to question whether we were really done for. I have since found out the some of the other guys had made this personal decision quite a bit earlier so I was either late to the party or remained the eternal optimist. We made one more mayday call and through the radio traffic we could pick up that people were doing their best to help us – there was a tanker coming up the mountain but they had got to the Kinglake roundabout without seeing us.

7.15pm–7.30pm: I was looking out my side rear window noticing that the smoke had begun to clear when back up the hill I saw a flash of red-and-blue emergency beacons. We had been found and confirmed back to Vicfire that we could see the rescue truck but were not sure they could see us. I shut my eyes took a breath and waited. The rescue itself is a blur. I remember a lot of disjointed images: a face at my window before the door opened; losing my footing on jelly legs trying to run to the other truck; racing through the smoke and flame on the back of the truck, lots of yelling and shouting, a few tears from some, lots of panic; and finally seeing the light coming through the smoke and noticing that the bush was no longer exploding around me.

8pm: The rescuers were on a tanker from Wonga Park, one suburb across from us. When they heard it was us stuck on the hill, they came after us. They started coming after us from the time we issued our PAN message. I want to buy them a beer and say thanks. Thanks Wonga Park, you are truly firefighting life-saving rock stars and I love your work.

**Kind words: Shane Warne with Aiden Buchanan, 13, who lost his brother Mackenzie, 15, sister Neeve, 9, and uncle Danny Clark** Picture: Craig Borrow

**Cuddles: Jayden Henry, 5, in front of what is left of his house** Picture: Jon Hargest

# The only thing between me and the fire was a red truck

## Tim Cochrane on the Wonga Park rescue

Tim was in the fire truck that saved Dean. He put everything else out of his mind and focused on the issue at hand realising there was no going back as they had to get the North Warrandyte crew out.

"I've never been to a bushfire before, only local incidents, so going up the mountain [into Kinglake] was a very uneasy time. At first I thought, 'Do we normally drive in situations like this?' As it started to get much gloomier and the fire started to get hotter I realised that I really was in the deep end. I just remember saying to myself, There is no door I can walk through that will lead me out of this hell, I can't breathe properly, I can't see and the heat is so intense. It is human nature to always have a plan B but I think this is the one time in my life I have never had one. The only thing between me and the fire and smoke was a red truck. There was no escape. When I realised that there was no going back and we had to get the Warrandyte blokes out I put everything else out of my mind and focused on the [rescue] issue at hand. I really didn't have a lot of time to be scared! I tried not to look outside the truck too much; the devastation the fire had left behind was amazing.

"When we got to the Warrandyte truck I remember opening the back door and seeing three firefighters under blankets in the back looking extremely dazed and confused. It was a real eye opener to the dangers of [being a] firefighter. The trip back out was just as bad as the way in, with flames surrounding the truck. But we made it out alive and with five other firemen! I would just like to say I wouldn't change any decision that my crew leader and driver made that day. They got us to the North Warrandyte blokes and then got us all back out again, overcoming some fairly hairy situations."

**Via email**

# Looks of panic and sheer terror depicted what they had endured

## Grant Palmer, CFA volunteer, Kinglake

He knew the day was filled with danger when he felt its early morning heat but, even as an experienced CFA volunteer, Grant had no idea just how bad his day would become.

"I sat on the back of the tanker battling a blazing sun. My crewmate and I drank litres of water on the two-hour trip, but the sun just sucked it straight back out. As we approached Whittlesea, signs of the severity of the situation hit home. Lines of cars choking the roads, people hosing down property in the middle of town and fire trucks racing about, some in formed strike teams, others heading out on their own. Our tanker raced along the road in formation with our strike team, the fire enveloping house after house, and overwhelming those that could not be got to in time. Over the next couple of hours we saved what houses we could, at times working alongside residents battling valiantly to save their homes. But beyond what we were experiencing on the ground, the distressed call of 'mayday' over the radio sent chills through my bones and punched home that this fire was extraordinarily fierce.

"As members of the crew carried out the grim duty of searching destroyed houses for any casualties, others rested briefly, all quietly contemplating our situation, blank faces and the absence of banter being sure signs that, like me, others were probably battling with what we were experiencing.

"After leaving Humevale we returned to the Whittlesea staging area and after a quick feed we were deployed to escort the initial fleet of ambulances up to Kinglake, where it was believed incomprehensible tragedy had occurred as fire had torn through the township and its surrounds. The extent of the situation was largely unknown as communications were lost and road access denied by continuing fire, debris and fallen powerlines. In darkness our strike team, behind a front-end loader with road-clearing duties and guiding around 15 ambulances and numerous police vehicles, laboured up the climb, the road almost impassable with debris. The enormity of the situation escalated as we climbed higher, passing car after burnt-out car that had run off the road. There were piles of three and four cars jammed against each other or blocked by fallen trees, just eerie metal shells.

"Through Kinglake West and Pheasant Creek, all the while the fire still burning behind the main front, the devastation to property after property was astounding, it was like none had survived.

"It couldn't be fathomed, even while staring glazed-eyed at it; a service station, church, school, all just ruins, and fire still consuming more. On that approach to Kinglake, I took stock of our situation. What was to be found in Kinglake? What must I brace myself for? On rolling into the town proper, I was instantly heartened to see people, lots of people. But the looks of panic, of dread, sheer terror and of utter devastation depicted the horror of what these people had endured, their faces now etched in my mind.

"How could one comfort these people? Some wandered aimlessly, others sat hunched and many stared blankly from the shelter of their cars. Looking around at cars burnt out on the street, at buildings still alight and at burnt ground surrounding cars haphazardly parked on any clear ground where people, families, had sought refuge, I couldn't begin to imagine what they had been through; for many their very survival seemed remarkable.

"Escorting ambulances with the more seriously injured down to Whittlesea, the crew were largely silent, broken only by confirmation-seeking mumblings of the unbelievable things we were seeing. Once back in Whittlesea we were sent towards Kinglake to perform house searches along a stretch that was home to many rural-style dwellings. Our strike team leader briefed us on the nature of the task and that we must prepare ourselves for what we may find, but how could you prepare? As a CFA volunteer, you soon become accustomed to focusing solely on the job at hand, no matter what it may be, but this task was beyond any other challenge. All houses our crew inspected were destroyed.

"Signs of the lives lived here were evident amongst the ruin. Kids' bikes, chook sheds, fish ponds, trampoline frames, cars, fire pumps all blackened, partially consumed by fire, but recognisable. The homes had burnt with such ferocity that they were often completely flattened.

"Through the night we searched one house after another and continued as the sun came up. The rising sun threw a new light over the area we were working in. Such extent of damage had never been witnessed, and it forced the realisation that the aftermath of this event would be significant, both in the loss of property, but more dreadfully in the loss of life.

"By early morning our relief crews had arrived and we were bussed back home, an entire bus load of around 20 people just silent."

**Via email**

# No matter what, the Australian spirit will still survive

**Shane Warne visited Kinglake and the Whittlesea relief centre on Thursday, February 12. He played cricket with young families, spoke to children and listened to the stories of volunteers and CFA heroes.**

"We met [a man called] Andrew who lost everything, but he's still helping out. All he's got is just the shirt that's on his back. He's had four hours' sleep in four days and he said, 'If I stop, I'm gone. I'm not going to stop'," Shane said.

"These stories are just unbelievable. The Australian spirit is alive, no matter what happens, the Australian spirit will still survive and be strong. You come up here and you can't really be sure what to expect. You have seen the pictures, and I think all of us in Australia and around the world have had a tear in our eyes watching and hearing some of the horrendous and heinous stories. [It's] just horrific.

"To actually witness that with your own eyes is something different. We have been up to the mountain and seen the devastation that the fire has actually caused and you can't comprehend what it's actually like.

"Our purpose for the whole day was just to be around – whatever they wanted us to do, whoever they wanted us to see, we were just here to try to help out. That's why we all wanted to come up, to try to help out and lift some spirits, and say they are not alone, they are here but they have a lot of support here and all over the world.

"There are a couple of things I have noticed being here today. One is the spirit – that's alive, no matter what. The other is just the people who are helping out. Some of them are so brave."

Aiden Buchanan had not shed a tear since the Kinglake fires took his brother, sister and uncle, but it all came tumbling out when the 13-year-old saw his cricket hero at the Whittlesea relief centre. A touch on the shoulder and a tender, "How you going, buddy?" from Shane triggered a flood of emotion.

"We are going to look after Aiden, we are going to get some stuff we are going to try to send him. I think he crawled out a window and he lost his sister and his brother. It's really unbelievable," Shane said.

"We said, 'We like your beanie, mate', and he said his 15-year-old brother gave it to him and he died in the fire, so we gave him a bit of a hug and he got a bit upset. We said, 'Hang in there mate', and we were just trying to lift the kid's spirits'.

"I'm proud to be Australian like the people who are just trying to help and doing so much. Everyone just wants to help.

"We met Carole Wilson, and she lost everything and she lost her husband 12 months ago. She doesn't have anything bar the clothes she was wearing, and she's been there [at Kinglake] helping out since it happened. She hasn't slept, she hasn't done anything except help out."

Shane said the children who lost loved ones and had nowhere to live were happy to forget their troubles for a few precious minutes. "For some of those guys, they were pretty excited to have a bowl; one of them wanted to be a leg spinner. They were all asking questions and it was just good to have a kick of the footy and play some cricket. If that can help in some small way then that's great.

"Your heart goes out to those people who have lost everything. The bravery is just unbelievable.

"Everyone in Australia is trying to help, which makes you pretty proud to be Australian, too. We have been ringing backwards and forwards, trying to organise more drinks and equipment for the kids. Everyone's doing what they can."

**Matt Johnston and Georgie Pilcher,** *Herald Sun*

# It felt like we had shared something very special on that awful day

## Phil Wall, SES volunteer, Kinglake

Manning checkpoints in the days after the Black Saturday fires, Phil watched grief and sorrow mix with joy and elation as communities recovered after the fires.

"The fires hit so quickly and with such ferocity that there was nowhere to go. We were assigned to a checkpoint in Whittlesea at the community centre, which was the main assembly point for resident registration and for people searching for loved ones. For 12 hours we had a steady stream of stories, from absolute tragedy to amazing survival and everything in between.

"I spent a lot of the day speaking with people and listening to their stories, including a couple who had just flown in from their honeymoon and came back to find they had lost everything. Another couple had flown in from Darwin where they live, looking for their daughter and three grandchildren who lived in the area and hadn't been heard of since Saturday evening. By the end of the night, though nothing had been confirmed, the news for them was looking very grim indeed.

"The next time I saw their son-in-law was on Monday morning's *Sunrise* program where he had still heard nothing. A short time later it was announced that, unofficially, his wife and children had been seen by a neighbour running back into their house as the firestorm hit and that sadly the house had then been destroyed.

"Sometimes as an SES volunteer we have to attend terrible

tragedies, but in most cases you are dealing with an individual case, one person and one family and even though there is the obvious ripple effect it is still created from a single stone hitting the pond. In this situation we were dealing with literally dozens of individual cases, each more devastating than the one before.

"As each story unfolded there were some fantastic good news stories too, like the lady desperately looking for a friend who she had not had contact with since the fires hit.

"As the hours passed and with each contact I had with her as she passed through our checkpoint, our positive outlook began to wane, and although we were saying all the right things, I think in our heads as well as our hearts we felt it may not end well.

"About 10 o'clock she came through in her car, stopped, wound down her window and with a huge smile yelled, 'Phil, I found him!'. We hugged, and there was a feeling of elation for a person I'd never met before, and probably would never meet again. But it felt like we had shared something very special on that awful day. Sadly, that feeling was to be shortlived as the very next vehicle was a man who had lost two family members. For each happy ending there are going to be many more devastating conclusions.

"At the end of our deployment, and as we headed back to Chelsea, it felt a little weird to see how normal life seemed to be going on. How could that be when a relatively short distance away, life was never going to be the same again for so many people? I arrived home in the early hours of Monday and as I climbed into bed I had a strange uneasy, guilty feeling. I was able to come back home to my family yet so many of these people who had so recently touched my life could not. Sometimes you can't help but question the fairness of life."

**As told to the *Moorabbin Leader***

# I'm not a believer but I owe my life to someone up there

## Ray Keating, 58, Kinglake

Sitting inside Whittlesea's St Andrews Presbyterian Church, Ray reflected on Black Saturday. He had rescued a woman from the side of the road as he escaped the Kinglake inferno but he says he's not a hero. Anyone would have done the same.

"I'm not really a believer … my family would laugh to think I'm here. But I feel I owe a thank you to someone." The 58-year-old hobby farmer tells a story of helping save homes and rescuing animals before jumping in his 4WD and out-running the firestorm. On his way down the mountain to the safe haven of the Whittlesea community centre, Ray picked up a young woman screaming for help on the side of the road. He doesn't want any thanks. He would like to know what happened to her, though.

"That's probably all I would ask for … to know if that woman is all right, is her family all right, that kind of thing," he said. "I got her to the community centre, so I suspect she is OK … but emotionally, well, no one escapes this without scars, do they. I don't think I'd seen her before. But it's hard to recognise anyone in that sort of hysterical situation. You will never understand what it was like. I could barely see a foot in front … I just knew we had to get out."

He leans down and pats his cattle dog, Digger, then glances back at the church. "None of that matters though, not when you look around and see what has happened. No, no. I didn't do anything more than anyone else would have. The difference is, though, I am here. Plenty are not."

Pointing to a series of pictures published in a newspaper of the Kinglake missing he says: "I think she is the wife of a man I helped tie his horses up ... the horses were going mad, frightened, obviously, by the smoke and the noise of it. The noise was like an aircraft landing in your front yard, this blasting, blasting noise. You know how dogs don't like sirens, well the horses were like that with this fireball rolling in. I saw the old farmer trying to round them [the horses] up, so I pulled over and lent a hand. It's what you do in the country ... it's what you'd do anywhere – mateship.

"I can't say for sure if that is her, but I've seen her somewhere. It's all a blur. I needed time out, some solitude, maybe. I think mainly I just needed some space, to clear my head. Isn't that what you do at a church?"

**Clementine Cuneo,** *The Daily Telegraph*

# I'm not religious at all but I've never prayed so hard in my life

## Vicki Ruhr, Kinglake

When her house burned down, Vicki, 47, didn't lose the pluck which won her the 2006 Pride of Australia Community Spirit medal. Days after losing everything, including her laptop, Vicki was living with relatives and using Post-it notes and note pads to get organised. She was with husband Cris, son Lachlan, 11, their dog Sailor and a friend when the inferno hit. They lay covered in wet towels in a paddock mown short by Cris, which saved their lives.

"There was no warning at all. We only had one fire truck on the whole of the mountain. They were all elsewhere. The power went out about

3.30pm. As the power went out my laptop battery decided to go. It started to get quite dark. My friend rang me and said he had heat stroke so I went to pick him up. As he's getting in the car he says, 'Oh, that's on fire over there'. This fire's coming across the road. I just floored it and the amount of s… that hit the windscreen. Very, very frightening. We tried to defend the house because we had no idea of the ferocity. It just got worse so I went in the house and said, 'It's not looking good out there'. It was just second by second. We had wet towels in a bucket by the evacuation point. The smoke alarms are screeching.

"I couldn't even get outside because at that time there were actual showers of fire. My husband was out there and I couldn't see him. The noise was just deafening. We went and lay down in the centre of the paddock with the towels all over us. I'm not religious at all but I've never prayed so hard in my life. Probably within seven minutes the house was fully ablaze. My husband watched the house burn down. I couldn't watch it. He was in tears and really upset. We've lost our home [but] the family are fine. We're going to stay. We're just rolling our sleeves up. Everyone's like that up there. A lot of people don't realise how heavily populated Kinglake is. Maybe something positive will come of this if there's a complete rebuild and it's rebuilt appropriately and sustainably."

**As told to Cheryl Critchley, *Herald Sun***

# It's just like Armageddon driving up there. Kilometre after kilometre of burnt-out trees

## Peter Hitchener, newsreader

**Comfort: Bernie and Jan Hansell return to the embers**

Picture: Ian Currie

# We thank them and listen to them, that's all we can do

## Graeme Scorringe, CFA chaplain

**Graeme arrived at Whittlesea on the night the Black Saturday bushfires ripped through the area and was one of the first to Kinglake the next morning.**

"It was bedlam as you can imagine on the night of the fire. And then going up to Kinglake, seeing the abandoned cars and the vast areas of blackened ash, like a moonscape – you weren't prepared for that, nobody could be prepared for that." He deals in what he calls "psychological first aid".

"In those first days people were naturally shocked and in some cases in a daze. We gave them a chance to tell their stories and process what they had seen and then the psychological support kicks in. We tell people not to be overly concerned with how they react. We tell them that everything is normal in an abnormal situation. One woman who had lost her house lost everything, but she just kept on cooking for everyone. She just cooked and cooked.

"Another firefighter, a volunteer who lost his house while he was with his brigade, turned out each day for work and just refused to go home. It was four or five days until he said he was going home to sift through the rubble. I don't think he could have coped with that until then. All we can do really, is focus on their achievements, these people who are prepared to sacrifice so much and jump on the back of a truck in the middle of the night and go out to help others. We thank them and listen to them, that's all we can do." As a chaplain he is sometimes confronted by people questioning God's will. "I tell them they will drive themselves insane talking about ifs and buts and maybes. I think when people face death, they prioritise what's important in life."

**Ross Brundett,** *Herald Sun*

# Delayed reaction, delayed responses are not unusual

## Michael Clarebrough, consulting psychologist with the ambulance service

"Psychologists aren't freaks, we're just normal human beings … I was in New York after September 11 and it brought back a lot of memories. I've counselled about 30 paramedics and I'd say almost half of them would be locals, people who worked and lived in the area.

"Some of them were first-line responders so they copped a double whammy – they lost homes and had to deal with the fact that they knew some of the people who died. It's very distressing for everyone. These people have seen the victims of hangings, and suicides, and road trauma, but this was something so unexpected.

"They've seen the victims carried out. You couldn't help but find that traumatic. The Kinglake team did a fantastic job. To have responded the way they did while some of their own homes were in jeopardy was just incredible. Not everyone will need counselling; we all have our own level of resilience. Quite a few will not need any more contact and, for some, it might be another six months or more before they feel the need to see someone about it. Delayed reaction, delayed responses are not unusual."

**As told to Ross Brundett,** *Herald Sun*

# It's not the house I've lost. I've lost the place where the kids grew up

## Ron Parsonage, 59, Kinglake

Ron raised five children in his home, which was reduced to a pile of ash by the fires. Sometimes he had to go on the dole; sometimes he took jobs in the local chicken sheds. If there's one thing he misses, it's the idea that his kids will always have a home to come to.

"It [a bushfire] kind of goes with the territory, so you think about it. Then it happens. I always thought I'd be right but now I'm thinking, it's not the house I've lost. I've lost the place where the kids grew up. I've lost the home.

"I don't know if I can explain this. It's like, it's not a house. It's where I raised them. It's the place they can always go. If they've got trouble with a boyfriend or a relationship breaks up, they can come home. If they need somewhere to go for any reason, it's their home."

**As told to Caroline Overington, *The Australian***

# There just aren't enough hugs in the world to make this pain go away. But hugs are good

*MX* reporter Marion Taffe lost her cousin and his family in the Kinglake fires.

When the phone rang at 1.30am on Monday, I knew it was bad news. It was my sister, Anne, and she couldn't even talk. "Is he gone?" was all I could manage. "Yes." "And the girls?" Anne just cried. "What, all of them?" She didn't have to say anything. We just cried and cried.

Our cousin Rob Davey, his wife, Tash, and their two little girls, Jorja, 3, and Alexis, eight months, had all died in the fires at Kinglake where they lived. At that stage we didn't have any more details – just, horribly, that the bodies had been found. We were later told the family and the dogs were found in what was the bathroom.

Rob had hooked the dog trailer up to the back of the car and it appeared they were preparing to evacuate but they didn't make it. It hit so hard and so fast.

For me, the wait for news started early on Sunday when Dad sent me a text: "Still no news from Robert." Rob had phoned his mum on Saturday to say they were evacuating. When the family hadn't heard anything by Sunday, we all feared the worst. But until Anne rang, I couldn't let my mind do anything but think they'd be fine, probably among the thousands of people who were now homeless and trying to get word out. It's too horrible to imagine that a whole family can be wiped out. All those memories, all that life, all the happiness over the new arrival of little Alexis – all gone because it was a hot, windy day. As kids we'd spend holidays and weekends swimming in Warrnambool, playing on the Daveys' trampoline. They were the coolest family, with the coolest stuff, and the first people I knew to have a VCR.

We'd hang out, listening to music and later riding in Rob's friend's bogantastic Torana. Then we grew up. Holidays with cousins became less frequent, people got married, had families and we'd only see each other at weddings and, sadly, funerals. The last time I saw Rob was at another cousin's funeral and we talked about how we had to try and stay in touch more and not keep meeting at funerals.

I know so many people have lost loved ones this week and I'm not alone in looking at photos of burnt-out cars and piles of ashes that used to be houses, wondering which one is Rob's house or car. There just aren't enough hugs in the world to make this pain go away. But hugs are good. People are amazing – work colleagues picking up the slack, friends lending an ear, buying a drink – it all helps.

With the massive task of dealing with so many deaths, we don't know when we'll all be able to say goodbye to Rob and his gorgeous young family, but four coffins at one funeral is not something anyone imagines seeing in their life. I can't get the thought out of my head and my thoughts are with Rob and Tash's parents and siblings. People are so precious. We need to hold our loved ones close.

# I've got lots of toys. If they get burned I'm going to be sad

### As the smoke began to clear in the days after Black Saturday, Paul Kent reflects on the effect the fires had on the children.

If Lachlan Berns was fighting the fires they would be out by now. He would use a hose and just hose it down. He would fight the fire in more than one place. His mum would be OK and none of his toys would be burned. Nobody would be upset and nobody would have had to hide under tables any more and, best of all, people would be able to go home now. Lachlan Berns is six years old, and he has the answers. I found him outside the Whittlesea Community Centre, ground zero for the survivors and the displaced, playing with his dog Bridle in between being interrupted by his brother Leigham. "There was a lot of fire and that made me upset," he said.

When the fires went through Kinglake on Saturday afternoon Lachlan's mum Lynette grabbed him and her three other boys, Dylan, 13, Jayden, 8, and four-year-old Leigham, and tried to escape, only to be turned back by the fire. What horrors they saw as their parents packed them into cars can only be guessed at: some saw friends left behind, friends they'll never see again. Some have no homes, all those Christmas presents are gone, their pets are gone. They saw the horror of the fire and felt the fear it evoked. These are emotions too complicated for children, and parents have been keeping a close eye on them, but there is an unconquerable spirit in children.

Unable to get through the fires, Lachlan's family headed back home and climbed under the kitchen table with wet towels.

"I was hiding under the table because there has been all these fires," he said. "We had a towel and it was wet, because when the fire goes in the house the towel does something and so there was only smoke in our house …"

"And we had no power," Leigham said. "Leigham, shush, I'm talking," said Lachlan. "We had no power."

If Monday was about grief in Whittlesea, survivors gathering and hoping, Tuesday was about resilience. Already people were rebuilding. Planning for the future. Insurance companies set up temporary offices, Centrelink was zipping through paperwork, plans were being made for temporary housing. A little way away, Keith Chasemore was hoping to get back up to Kinglake to get his truck.

In a brilliant piece of plumb luck, Keith had towed the caravan to Whittlesea last Thursday to get a showground spot for the cancelled country music show. Now, with his home standing less than a metre high, he and wife Sigrid have set up home at the showground.

Already the insurance company has told them they will move a portable residence on to their home as soon as it is safe. All about, people were on the move, getting their lives back. Meanwhile, those who remained at Kinglake and Pheasant Creek and other affected areas were running out of supplies. If they headed down the road to replenish they were not allowed back, so they stayed there. But they were running out. Mostly, fuel to run generators had all but gone. It meant no power at night and no power to pump water into homes. They had no batteries and, worst of all when the cupboard is stocked with emergency tins of food, no can openers.

All the while, the special resilience of children showed through. They played and found their way to ice cream, and skateboards and scooters were shared.

Lachlan's father, Nathan, called the family on Saturday afternoon to hear they were trapped. As the fires moved over the mountain, the fear gripped; he couldn't reach them. "It ripped my heart out."

For Lachlan, escaping the fire wasn't as difficult as it might seem. "Do you know that paddock where there's some rocks and some glass?" he said. "We had to go there … that's a safe place. But the shop got burned, but only at the back.

"We're going to move in there soon when all the fires have gone out. I want to move in now. We've got Christmas stuff still there …"

"I've got lots of toys," said Leigham.

"Shush Leigham, I'm talking," Lachlan said. "If they get burned I'm going to be sad."

**Skeletons: What is left of Silver Creek Cres, Flowerdale**    Picture: David Caird

# Chapter 5

# Flowerdale

- **Origin**
  The tiny homestead of 320 houses is defenceless when fire hits at 5pm. Its only tanker has been sent to fight fires in nearby towns

- **Destruction**
  A southerly blows the fire away from Kinglake and engulfs Flowerdale, destroying 200 homes

- **Toll**
  Four people are killed either trying to defend their properties or flee the area. More than half the town's homes are destroyed

f there is a theme emerging it is in Flowerdale. It starts slowly in the little town, like it will in most places, yet before their day will be over the men that stay behind in Flowerdale will have defined themselves. By early morning that Saturday the fires are further west, the radio says. The other side of the Hume Freeway, pushing into Hidden Valley.

Most people in the town know the fire is there but is also far enough away, if that sounds right. So that's how the day goes, really. People just going about their business, until mid-afternoon. News comes in that Hidden Valley is under ember attack. A family travelling through to the valley happens to stop by at the pub and they are warned to rethink their plans. About 3pm Reece Warren calls in to the local pub to see if anybody has any news. No, they say. Still the same. Well, he says, he is going up Collins Rd then, across from the pub, to see if he can see anything. Collins Rd is a dry gravel road that winds up a hill and gives a pretty good view of the valley.

Slowly, and with purpose, Flowerdale is proof of what a

community is capable of when it cares. Reece goes away and comes back to the pub pulling a generator. He also has a fire cube, filled with water, on the back of his ute. On the trailer with the generator are shovels and picks and other stuff to build firewalls.

The people of Flowerdale are on their own. They know it and are getting on with it. Their CFA tanker has left to fight fires elsewhere. A local policeman called in to say they should consider leaving, then left himself. It is some time around 5pm now and many of the townsfolk are aware the CFA is gone and that the fire is heading for Whittlesea to the south. It is also attacking Mt Disappointment. They can't get any information on the radio other than the Hume Freeway is cut off. Information that, by now, is old enough to shave.

People are starting to worry. They need to know so they begin gathering at the pub, sharing what they know, discussing what might be possible. Forty or 50 of them.

A CFA volunteer walks in and there is great relief. For as long as he takes to speak anyway: "If you don't have any plans," he says, "then get to Yea for safety." It has a finality to it that makes people think seriously about heading for their cars, getting out of Dodge.

One of the men in the pub says he isn't going. "I'm staying to defend the pub." A handful of blokes look at each other. "I'm in," says Peter Byrne. "I'm in," says Reece. "I'm in," says Crash, something of a local legend. "I'm in." "I'm in." In all, nine are in.

Quickly now, the women and children are put into cars and sent to Yea, about 30km further north. The remaining men buddy up and make an action plan. They set to work around the pub, filling wheelie bins and buckets and whatever else can hold water. They wet down the roof and soak the ground around the pub.

By now, the southerly is well and truly in. The fires are turning back from Kinglake, about 20km south, and are coming for Flowerdale.

The men just finish preparing to fight the approaching fire when, in something of a rush, about another 40 people descend upon the pub. Initially planning to stay in their homes, the fires have spooked them enough they now want to flee.

There are grandparents and their grandchildren. Families. They are at the pub because they want to know what the latest news is but, in truth, they are caught in between. The men believe the road to Yea is now too dangerous. The Murrindindi fire has closed in on it and so they tell the people to stay and quickly start work on a new plan.

Initially, the plan is to stay in the pub as the front hits but now there are all these people. And then a bloke they call Stylesy says it might be smarter to line up the cars on the gravel patch adjacent to the road in front. The trees alongside the pub might catch alight, he figures, making them vulnerable, to say nothing of the 90-year-old pub itself. If nothing else, the gravel patch is clear.

Good idea. They line up 15 cars, nose to tail, and everybody leaves the pub and gets inside a car. They do not have to wait long. The fire comes from the south, up Whittlesea Rd, with a whoosh of heat and power. This is it, this is their moment. So long as everybody in the cars holds their nerve and doesn't panic, the men believe, they will be OK. The greatest threat to the plan is if somebody panics and breaks the line, peeling off to make a run for it themselves.

And then they strike some luck.

Just as the fire reaches them the wind changes. The fire blows back on itself. At that, these men, going beyond themselves, jump out of their vehicles and hit the fire with their hoses, their buckets, whatever they can get their hands on. They push it away from the pub and the line-up of cars. It is a small victory, but one they are able to maintain. For several more hours the fire comes back in spot fires. As each spot fire finds a vulnerable place to settle they stomp on it,

**Standing sentinel: Gas bottles amid the ruins of Flowerdale**  Picture: Matt Turner

**Twisted mess: Peter Byrne is daunted by the scale of his loss**  Picture: David Crosling

keeping it from spreading, keeping the threat down. They do this for near on three hours.

Indeed, it is as this is happening that a resident comes driving through the fire path in something of a mad rush. In the back of his car is Bob Harrop. Bob is his neighbour and after the front moves on and it is safe to poke your head up, the neighbour finds Bob at home unconscious. It seems for the past couple of hours Bob, 83, fought the fires by himself. Tried to, anyway. He is still unconscious, suffering smoke inhalation and third-degree burns. He is in a bad way. They take him inside the pub and quickly people try to make him comfortable. They take out his false teeth so they can rub water on his lips and drip water into his mouth. They put cool towels over his burns to soothe him. Women begin taking shifts holding his hand, whispering to him, encouraging him. "Come on Bob, you're OK." Some wonder why he was even fighting the fire in the first place. The answer is simple – and noble. His wife Elizabeth is in hospital recovering from an aneurysm. The brain operation she has can cause all manner of side-effects and one of the side-effects that clutch at the heart before a patient turns in is the risk of memory loss. Bob simply wanted her to have some memories to come home to.

It would be nice if it all ends here. The fight fought, the fire defeated, Bob making a terrific recovery. If this was Hollywood, it would be a perfect place to fade out and roll credits. But the people at Flowerdale are not finished. Not by a long shot.

Another front comes, this time from the west. Men jump into utes and head into paddocks, in the direction of the fires, extinguishing spot fires. They fight to keep the fire as far away from the pub, and the people in it, as they can.

This threat ends. Quickly they begin wetting roofs down again. Start spraying water over the ground around them. And as time passes

**Quick thinking:** Nineteen people escaped the flames in the Murrindindi River

**Take cover:** Terrified locals and firefighters protect themselves from the fire

they begin sticking their heads up wondering when someone might come and check out if they are OK. They do not know, although they are beginning to suspect, that Flowerdale has become the town the state forgets.

It is approaching midnight and the worst has hit most townships. Elsewhere, the news is reporting 14 dead at nearby towns like Kinglake and St Andrews. That is where those on the outside are focused. Never mind that the figure throughout the region is already much, much more. Right now the people of Flowerdale do not know that nobody is coming. The situation is simple; with nobody getting out, nobody knows to come in. More, rescue services are unable to get in simply because of the ferocity of the fires. Flowerdale knows as much.

Of the 320-odd homes in the area, more than 200 are gone. The town, a small mixture of treechangers and hippies, numbering no more than a few hundred people, has been decimated. Before the night is over another front comes through, this time from the east. It is the Murrindindi fire. Again the men at the pub fight it back, with mops and buckets and hoses. "These guys are bloody amazing," says Megan. "They should be given a medal."

It is not until 36 hours after the first fire hit that an outsider sees the devastation of Flowerdale. A mother is found dead huddled beside her car, her two daughters huddled alongside her. Why they got out of the car nobody knows. Another two women are also found dead, also by their car. At some point during the night, the people at the pub tell them, Bob Harrop also becomes one of the town's fatalities. The injuries are simply too much for the old man's body. He is the only fatality at the pub, where exhausted men have finished the job. Three times the fire comes at them. Three times they push it back. They save 40 or 50 lives, in what is their finest hour.

**Paul Kent**

**Flattened: Ken and Liz Mival with son, writer Al Mival (right)**   Picture: Mark Cranitch

# I could see burning pine needles 20m above the roof. A million sparklers flying through the air

## Alex Jones, Flowerdale

He fought the flames that endangered his house until the early hours but even after thinking he had it under control, Alex was woken from his sleep by his wife screaming that a new fire had started on their property and was racing towards their car.

"The whole horizon around us glowed red. The wind started to pick up again from the southwest and smoke puffed up from the creek where pine trees, blackberries eucalypts and scrub had been left untouched for years. A large dead tree suddenly burst into flames, and another one near it. The flames lit up the hillside and the wind became stronger. Embers blasted over the hill and towards us. I stood there with my wife and oldest son, all we could do was point our hoses towards the approaching attack. Thick smoke blew down at us and my wife screamed out, 'This is madness get inside'.

"I stood there for maybe a minute longer and couldn't see my house which was only metres away. I closed my eyes and stumbled around to the back door and went inside for clean air. Inside all the smoke alarms in the house were beeping. My two girls were on the floor screaming in terror. I yelled out, 'It's going to be all right'. My wife Tanya replied, 'No it isn't'.

"With only five breaths of air from inside the house I turned, faced the door and ran back outside again. The pump was still running so I grabbed the hose and squirted the house underneath, on the roof, on the decking, everywhere that the embers blasted. The wind seemed to get stronger. I knelt down and held the hose in a fan style. Embers blasted my whole body.

"I turned the hose on myself many times. Looking upwards I could see burning pine needles maybe 20m above the house roof. A million sparklers flying through the air.

"I looked over to the other side of the house and it had begun to move into our property. We quickly moved the pump down to the water tank because the hoses wouldn't reach and put that fire out. Then we moved the pump back to the pool to keep fighting the other fire on the other side of the house.

"We could hear explosions from our neighbours' property over the road, but there was nothing we could do until we were safe. Four o'clock in the morning and we had done it – saved our home and our neighbours'.

"Tanya and I wandered back home, walked in the door and sat down. My four children were so tired and relieved at this point. Water flowed out of my eyes, my sinuses were blocked and I could hardly talk. We all went to sleep. At 6am my wife screamed out, 'Quick, get the hose, there's a fire near my car'.

"I stand up and run outside to the pump, my head is thumping and my eyes burn but I put that one out easily."

*Via email*

# We've had bushfires before but never like this

## Margaret Mahon, chairwoman, Yea Red Cross

# The fire spotted ahead, leaving us all in the middle of the blaze. It was absolutely howling

## Andrew Collard and Brian Lawry, firefighters

With 100km/h winds, the quick thinking of Andrew and Brian helped them save the lives of 19 people. They led the group, including seven children under five, to water and kept the fires at bay while the children sheltered under wet blankets in Department of Sustainability and Environment Toolangi fire trucks.

Andrew: "We had a call from our tower for a fire that had just started at the Murrindindi Mill. We responded and when we got there the fire was pretty well as enormous a fire as we have ever see, it had grown in 10 minutes to a massive size. It was the fire that eventually reached Marysville. There is an area, the Murrindindi scenic reserve, where there are a lot of camping areas so we pretty well knew there would be people in there with the fire burning towards them. The CFA had just arrived, they were trying to attend to houses around the mill so we went through the fire and went up to try and evacuate any campers that were in there.

"We found a group and once we started to advance the campers out, the fire spotted up ahead of them so they came back to us, leaving us all in the middle of the fire. There was a total of 19 campers, seven were kids aged under four or five. One of our rangers, Mike Lauder, quickly made a decision that we were basically trapped and decided everyone should go to the Murrindindi River.

"We parked our fire-fighting units in the river and put the kids, some of them were only six-month-old babies, and their mothers in one car in the river. Some other kids were in another car with fire blankets over the top. We had hoses set up so we had a constant water supply on the cars. The fire was around us on all four sides.

"It was absolutely howling, it wasn't a fireball as such but it was burning all around us, we were surrounded. We were constantly having embers landing on us. We stayed in the river for two hours.

"Our colleague, Brad Sexton, tried to get in with a bulldozer early on, the fire was too big. He later found out he had lost his house at Kinglake. Once the fire had died down some other crews got into us and cleared the road for us. For us it was stressful but we spend so much time around fire with what we do.

"The people we were with were brilliant. They helped us and were spreading as much water around as they could. When we got ourselves organised, things seemed to go very well. It was our instincts but we do spend such a lot of time around fire so it wasn't as daunting for us as it would have been for the people with us who had no idea."

Brian: "There were 100km/h winds and fire behaving like we had never seen before. The campers would have been trapped, they wouldn't have got out. We couldn't drive back through to get out, so they certainly couldn't have. They got very panicky at the start, they asked for reassurance.

"They wanted to know: 'Are we going to get out of this?' The obvious answer is yes. You're not going to say no. That would create panic. We were going to do our best. Mike Lauder deserves a fair bit of the credit. It was very quick thinking on the spot that got us into the river. I went through Ash Wednesday as a 19-year-old; this was worse."

**As told to Gemma Jones, *The Daily Telegraph***

# We had a buddy system going

## Peter Byrne, Flowerdale

As dozens of residents fled, the publican and eight others decided they were going to stay and fight. They used hoses, mops and buckets to save the hotel and the local community hall. They kept devastated residents calm inside the pub. About 40 were at the hotel and they sent all the women and children off to Yea.

"After we evacuated the women and children to Yea, there was about eight of us who decided to stay. We are such a small town, there are no shops or meeting place, we don't have a town centre. We only have the pub and the town hall so it is pretty important to us. It may be a bit Australian trying to hold on to the pub, but it means a lot. We allocated tasks and had a buddy system going and that seemed to work. We had three fires bearing down on us at the one time. They converged on us all at the same time. The fire went through here like a bomb."

**As told to Milanda Rout, *The Australian***

# I don't think I can describe how happy I was to hear they survived

## Kathie Crocker and Diva the cat, Flowerdale

Among the devastation there was life too. Kathie returned to the ruins of her Forest Rd home she shares with Lucky the sheep and his friends – five more sheep, three dogs, three alpacas, a calf and a cat.

"When I left at six o'clock, the only thing that worried me was that

**Lucky ones: Wayne and Laine MacDonald and family have opened their home to the less fortunate**
Picture: Craig Borrow

**Residents return: Kathie Crocker's cat Diva survived the fires in a wombat hole**
Picture: Darryl Gregory

they weren't going to make it. I had to leave them behind. I don't think I can describe how happy I was to hear they had survived. They were scared when I left, running around. It was sad to leave them, but there was just nothing I could do."

When thick smoke started tumbling across the sky, she knew it was time to leave. Kathie rounded up her three dogs, but her feisty cat, Diva, fled. "She scratched me and took off."

Finding 10-year-old Diva was Kathie's main priority when she returned. She walked the property, calling the cat's name, before she found it cowering in a wombat hole. The distressed pet was finally coaxed from its hiding place, before that feistiness returned.

**Ashley Gardiner,** *Herald Sun*

# We wanted to help best we could

## Wayne and Laine MacDonald, Flowerdale

Their home survived the bush fires but Wayne and Laine MacDonald wanted to help others less fortunate. They erected a sign outside their home inviting people who needed to call a loved one, have a shower or wash their clothes to come in.

"We still have a house, so we thought we were much luckier than a lot of the other people in town. We just wanted to help as best we could. We have had more people for the phone because that was a big issue for people wanting to get in touch with family members. We have had some showers, but it has mostly been for the phone."

**As told to Emily Power,** *Herald Sun*

# All that remains are memories

Al Mival, a writer with *The Sunday Mail* in Brisbane, returned to the home of his parents, Ken and Liz Mival, to see what was left of their home in Flowerdale.

As I walk down the driveway of my parents' house, a torn strip of blue-and-white police tape, tied to a scorched bush, flaps in the gentle breeze. "It means they've already checked for bodies," my dad said as we arrived. We shuffle towards what had been their beautiful timber home at Flowerdale – now reduced to a flattened mess of ash, melted glass, cracked concrete stumps and twisted sheets of roof iron.

Mum is determined not to cry, but understandably, she can't help it; tears roll down her cheeks. I put my arm around her, but there's little I can say as they attempt to understand how all the work and sacrifices they made for the tree-change house they built 10 years ago have suddenly been reduced to a pile of rubbish a few feet high. "Well, now we know," Mum said in that pragmatic way that mothers use to signal it's time to begin dealing with a situation.

My parents, Ken and Liz, saw their house for the final time about 7pm on Black Saturday when they opted to flee in the face of what became the nation's worst bushfire disaster. As the fire swept quickly towards them from the south, they took their border collie Molly, some precious photo albums and my late grandmother's jewellery, attached their camper trailer to the car, and drove towards safety. Unlike scores of others who tragically became trapped, they had an escape route to the north that took them away from the fire, past the local store at Hazeldene, the Flowerdale pub, and on towards Yea where they spent the night with hundreds of other fire refugees.

"We're safe," Dad told me when I finally made contact that

night, "but don't be counting on that inheritance." Dad's a realist. But even he surely could never have imagined at the time that absolutely everything would be lost by the time he and Mum next came down that driveway. Our old Subaru is just a shell. The driver's side window has melted and folded inwards. A stalactite of melted glass stretches down to the floor. The alloy wheels have liquefied before cooling as shiny puddles in the gravel. Nearby is the charred shell of the Triumph Spitfire convertible my sister used to drive. Just a few metres farther away, the clothesline is still intact with the peg basket swinging on the wire. The pegs on top are relatively unscathed. The veranda posts that helped define the home are reduced to lines of charcoal on the ground and are all that remain of the house's many timbers. There's no trace of the mountain-ash floorboards nor even a fragment of their beloved oak dining table.

As we pick our way through the rubble, we resort to weak jokes about decluttering. It's all we can do to counter the shock. Over the years, Dad had built up a collection of wines, many from nearby Yarra Valley. "Just waiting for retirement," he used to say. The wine was stored in the cool under the stairs. There are no stairs now, nor is there any sign of the 1989 Grange we gave him on his 60th birthday. But among the melted and broken glass are a few intact bottles. Dusting off the ash, we find the caps are still on tight, but there's nothing inside. The wine has vaporised and escaped through the seal.

There is nothing to salvage from the upstairs bedroom where my sons slept when visiting their grandparents. Nor is there anything left of my parents' bedroom except for a metal case containing scorched steel frames that were once a spare set of glasses. Where the kitchen once stood are the remains of some "ovenproof" cookware. It falls apart in my hands and lies among what could be broken tiles from the upstairs bathroom. As we head back up the driveway, I remember how the bush around the house once echoed with bird calls. Now there is eerie silence, except for a loose piece of tin banging in the breeze against the chimney of the ravaged pole house up the hill. As Mum took one more look, she noticed the birdbath was bone dry. We all agree we should tip some water in it – just in case.

As we pass kilometre after kilometre of scorched land and black, skeletal trees, we wonder how these communities will ever recover. Can people who loved to live in the region, like my parents, ever return? "I really don't know if I'll ever be comfortable there in summer again," Mum says. And then reality sets in. "We're lucky," she says. "We're alive. We have family we can stay with until we can sort out our lives. So many people we know keep offering us help, but we don't need help. Let's worry about the hundreds of other people who are so much more worse off than us."

And as we weave our way down the mountain road, away from a community in ashes, there is nothing more to say.

# She's doing well but a bit stressed

## Krispy the koala, Yea

Amid all the misery, Krispy the koala put a smile on the faces of staff at Yea Veterinary Hospital, owned by vets Tomi and Anthony Dredge. The family who found her after the Murrindindi blaze couldn't resist having some fun with the name. Krispy seriously burned the pads of her hind feet and had minor paw burns. Anthony and Tomi hope to release her when enough vegetation returns.

Anthony: "Krispy was found in the Murrindindi area. She was just a couple of kilometres from there. The people who brought her in had stayed and defended their house from the bushfire. When it all settled down they found her just coming out of the bush on their property. They're kids with a bit of a sense of humour. They named her Krispy. She's got burnt pads on her hind feet. She's got moderate burns. The plan would be to keep her until her wounds heal. [If she wasn't found] she'd have a little trouble with mobility. She'd be prone to predation from other animals."

Tomi: "She's a good patient. She's pretty good actually considering what she's been through. She's left her bandages. She's doing well but she's a bit stressed about everything that's going on. If we can save a female and release her, that would be great."

**As told to Cheryl Critchley, *Herald Sun***

# This is by far the worst disaster I've ever been involved with

## De Villiers Smit, physician, The Alfred Hopital

De Villiers worked in the aftermath of the Bali bombings and was always optimistic that burns victims from the bushfires stood a good chance of survival.

"This is by far the worst disaster I've ever been involved with. These patients that we are seeing right now are major burns patients, whereas with the Bali bombing there was more trauma involved – broken bones, blast injuries – because of the bombs going off."

**As told to Stephen Lunn, *The Australian***

# You have down days, you have up days. But there is light at the end of the tunnel

## Ranald Webster, 87, Pakenham

His blackened and swollen face photographed in The Alfred Hospital's burns unit as he recovered from the Ash Wednesday bushfires made Ranald the unfortunate face of Victoria's previous worst bushfires. Twenty-six years later, the former CFA volunteer was back in the burns unit to visit the victims of Black Saturday to share his amazing story of survival and let the most seriously injured know there is light at the end of their tunnel and a wonderful life to live post-recovery.

"I've got two horrible-looking photos of myself and I say: 'This is what I looked like when I came in, this is what I look like now. If I can do it, you can do it'. They are going to go through a lot of trauma because they are away from their home, away from their loved ones and haven't a clue what is going on.

"They could have lost their house and/or friends and relatives, so when they think about it they are going to feel very isolated. You have down days, you have up days. You think about yourself because you have a lot of time to lie there and think, but there is light at the end of the tunnel. I always tell the people at The Alfred – because some of them feel real sorry for themselves, which is quite natural – 'Life goes on. It's up to you if you want to be in it or not and you're the only one that can do that'."

**As told to Grant McArthur, _Herald Sun_**

# People shut themselves in, too frightened to come out

## Bill Brown, area manager, Goulburn Valley Area Mental Health Services

Bill was one of the first counsellors into Marysville and Flowerdale after the fires.

"When we first got in, a number of people were just in a daze while others were excitable, still pumped with adrenalin. We had people who shut themselves in houses, too frightened to come out. We went with the combatants [emergency workers] house to house trying to develop understandings with the survivors – and some of our conversations are still ongoing – and draw them into the larger community. There were terrible things that the workers would have seen, but the support network for emergency services was first-class. Really, the hardest group to reach were the adolescents who have a tendency to pull back from their family and withdraw, but we're trying to reach out.

"Every day the story builds and builds. It's not until you drive and drive and see kilometre after kilometre of blackened trees that the enormity of it hits you. We are more confronted by people ready to defend their property than by people asking for help. One of our team was confronted by a man waving a wrench. He thought she was a looter. The purpose of our engagement right now is to at least get people talking and lessen the impact of what will happen in the weeks and months to come. We don't expect that we will be exercising serious grief counselling and specialist mental health treatment until months from now."

**As told to Ross Brundett, *Herald Sun***

**Ashes: Little remains of what was the township of Marysville**  Picture: Norm Oorloff

# Chapter 6

# Marysville

- **Origin**
  By 6pm the fire charges into Marysville, population 517.
  Within 30 minutes the town is razed

- **Destruction**
  Nearly every building in the town, including the school,
  is destroyed and 57,000ha are scorched

- **Toll**
  As many as 100 people are feared dead. In neighbouring
  Narbethong·at least nine are killed. Marysville ceases to exist

For John Munday, it starts shortly after he wakes. It is 6.30 and, first thing, he goes outside and runs his hand across the grass. He feels no dew. He lifts his face for wind. There is none. Then he looks into a clear sky. We might get lucky, he says to himself, although not really believing it.

He goes to the back veranda of his Acheron home and starts going through his preparations, checking his firefighting gear he has laid out in preparation: goggles, facemask, gloves. His frozen water bottles in the fridge, some fruit. Then he goes outside and waters his vegetable garden, giving the plants a drink.

To the south, the people of Marysville are also going about their business. Lucie O'Meara, just 20, spends the morning making pancakes for her husband, Luke. The Marysville Bowling Club is open. Closed for a year, this morning they are rolling on the new green for the first time. Already it appears the extreme forecast has deterred many of the tourists that normally head to Marysville on a weekend.

John turns his laptop on and logs on to the CFA site, calling up the incident management system that logs where jobs are being reported. Shortly before midday it begins. "A job came up at Kilmore, where the first major fire began," he says. He gets a ruler out and follows its down-line – the expected path the head of the fire, the hottest part, will take – and has only one thought: "This is horrible." He monitors the Kilmore fire until word comes through that they have lost control of the Bunyip State Park fire. For John, it is time for action.

Back in Marysville, though, life is still normal. John Cartwright, 78, has left the bowling club and is home watching Gregory Peck on TV. Nora Spitzer and Kay Menzies are thinking about an appointment they have at Lyall Cottages. They are masseurs with Cathedral View Natural Therapies. Even with John Cartwright no longer looking on, the new bowling green, with the drought-resistant grass, is still rolling terrifically.

For days afterwards, nobody will really know what happens in Marysville. By the time ABC radio starts issuing fire warnings, the town has already burned down. By the time CFA boss Russell Rees and other emergency services co-ordinating the fight in the war room think Marysville might be next, again, it has already burned down. Indeed, it is not until 8.57pm that Russell is told, somewhat hopefully, there might be fatalities from the day's fires, but something "less than 14". It is terribly optimistic. By then, 45 are dead in Marysville alone. The town is virtually wiped away and so many townsfolk are so upset it is days before they really talk, if at all.

Nobody really knows what happens when the fire hits, except John. It makes hard listening. His Acheron crew, which forms part of the Alexandra group strike team, are on their way to the Kilmore fires when they are turned around at Trawool. The Murrindindi sawmill is alight, they are told, most likely lit by arsonists, opening a new front. The fire is running south, parallel to the Kilmore fire, and John's down-line contains more dark warnings. As the Acheron crew head back, travelling west to east, the southerly starts whipping in and John is surprised by its strength. Such is the buffeting from the right, he is wrestling with the truck. As they head towards Yea, they find themselves on a ridge that reveals the full job ahead. "A huge convection column of smoke," he says.

The smoke from the fires will climb 15km into the sky, 5km higher than the clouds in a severe thunderstorm. Word comes across the radio that the fires have reached Narbethong, houses are being lost. Before John and his crew arrive in Narbethong, though, they are stopped at Buxton and told they are needed in Marysville. This is some time after 5pm, when the people of Marysville are starting to watch the smoke rising on the ridges to the south.

In Narbethong, Faye and Bill Walker get a phone call from their neighbours at 5.30pm, telling them to get out. The Walkers have their son with them, Geoffrey, 53, who is in a wheelchair. They prepare to get out and at 6.30pm call one of their daughters, saying smoke is over the back shed and they are getting out now.

Over Marysville, birds soon begin dropping out of the sky, stone dead. Elaine Postlethwaite, 72, and her husband, Len, are having an argument at the top of the hill at the corner of Martin and Falls Rds. Elaine wants to flee. Len, 82, says no. "Come on, Len," she says, saying it twice. You just can't imagine it. The town's longest-serving resident, no fire is going to run Len out of town. More, when Elaine finally leaves with neighbours, to be saved, Len sits on his veranda and stubbornly turns his back to the fires.

Nora and Kay are midway through doing their massages when they hear a crash outside. A tree has fallen onto a car and the sky is dark. They get into their cars and leave. As do the couple being massaged. Lucie and her family head to the five-star resort, Cumberland Spa, to find safety. There is a swimming pool there. Then at the last minute they are convinced to leave the resort and head to the town's oval, Gallipoli Park. It is about this time, shortly before 6pm, that John and his fire crew reach town. The cars on the Buxton road are nose to tail, jammed, and hardly moving. It is the only working road out of town. The main fire is still about 15 minutes away but already spot fires are running ahead, causing small outbreaks. Embers as big as dinner plates are landing around them.

John and his crew – Jamie Walker, Dale Wakefield, John Stephens and Garry De Klijn – put out a spot fire and are stunned by the wind. "Hurricane-strength," John says, knowing the fire is coming close behind it. And right here is where experience outweighs preparation. For all his preparation, the fire chief knows they cannot beat this fire. They begin to retreat to Gallipoli Park, stopping briefly to chaperone cars along the Buxton road. Visibility is no more than 10m and soon the cars are in gridlock.

Now they all head to Gallipoli Park and it is now John's heart begins to break. A man approaches him telling him an elderly couple are trapped in a home. The house is in the wrong direction, towards the oncoming fire. He has to say he cannot save them. Residents bang on the side of his truck, begging for help. The truck is retreating. John looks up the road. "A father and two small children, under 10, standing in the middle of the street in shorts and light clothing," he says. "They had a look of bewilderment. I knew they were there. I knew there were people all around us." Asked later what happened to the father and his two children, his answer is brief: "I don't even want to think about what's happened."

The noun remains long after John stops speaking: bewilderment. What an awful place it must have been. When the fire finally hits, there is nothing they can do at Gallipoli Park but seek cover. For about

30 minutes no one moves. People remain in their cars. Lucie huddles down with her husband and small child, and the town dies around them. Houses are burning down, cars are aflame, it is all going. The Cumberland Spa goes, estimates later saying as many as 100 people dying inside.

There is no gas line to Marysville, so all around the gas cylinders begin venting. This is what they are designed to do in a fire. A seal breaks and the gas slowly escapes. Now alight, it shoots into the air like a flamethrower. But this is different. The extreme temperature causes the gas to expand quicker than it can escape and so the cylinders start exploding.

Gallipoli Park is a natural amphitheatre, meaning on the ridge around them every single house is on fire. There are 40 to 50 firefighters there, along with about 60 locals. John and his crew spend the time going from car to car, checking that people are OK, that they have water. All anyone can do is sit and wait. Around them the little town is gone.

For 146 years it has stood there, virtually untouched. Industry has long since moved on, meaning over a century Marysville morphs from a timber town that boasts 14 mills – "the gateway to the forests" – to a town of arts and crafts, of English-style guesthouses and weekend getaways. A popular destination for tourists, they like to say. Now it is gone.

There are as many as 100 deaths from a town of just 517. And the thing right now is, nobody knows. Marysville is not listed among the affected towns until the day after Black Saturday. So comprehensive is the destruction, so complete is the job the fire has done, those who know are too busy fighting for their lives to bother with such trivialities as informing anyone. Lachlan Fraser breaks this mould. He is on the side of the road, hugging his dogs and weeping softly. His fruit trees have gone up, along with his house. Finally, he calls his mum on a satellite phone. "I'm alive," he says. "The dogs are alive. The house is gone. The town is gone." His mother, Barbara, gives the only rational response: "What?"

The main front passes and people concentrate on putting out what fires are left. They are finally manageable. It takes hours, but it seems like minutes. Which is only fair, because when the blaze first hit, the minutes seem like hours.

There is no let-up, though. While they wait, the Murrindindi fire merges with the Kilmore fire, creating a 100km-long firefront. Then John and his crew hear the fire has now turned and is racing north, towards Taggerty, and Acheron. Towards home. "We were absolutely trapped and helpless," he says.

Already Narbethong is ruined. Nine are dead. In a town of 281. In any other time such numbers would numb a country but on this night they are just details. There are three dead in Taggerty, houses are burning and John and his crew are trapped. Eventually, the intensity drops off enough that they decide to take a chance. "We thought we could fight our way out of Marysville and get to where the head of the fire was to fight it off," he says.

So they try and find nothing is easy. The road is blocked by trees and branches and debris. Then someone remembers there is a D4 bulldozer, virtually untouched, in town.

It takes hours but, branch by branch, tree by tree, burnt-out car by burnt-out car, they clear enough road to get their trucks by.

Back up the Maroondah Highway they go, towards Acheron, finally over-running the flames a few kilometres short of Taggerty. And there they make their stand, stopping the fire. By the time John and his crew make it home the destruction is absolute. Marysville is flattened. A dark footnote in Australian history. It creates headlines around the world. The little historical town wiped from the map. For days afterwards ugly rumours swell about the town. One hundred people have died in an Anglican church, goes one. No, they didn't die there, that's where the bodies are being taken. Nobody knows. Everybody hears something. What is true is police shut Marysville down, declaring the whole town a crime scene. It fuels more rumours. Everyone, it seems, knows someone who has died.

At Narbethong, Faye and Bill Walker are found dead in their home, along with their son, Geoffrey. Their car is in the driveway, the keys inside and the dog in the back. John's son, Angus, loses his best mate. He is 18-year-old Stuart O'Gorman, the son of Allan O'Gorman, who ignored his business partner's flashing lights to streak up the mountain in a futile bid to save his son and wife. John does not know this yet. Instead, he makes it home about 3am, after other crews relieve his team at Taggerty, and climbs into bed spent.

Meanwhile, back on the oval – Gallipoli Park, at Marysville – many are only now beginning to understand the depth of what has happened. Len Postlethwaite, once a champion woodcutter and the town's oldest resident, is gone. Not even Len's broad back could withstand what came.

Glen Fiske is there with his son Kellan. Kellan is told his mum, Liz, and his brother, Dalton, are dead. He collapses to the ground, struggling to breathe. The following morning, Liz and Dalton are found wrapped in each other's arms.

The fire has passed, but there is no joy. Rod Liesfield is on the oval. "My wife and the kids are gone," he says to someone. "That's good," the person says. "No," says Rod, "they're *gone*."

**Paul Kent**

**Home safe: Judy Jans lost a cottage but her house survived**   Picture: Norm Oorloff

# Cats in cat boxes. Dogs on leads. All strangely docile, as if they sense the vibe

## Julie Bell, Warburton

*Julie escaped the bushfire in her car. As the convoy crawled through smoke her children prayed. The determined spirit of her fellow refugees has helped her cope.*

"I bustle my daughter into the car, asking her, 'Hear that? What's that?' It's a huge roaring sound. Eyes huge, she says, 'That's the fire'. In the car, reverse, we're on the open road. Grandma and Bob not far behind. Mum later tells me that as she got into their car she could feel the updraft. Mum was in the 1969 bushfires, when I was only two. She says, 'Once you have smelt a bushfire, you never forget it'.

"We are part of a convoy of about 50 cars driving out of Marysville in the smoke with our lights on. Safety in numbers. The girls yell, 'We can see the fire!' On the mountains to the left we see the flames. My eldest girl, aged 10, later wrote, 'I thought all of Australia would catch on fire'. The girls all start praying. I find their voices and requests of heaven comforting. It keeps us all calm and centred.

"At Buxton and Taggerty people are stopping and getting out of their cars, asking for info. We get to Alex and follow cars to Alexandra High School. There's a car with three massive paintings sticking out of the boot. Somehow it is this that finally makes me realise this is serious. Cats in cat boxes. Dogs on leads. All strangely docile, as if they sense the vibe. Cars parked every which way, new ones roaring up every few moments.

"The smoke is thick, like dense fog of a dirty yellow colour. You can hardly see a few yards up the street. We zig-zag through fire refugees into the hall and write our names on Red Cross registration paper. No power. People perch wherever they can. We have towels soaked in buckets of water – Mum's idea. I had thought, 'Surely we won't be in a situation in which we actually need these'. Now we thankfully wrap them round our heads and across our faces. My stepfather says, 'It's like the Blitz – only that was noisier'.

"Food and drink gets passed around. I cut up our rockmelon and watermelon and pass it round. Our throats are raspy, our eyes stinging. It's getting darker. I make nests for the girls on the floor. Sometimes when it's hard to breathe, I feel panic rise and quickly swallow it down, telling myself I'm OK, this is only momentary discomfort that we can live through.

"How frail we are. Yet everyone is calm and helping each other. Together we're strong. People are talking, a few hugging each other and sharing tears. A woman next to us says she does not know if her husband is alive. There are a few torches in the gloom, enough to help us pick our way to the toilets. Water bottles are passed out. It's stinking hot, oppressively hot. The doors to the hall are all open. It is too hot to close them and people would feel too claustrophobic anyway. All eyes are staring into the smoky gloom in the direction of the hills on fire. The SES brings a generator and now we have light. I sense people's anxiety levels drop as light filters through the smoky room. A large fan is started up, moving fetid hot air around. Evacuees from Marysville are realising they probably do not have homes anymore. Yet there is still a sense that surely we're exaggerating, being drama queens. When the smoke clears, it won't be that bad – right? It's unthinkable that anyone might have lost loved ones as well as homes."

**Via email**

# Sharen ... had gone home looking for me and she rang the kids, thinking she was finished

## Terry Donovan, owner of Dalrymples Guest Cottages

Terry quickly realised the fire was much worse than he had anticipated, and left. But he had to go back into the flames to find his wife before they both escaped.

"Like a lot of people, we were going to stay and defend, that's what we had learned. We got our guests to leave, a few minutes after that my sister-in-law rang. She lives in Kings Rd. She said a firefighter had yelled for her to 'get the f..... out' and he pointed to the bush and there was a wall of flames. She came around and got my wife, Sharen, but I said, 'I am not leaving'. It was against everything we were told to do. So after probably the biggest fight we have ever had in 35 years of marriage, I said, 'You go, I'll be right'.

"Just after they left it went completely black. I grabbed the ute and took off. I went to the main street and there were trees across the main road. As I was doing a U-turn I got a phone call from my son, who was in Melbourne. I said, 'I am in a bit of trouble'. Sharen had rung him to say goodbye, she had gone home looking for me and she rang the kids thinking she was finished. I went back and got her. We again went down in the ute and we crashed through a few branches and trees at the bottom of the main street and just got away; there were trees being blown all over the place. We got the headlights on, we picked up a couple more people and found them seats in the car with us. As we left we watched the church burn then everything else just exploded, one building after another. We all went to the oval at Gallipoli Park for the rest of the night. Our first duty and responsibility is to the people who have lost family and friends, then we will rebuild. I hope people can remain positive."

**As told to Gemma Jones, *The Daily Telegraph***

# It came right into the valley, roaring like a train

## Bruno Torf, 53

Bruno huddled in his car with his Jack Russell, Itchy, in the middle of the cricket oval, watching in disbelief as the town came crashing down around him building by building. He had narrowly escaped the roaring flames licking the back door of his art and sculpture gallery, which was engulfed as he fled with a handful of precious pieces.

"It came so suddenly, without warning and from all angles. It came right into the valley, roaring like a train going 100km/h. The heat was so intense. My friend Simone Ray said, 'Run to the oval, it's the place we're supposed to gather'. There were only 18 of us that made it. I could see the community building, Marylands resort and the Blackwood Cottages crumble one by one."

Seeking refuge at his daughter's Frankston flat, Bruno and his family are counting their blessings that they are alive.

Daughter Iris, 27, said: "It's incredible. The longer we hear about it the luckier we feel."

**Natalie Tkaczuk Sikora, *Herald Sun***

# I thought we'd sent them into a fireball. That's when your guts go

## Senior Constables Andrew Walker, Ian Hamill and Peter Collyer

A group of brave policemen evacuated hundreds of people with only seconds to spare in a life-or-death escape. The terrified locals' only chance was to follow the police out of town.

Senior Constable Andrew Walker: "You could hear the roar. When we got there the edge of the oval was on fire. We had to make sure the road was clear towards Buxton. I think people were still a bit hesitant. You think to yourself, 'Are we doing the right thing?'. But with that fire you had to do something. Pete and Ken [Dwight, colleague] then started shooing people out. I remember trying to get them to go quicker and quicker. I thought we'd sent them into a fireball. That's when your guts go."

Senior Constable Ian Hamill: "As we were driving into Marysville you could see the fire coming in and getting onto the flats. We knew we had limited time because there was only one road in and out. My sister-in-law rang and said, 'Don't be a dead hero'. It spooked us even more. We decided we wouldn't separate and we'd do the safe thing. When it went black, and with the roar of the fire as we're leaving Marysville, I knew we had that one road and I thought we'd lost that. I honestly didn't see faces. It all happened in two minutes."

Senior Constable Peter Collyer: "[The approaching fire] was like a low bass note with a rush to it. I could only describe it as like a hundred steam locomotions coming over. The harsher you were [with the locals] the better. You didn't leave them with any doubt. I've been in this job

27 years and I would say this is the most fearful I've ever been. I felt our lives hung in the balance of whatever decision you made. If you made the wrong decision you were a goner."

**As told to Anthony Dowsley, *Herald Sun***

# I've got my family and that's all that matters

## David Nicholls

The burnt-out petrol pump at the Tudor Lodge guest house in Narbethong reads $6.66. Devil's number aside, who does buy just $6.66 worth of premium unleaded? Someone in a hurry. Someone like David, who tore down his driveway in a burning ute with nothing more than a briefcase of his wedding photos.

"It was the only thing I managed to grab out of the house; when I drove out of my driveway my car was already on fire." Minutes before crashing into a tree, he passed a woman who refused a ride. "I tried but she wouldn't get in my car. They found her about 500m up the road." In the rush he hit a fallen tree that took the front wheel off his ute, leaving him no option but to dive for cover at the side of the road and shield his face with his briefcase. He rang his mother and told her, "If I don't get through, goodbye". "She just cried on the end," he said. After what felt like hours the fire passed and he was found by a CFA volunteer. The wedding photos are still in pristine condition.

"I only got a little burn on my cheek but I couldn't stand afterwards," David said. "I've got my family and that's all that matters."

**Angus Hohenboken, *The Australian***

# I looked at Paul and said: 'This is it. We're gonna die'

## Brooke 'BJ' Fowler, 35

Best mates for nearly a decade, Brooke 'BJ' Fowler and Paul Jones were trapped in the inferno which raced through Narbethong, Marysville and parts of Buxton. The two timber workers and self-described troublemakers decided to stay and fight for BJ's property but were soon fighting for their lives. Their escape took them through fields of flame, three burning houses and a 5km walk through hell before being hospitalised in Alexandra.

"We were hosing down the outside of my place near Buxton as the fire approached from Narbethong. All of a sudden the sky just turned orange and we heard this roar. Five minutes later there's a wall of flame coming over the hill in two separate fronts, from the south and east. Embers started landing and we moved inside to the cellar. We had 15 seconds to get in the house and then all the windows exploded. There was so much smoke in the house I couldn't see my hand in front of my face. With wet tea towels around our faces we lay on our backs spraying the ceiling with hoses but couldn't take more than a quarter of a breath.

"The roof was going to come down so we went out the back door to get to the vehicle but there was just this wall of fire. There was no smoke but you couldn't breathe and the heat was just so intense. We went for the wet towels we had outside but they were on fire. We collapsed outside, we couldn't breathe and we were just losing it, just drifting off.

"I looked at Paul and said, 'This is it. We're gonna die'. I said,

'I love you' and we hugged and said, 'Let's try our best to get out of here'. We ran to the neighbour's house, which was starting to burn but not like my place, and broke a window to get in. We were able to breathe easier inside but then the whole house went up in flame and we started to drift off.

"Again I said, 'We gotta get out of here or we're not going to live. We've got to run into that paddock'. There were round hay bales burning around us and we collapsed again for 15 minutes. I said, 'We're gonna die again. We've got to get to the highway'. Both sides of the highway were on fire and it was like a ghost town with tornado winds around us. I could feel my hands, nose and ears burning from the heat. After walking for about a kilometre along the road to Buxton we found a shallow dam and covered ourselves in mud. We kept walking to Buxton, having to go right around logs across the road. We finally found refuge in a farmhouse but then flagged down a convoy of people in cars fleeing Narbethong, who drove us to a hospital in Alexandra. The cars had to ram about five logs out of the way to get there and we arrived about four hours after we started our escape.

"I was hospitalised for burns from the radiant heat. We were put on oxygen pumps for smoke inhalation and could not open our eyes for two days from the pain. Emotionally I've been a wreck since but glad to be alive. We can't believe we've survived it but we're great mates and battlers. Everyone knows we love a rush and get into trouble but we had to have a go of saving the house. We wouldn't do it again though.

"We will have to be friends for life now – with smoke inhalation problems in common. We've worked together, go four-wheel-driving every weekend, drink a lot of cans together, have camp fires together. I don't think we'll do the camp fires anymore."

**As told to Liam Houlihan, *Sunday Herald Sun***

# Bugger it, I'm not going. I'm going to stay and try to save this place

## Greg Cherry, Crossways Country Inn

After sending his wife to safety in Alexandra, Greg chose to stay and fight the fire, bucket by bucket. That's all he had to douse his property and, against impossible odds, he won.

"I just thought, 'Bugger it, I'm not going. I'm going to stay and try to save this place'. We'd put too much into it to let it just go up in flames. I reckon I was there for about an hour and a half and at times it got pretty hairy as I couldn't breathe but I just covered my mouth with the towel and that got me through the worst moments."

He put on sunglasses and sunscreen – and amazingly, this helped. Even so, the radiant heat was intense. "It got pretty warm up here and the buildings were too hot to touch."

**As told to Julie-Anne Davies, *The Australian***

# I looked at my husband. I felt powerless

## Vicki Moritz

Vicki and her husband, Russell Glenn, lost three pets and a home while cowering in their car.

"We didn't know if our vehicle would hold up. There was a massive fireball raging around us. I think the word is conflagration. For 90 minutes we sat and waited. We couldn't touch the windscreen.

I looked at my husband. I felt powerless. He kept saying, 'We are not out of this yet'. He backed the car into a steel shed but the front of the vehicle was poking out. The fire melted the front headlight. That can only happen at 1100C. The loss of life is the hardest thing to deal with. Our pets [two dogs and a cat] were our little family. We have a huge sense of loss over our animals. The loss of real estate is minor. We lost friends and we lost the beauty of Marysville."

**As told to Nui Te Koha, *Sunday Herald Sun***

# The wall of flames followed me

## Alan Ryan, 59

With embers raining down on his car, Alan was one of the last to escape the flames.

"I drove out with the firestorm actually coming over the ridge at the top of the town. The wall of flames followed me. With the debris that was flying through the air it was dark. It was like Armageddon. Mine was the third-last car out of Marysville. I had the windows up but it was horrible, there was so much turmoil outside. There were exploding sparks around the car. I actually managed to get out of town, not through the ability of my headlights but by the reflective road markers. It was like I was coming in to land a plane, with landing lights on the runway. There was no official warning, everything happened so fast. I have sat by myself quietly and looked back on it. I reckon if I had been a minute later I would have been enveloped. Then I think what if the car had stalled? What if a tree had fallen on the road? What if there had been an accident blocking my way?"

**As told to Gemma Jones, *The Daily Telegraph***

# I was concerned I hadn't done my breakfast dishes, which were in the sink, nor made the bed

## John Kennedy, Buxton

John had only just finished renovating his dream home the week before the fires hit. He escaped thanks to a friend who insisted he leave as the flames roared towards them.

"I was armed with a CFA frequency scanner and I had an engine-powered fire pump, hoses and plenty of water. I had always had the view that in a bushfire situation I would stay and defend. I had watched the fire for a couple of hours as it was burning along a ridgeline about 10km to the west. From the time I first noticed it about 2pm it had got alarmingly larger but it was burning southwards – away from me and only occasionally I could see flames.

"So I was bunkered in and had given the pump a run and fully fuelled it. [The fire] switched direction and completely changed course, coming back at me. I'd heard on my scanner that it had already taken out the Narbethong village to the immediate south.

"The air was smoke-laden and blowing a gale and it was stinking hot. But I had the fire pump warmed up. Then my mate David arrived. He insisted I leave but I remember saying, 'No way, mate, this is my dream and I am staying to defend it'.

"Just then there was an exploding roar from the south and a huge windstorm. 'Nope, be sensible, grab something and go,' I thought. I put a note on the front door, '6.05pm John Kennedy left with David Wilkinson' so the CFA fireys, when they come to check, will know

I am OK and will be back soon when this is all over! I remember grabbing a favourite pen, my sunglasses, scanner, wallet and small change and we bolted. I was concerned that I hadn't done my breakfast dishes, which were in the sink, nor had I made the bed!

"We went back south, with the firestorm in view along the highway, convincing another retired couple to follow us in the smoke in their vehicles – and they did, fortunately, but now their house is gone, too. We headed to another mate's place, about 15km up the highway. He had no power and thus no means of running his sprinkler and pump system, nor did he have a fire pump. There were five blokes, some rakes and shovels, and a house which had filled by then with three women and about seven or eight young children, the youngest a babe in arms. We knew we were in the direct fire-line and it was coming. So we waited – by now it was after midnight. I'll never forget the glow and the distinctive roar in the air and the exploding sounds every 10 minutes or so. And then it came at a phenomenal rate and we waited until it got close. We had no alternative – we had no equipment, save for the rakes and shovels.

"The house had a circular, well-used gravel driveway so we figured that gave us a natural firebreak. David Deal, the owner, had a Bobcat so his idea was to get into the paddock next door and [bull]doze a fence-line firebreak, say two buckets in width. We cut the fences and he got one pass done and then the hydraulics on the Bobcat failed. The fire streamed across the grass paddocks, igniting anything of substance as it came, and even though the lawns were well cut they still burned. We managed to save the Bobcat though.

"But between the driveway and the house is a well-established garden with timber sleeper beds and a number of ornamental conifers. And one of these had burst into flame and the embers were adding to those already falling on the roof of the house, creating a grave risk of igniting whatever was in the spouting. With the first conifer flaring, a couple of blokes managed to pull the tree apart and while it burned to destruction, it didn't extend to many of the others in the garden.

"Thankfully the wind, by this stage a northern one, was actually blowing the fire alongside the property and it was rolling. As long as we could hold it at the driveway we looked safe. Whenever it flared into the lawn and grass area beyond, we managed to put these out.

"By now it was after 4am and we had survived, lit only by the flames, and then the CFA trucks arrived. The property has a large dam at the rear and I counted 10 CFA trucks, many from distant towns, which backed up to the dam and refilled their tanks.

"We sat down in the deckchairs outside and waited while we watched the fire burn around us. Warm and tepid cordial was all we had as the fridges and a few light stubbies had gone hours ago.

"At first light David and I decided we'd try and get back to my place. The road was littered with many fallen trees, a lot of them still burning. I'd realised by then there was no chance that my place would still be standing. When I arrived back at the estate the gates swung jauntily as all the treated pine fence posts were gone. I could see that the ground was baked like concrete, not a square inch had been missed.

"We got halfway up the driveway until the debris stopped us, and walked the rest. I could see that the ruins of my beloved house, shed and cottage were still burning.

"The 18 magnificent 250mm x 250mm timber posts I'd bought from Barry Donchi at Nullarbor Forests were still ablaze and the stonework had obviously exploded. The roofing we had screwed down ourselves lay collapsed, bent and destroyed. I was there for about 30 seconds only, no need to see more. Everything is gone. On the way out I padlocked the remaining gates shut. Maybe I'll be back some day."

**Via email**

**True blue: Police heroes Ian Hamill, Ken Dwight, Peter Collyer and Andrew Walker**
Picture: Rebecca Michael

**My patch: Bruno Torf, pictured with grandson Jaelan, survived by huddling in his car with his Jack Russell, Itchy**
Picture: Nicki Connolly

# Time. There isn't enough of it before the fire hits Marysville

**Patrick Carlyon, of the *Herald Sun*, revisits Black Saturday in Marysville, a town that died in 30 minutes.**

The Marysville Bowls Club hums with chatter. It's open, finally, for the first time in 12 months. About 15 bowlers roll on the new drought-resistant grass. Colin Paul, 83, a crack rifleman who served in World War II, looks on. He is armed with walking sticks. A recent fall has slowed him down. Colin is the oldest club member. Like the youngest member, a Year 9 student, Colin has less than eight hours to live.

The bowlers play a couple of games. It's 11am on Saturday. The sun is heating up. John Cartwright, 78, goes home and gazes at the photo of his wife, Jean, on the loungeroom wall. This is his daily ritual. She died from cancer a decade ago.

In the shot Jean is 19. It was taken when they first met. He has never really recovered from her loss. They were married in the 1950s, two locals in the honeymoon town that Melburnians would head to for a weekend of tea and scones at English-style guesthouses. The relics of the era endure. As does the mood. Marysville, according to the official guff, is "a place to relax and unwind".

Once a sawmilling town that was a gateway to forests of mountain ash and waterfalls, it has also come to embrace tourist lurks, such as arts and crafts. Still, it sags in the wider rural malaise. No jobs for young people. The footy and tennis clubs are gone. The local CFA boasts a tanker, a pumper and a dozen-odd volunteers. Once there were 14 timber mills and a big bell in the middle of town that rang terror in children's imaginations when smoke was spotted.

Nature had been kind to the hamlet. Even the 1939 fires flew over the leafy basin. Now there are no mills and a CFA siren in Barton Ave that, for reasons not yet clear, will not be heard by many residents this afternoon. Today, it's too hot for tourists or anyone else. Lee Jowett, 56, has been fixing a neighbour's door. The builder goes home to do some paperwork. His son-in-law and a mate pop in to borrow something. He can't remember what. They go to leave, walk out, then walk straight back in. It's about 4pm.

"Oh, s.....," they call. "Come and look at this." No one guesses at the twilight ahead. How could they? History offers no precedents.

The storm that will blow and burn Marysville's 146-year history to rubble, sparing only a crooked chimney here and there, a bakery, a motel, a cafe and the odd house, passes before many people grasp it has arrived. After bowls, John watches a Gregory Peck flick. He'd prefer the races but the Caulfield meeting has been postponed until the next day. Damn heat. At about the same time town doctor Lachlan Fraser has returned from puffing up a nearby hill. Like all ultra-marathon runners, he's a bit mad. Not long ago, he finished a 220km run to Mt Kosciusko. Fit, 46 and "looking for a lady", Dr Fraser is training for a 50km jaunt the following Sunday. Training partner, his blue heeler, Indi, is starting to tire. Dr Fraser doesn't push. He, too, is feeling unnaturally hot for the morning.

He goes home and measures the house for insulation batts – paid for by the Federal Government – which would be welcome on scorchers like today. He flicks on a taped episode of *The Simpsons* but never finishes it.

Mark Simmons, 48, president of the bowls club, fills up the car with petrol then settles in at home. He notices the smoke at about 3pm but it's a long way off. Still, he'll keep an eye on it and he cancels a trip to Werribee. Just in case.

The local radio station gives regular fire updates, interspersed between country music. The tunes frustrate Dr Fraser. They lack the requisite urgency demanded of the threat. He drives to a higher point to gauge the smoke then rings the bushfire hotline and waits 20 minutes before someone comes on the line.

Murrindindi, 30km northwest, officially starts burning at 2.57pm. Its flames fly southeast, towards Narbethong, fuelled by towering mountain ash, thick undergrowth and winds that some say gust to 120km/h. In Marysville, as ex-CFA captain John Cartwright suggests, people try to look on the bright side. "You always believe the worst will not happen," he says.

Others aren't as convinced. Dr Fraser takes another drive after the power goes out at about 5.15pm. He has watched the Channel 10 news, which led the bulletin with the Bunyip fire. He looks across to Narbethong, 12km away, from Keppel Falls Lookout, about 10 minutes from town. Narbethong is spotting with flames.

The wind rises in Marysville, hot and roaring, like a million hair dryers set on high. Dr Fraser returns to discover a road accident on the corner of Lyle and Sedgwick Sts. A gum tree has squashed Beverley McGearie's car. She's all right but in shock. She keeps asking how she got here. Dr Fraser notices the advertising on her car: "relaxation therapist". Two masseurs stop at the scene, fresh from jobs. Dr Fraser can't compute this. Fire threatens to destroy a town and people are getting massages?

Marysville has had fire warnings, of course, but it appears that confusion shrouds the town before the smoke rolls in. The supermarket, for example, remains open after authorities start plotting evacuation strategies. Pauline Harrow, the CFA radio operator, has taken a call from the Mt Gordon spotter, 3km to the west, about 4.30pm. Flames are still three mountain ridges away but it's suggested the evacuations begin. "I said to [the SES], 'You better start evacuating', but she only had three members there," Pauline says. "People could see smoke coming into the town and I think they were starting to evacuate their families." How many get away is unknown, but the SES and police get around to many residents, who head north to Buxton.

By 5.50pm a convoy of cars is banked back into town. For the CFA's John Munday, of the nearby Acheron crew, it suggests people have, belatedly, decided to flee. He glimpses a vision that will haunt him – a father standing in the middle of the road with two small children. They wear shorts and T-shirts and expressions of utter bewilderment. Behind them, the smoke darkens and that orange glow everyone will talk about starts to show. "It was pandemonium," Munday says.

A man in a 4WD stops and begs the crew to save an elderly couple trapped in their house up the hill. Munday has to refuse. He knows the full blast is about to hit. He cannot think about saving anyone else. Saving his crew will be tricky enough. He says it was clear-cut that Marysville was doomed from the start. "There was no way anything was going to get through it."

Pauline bunkers down with Marysville CFA chief Glen Fiske and seven others. Glen's son Kellan, 18 or 19, is in a tanker crew that heads to Yea about 4.30pm. The family is well liked. Glen's forebears, who arrived in Marysville in the 1800s, used to run the Marylands Guest House. Married to Liz, with two sons and a daughter, Glen works in a nearby timber mill. They're good people.

In the corrugated iron CFA building, cut into a hill, the smoke pours in. Pauline peeks from a window when "everything" catches fire in Barton Ave. Her wider family will lose six houses in the next 15 minutes, including her daughter Leah, who, with husband Luke, is supposed to move into a new house in Steavenson Close on Monday.

"I just started panicking," Pauline says. "The urge to run was pretty strong. We did the best we could but lives were lost and obviously it wasn't good enough. [But] I don't think it would have mattered if we had had 100 trucks there. It wasn't going to stop it." The sun is about to hide. Birds are about to fall out of the sky. And something wicked is about to roll down the hill from the west, engulf Our Lady of Snows church and rumble through a town so shaken it may never breathe again. It arrives at about the time Jo Hall introduces the 6pm Channel 9 news, and leaves before she signs off. Its roar will be likened to jet planes and freight trains. There will be reports of the sorts of fireball that visited Dresden and Tokyo in 1945. Embers swirl like lit matches in a clothes dryer, lawnmowers spontaneously combust. Tyres pop, gas tanks blow and gums 30m high and a metre wide will be ripped out by the wind. People will draw smoke for their last breaths and perhaps wonder how and why they could be taken so fast. Some, it seems, will fall where they stand, to resemble those petrified bodies at Pompeii. What emerges in these tales of survival at Marysville is that no matter how thorough the preparation, no one could prepare for the fire ahead.

Something else becomes clear, too. Luck is not only handy. Today, in Marysville, it is everything. Untended houses still stand, defended houses burn down. And conventional advice, such as staying inside the house and filling baths with water, is shown to sometimes offer the thinnest veneer of protection.

Time. There isn't enough of it before the fire hits Marysville. And once the fire does, time distorts so that 10 minutes feels like a day, and the rest of your life hinges entirely on getting that next bucket of water right bloody now. "We knew it would be a bad day," John Cartwright says. "Everyone was warned the day before. But if you took notice of every fire-danger day, you'd be leaving every week in fire season. This wasn't a fire, this was an inferno."

Dr Fraser has a methodical way. Patients like that in doctors.

He fills the bath, wheelie bin, sinks and bottles with water. He is as prepared as he can be, yet his frantic efforts, which lead to a burnt face and sliced tendons in his hand, will be futile. He runs about with a bucket of water dousing spot fires at the front and back that spark and multiply when he puts them out and looks the other way.

The home of his absent neighbours erupts like a blowtorch. He ties his dogs, Indi and Lani, to furniture inside. He is armed with a hose when the jasmine trailing up the side of the neighbours' house catches light. Embers shower. He tries to splash the neighbours' home. Too late. The eaves catch alight. Dr Fraser slips on the veranda and puts his hand through a window. Toilet paper stems the flow of blood but he knows it will need surgery – assuming he survives. He wets his windcheater and breathes through it. He grabs the dogs, telling them over the roar that they will survive. And, right then, Dr Fraser gives up on saving his house.

Mark, the bowls club president, leaves a tap running before ushering the family into the hallway and donning a tea towel like a baddie in a cowboy movie. Mark, his partner Sue and their sons, Ben and Beau, get on the floor. "It was like a foundry, when it actually hit; the amount of embers and sparks, it was just like you see in the movies or working in a foundry," he says. "You could hear the windows shaking and buckling. At one point when it was really ferocious I could see smoke coming off our drapes."

They play a waiting game. If the brick house withstands the blast outside long enough, they have a chance. If toxic fumes enter too soon, forcing them outside, they will die of radiant heat or smoke inhalation. The fire box, an opening for gathering wood, becomes the fear. It burns and smoulders and finally, after maybe 20 minutes, opens. A window finally shatters. They will die if they stay in the house. They will probably die if they dash for the lawn, where they can hose each other in water.

Mark notices a neighbour's weatherboard house. The couple are home, their daughters not. Mark comprehends that the house is no longer there. Its raised floor presumably allowed ember slurries to form underneath. Nothing anyone could have done.

The family takes turns spraying one another on the blackened lawn. Beau almost collapses, but revives. The house crackles to a pile. They move to the horse paddock next door, chattering about the fate of others, and ready themselves for the next perceived threat – lightning.

John Cartwright is hoping his good friends, the Simmons, will swing by to pick him up. There is a problem. Their three cars are destroyed, including Beau's 2004 Commodore, which presents the family with a fireworks display that all, except maybe Beau, find rather intriguing. John has stayed inside, watching fence palings flare like flaming matchsticks, one after the other. He ventures outside to put out the eaves. No outside water. He rings Wayne, his son, as windows crack. Wayne tells him he can't survive in the house. John says he can't survive outside the house. But it gets too hot. Ash whooshes in. Better to cook outside than inside. John is making it up as he goes along.

This is how it is when you're about to die, he thinks. Or is it? He's never been about to die before. John grabs a bucket of water and a tea towel, forgets his dodgy hip and staggers through smoke to the empty swimming pool of the motel next door. He sits on the bottom step and wipes embers when they settle on him. This is where he will be found four hours later. John has watched his house burn down. He has also pondered the loss of every photo he possesses of his late wife, Jean.

Six days after the blast, builder Lee Jowett still will not have checked a lottery ticket he bought on Saturday. He isn't hopeful of winning. He reckons he has used up his good fortune. "I don't think I have a chance as long as my bum points to the ground," he says.

His house survives the fire, perhaps because it is sheltered by a hill. He isn't there when the blast comes through. Fearful of falling gum trees, he parks at the golf club and waits an eternity before the radiant heat dwindles enough for him to open the door. He later sees the logging truck, abandoned beside him in the car park, melted to the ground. The newly laid neighbouring bowls green, a lingering source of community kinship, is untouched. It's not much. It's something. Lee's cat, Old Taz, leaps from the car during the worst of the blast. He gives up on him. Three days later, Old Taz will turn up meowing at the door, looking for breakfast and sympathy for a burnt paw.

Dr Fraser sits on the road, hugs his dogs and cries. The house, the fruit trees, everything, is lost. His phone rings. It's someone called Andrea asking about a planned group dinner in Melbourne tonight.

"The house is on fire, the town is on fire, speak to me next week, bye," he tells her. A few hours later, Dr Fraser rings his mother in Eltham on a satellite phone (all other communications are out). "I'm alive," he tells her. "The dogs are alive. The house is gone. The town is gone." "What?" replies Barbara. Like the rest of Australia, she doesn't know that Marysville isn't there anymore.

Through busted fences and around fallen trees, survivors head to the football oval at Gallipoli Park. It will be a long night of burning eyes and no sleep. It stings to blink. Dr Fraser treats people as best he can. He has replaced the toilet paper on his wound with a bandage. He checks the clinic: it's gone. He sees signs everywhere, signs marking piles of burning rubble. Television footage later shows a front door and nothing else, except a "No smoking" sign hung on it. These signs speak of a "before" that, regardless of rebuilding efforts, can never be recreated. But it's no time to start dwelling on the chances for an "after". Not yet.

Dr Fraser makes do with the medical kit he carries for marathons in his glove box. Eyedrops. Anti-nausea medication. Panadeine

Forte. He offers the worst piece of medical advice he will ever give to an overweight patient: "Eat as much as you like tonight." Around the oval, gas cylinders keep exploding, such as the big one at Marylands Guest House, which flames like fiery geysers. The pavilion smoulders. Someone, somewhere, somehow, starts snoring. Melbourne will not grasp the dimension of the tragedy for days. Dozens, perhaps more, die in Marysville before Victoria knows they are gone.

And over the coming week, Marysville will loom as the site of most deaths. The name will take on a sinister echo. The town is a morgue. How many dead bodies here lie untended under sheets of corrugated iron and on the sides of roads? Its crime scene status, which quarantines the town from visitors, will allow ugly rumours to baste, such as the supposed death of 100 people in the Anglican church. Yet right now, no one here at the oval munching on biscuits and cakes taken from the Marysville Bakery (the owners won't mind) is trying to grasp the magnitude of the disaster. They can't make sense of it. Not now. Maybe never. They have lost their homes. They don't know where their friends are.

Everyone knows everyone in Marysville. There are about 20 or 30 here (and a lot of dogs) from a permanent population of about 500. Where is Kirstie Nilssen, 39, the cheery mother of two who runs the Christmas shop? Where is Len Postlethwaite, once a champion woodcutter, who comes in heavier than 18 stone? Where is Marie Walsh, the tree-changer who moved here two years ago with her retired dentist husband, Dan? Where is Nicole Jefferson, the waitress two weeks from giving birth, and her fiance, Jamie Bowker?

Where is the wife of one of the local policemen? She got in the car, but then what? Where is everyone else? They must have moved fast, as Dr Fraser puts it, to have got out before the flames. Or …

Among the gathering are Glen Fiske and his son, Kellan. Kellan is told about the death of his mother, Liz, and his brother, Dalton, in their Lyle St home. Dalton, who is 14 or 15, is the bowling club's youngest member. His brother falls to the ground. He cannot breathe.

"Two people trying to save their town and losing part of their family," John Cartwright says. And then to see the boy puffing to survive, but still there wanting to save more people.

"That's bravery, isn't it?"

It's perhaps 2am at the oval. Earlier, Rod Liesfield had come, distressed. He and his family took over Nanda Binya Lodge a week ago. "He said to somebody, 'Liz and the kids are gone'," Dr Fraser says. "This person said, 'That's good'. And he said, 'No, they're gone'." It's unclear what has happened to his wife and their two boys, Matthew and James. Rod is inconsolable. In coming days, talk will move to a tree falling on the spa the family was huddling in.

It's after dawn on Sunday. Dr Fraser wanders the Marysville streets. He's strangely curious. He wants to search for any relics of his home. Others will later count 32 houses standing where there were once a few hundred. He wonders how long the rebuilding will take and there has to be a rebuilding. Five years? Ten years? Flames lick a couple of fence palings. Dr Fraser kicks them over to stop a carport going up. He walks past the Fiske home in Lyle St. Glen is in the driveway. He has been inside. His wife and son, it's said, have been found arm-in-arm.

Dr Fraser puts his arm around him. Glen does not, cannot, say anything. The doctor, too, struggles for words. "Oh God," he manages. The only memento Dr Fraser has found from his home is a Swiss cow bell, lying under ash about 10m from where it once hung in the kitchen. He keeps walking with the dogs, the cow bell clanging in rhythm to each step. "It's this lonely, grey, ash landscape," he says. "It's like a nuclear bomb has hit. And this cow bell keeps ringing. It's like for whom the bell tolls." Dr Fraser turns the bell upside down and chokes down on the hammer. "It's this lonely, grey, ash landscape. It's like a nuclear bomb has hit. They can't make sense of it. Not now. Maybe never."

# Bugger the house, maybe we should just think about leaving

## Jonathan Densem and Emma Smetham, Buxton

Caspar Densem became a ray of hope amid a state of despair when he was born in Shepparton hours after his parents Jonathan, 39, and Emma, 40, fled the inferno. The little boy was born a day early on Sunday, February 8, in Goulburn Valley Health's Maternity Unit in Shepparton, weighing 3.4kg and with a thick head of hair.

Jonathan: "It was 46.8C at our house. [The fire] was going to the left straight down to Marysville. We weren't concerned because it was clearly not coming towards us. Then the wind changed. The fire crested at the back of Buxton. I said, 'Bugger the house, maybe we should just think about leaving'. I just walked in and said, 'The fire's crested the ridge, let's go'. It was unbelievable. It looked like Mt Vesuvius. The smoke was just unbelievable. We had a bit of a hug and thought this could be the last time we'd see [the house]. All of a sudden the house and everything in it is not very important. We decided we would head up north. We turned the light off at 2.30am and within 30 seconds Emma goes, 'Johnny, I think I'm having a baby'. It was the only thing that had no drama. The hospital staff were incredible. The government services have been incredible. [Caspar has] been wonderful. He's a bit of me. He's got a long nose like me ... and heaps of black hair."

Emma: "I was going up and down ladders stuffing drain pipes and filling them up with water. We could see large flames cresting over the hill, which was less than a kilometre from our property. We were just going, 'This is crazy, we should just go'. The smoke got thicker … and it actually went orange. I was going, 'Don't tell me we're driving into a bloody fire'. We were worried about how much petrol we had because the towns that we had driven through didn't have petrol. I had a [caesarean] with [other son] Otto. If we delivered at Alex or Seymour and then got into trouble then we would have had to travel by helicopter to Shepparton. I think [the fire] helped me to focus calmly, ironically, on the fact that we're delivering this baby and that we were safe and sound with wonderful people. What more is there to life?"

**As told to Cheryl Critchley, *Herald Sun***

# I saw things on Black Saturday I could never describe to anyone

## Ashraf Doos, 56

Ashraf lost his house, business, friends and some customers in the blaze that ravaged Marysville. With his wife and two children, he was lucky to escape the inferno that reduced his hometown to ash. Except for his family, he lost everything.

"My home, my business, my friends, everything is gone. We thought it would be OK, we thought we could survive it but I saw things on Black Saturday I could never describe to anyone. It was horrific.

"We took refuge inside the patisserie; it was also our home and we really thought it would be all right. We held out as long as we could but then an SES worker ordered us to leave. Thank God she did – 10 minutes later our life was dust.

"But Marysville Patisserie will open again. I may have lost my recipes but I haven't lost the heart or the passion to cook. We will have to build it from scratch, but we will, we have to. We will need community support, we will need government support and we will need tourists to keep coming.

"The gem of Marysville was always the appeal of that old village charm and that will be hard to recreate. But it is also known as God's garden. It is beautiful and all that has survived so why can't we come back?"

**As told to Shannon Deery, *Herald Sun***

# We have to make sure the tourists come back

## Simon Hudson, owner of Kerami Guest House

Simon is determined to stay and help rebuild the picturesque town after his historic guest house was razed.

"My T-shirt is the only thing left of our business. It's very upsetting. We've lost our house and our business and our friends. [Kerami] was 90 years old and one of the original buildings. I think the fire was so hot … Marysville's just completely devastated apart from 10 or so houses. I think [seeing it] helped. We've been able to move on and get what we need up there and work out where we go now. We have to make sure the tourists come back. Everyone wants to rebuild. It was a beautiful town. I've never seen a fire before but [now] it just looks like ash and tin. You have this sinking stomach. You can't eat and can't drink.

**Gutted: Ashraf Doos lost friends, his home and his business**    Picture: Alex Coppel

**Smiles: Caspar was born hours after the Densems escaped**    Picture: Mark Smith

Everyone's sitting there quietly and looking for their [houses]. The Tower Hotel is there, a couple of houses, but all infrastructure is gone. Ten to 12 buildings remain out of a little bit over 200 buildings."

**As told to Liam Houlihan,** *Sunday Herald Sun*

# I'll definitely go back there

## Harley Ronalds, 17

"It was black and scary. I'm not in my own bed and my own home and some people get really angry and then I get angry. I'll definitely go back there. I'd have to stay there. It's one of those things where you do want to and you don't."

**As told to Liam Houlihan,** *Sunday Herald Sun*

# We didn't look back and I think it's good we didn't

## Reverend Ivor Jones, 74, and wife Yvonne, 69

Rev Jones and his wife lost almost everything they had when the fires raged – except their faith.

Rev Jones: "I was a young boy in Liverpool – devastated during the war. I was there for the May Blitz in 1942 as a boy but the Blitz went on for three to four years. This [devastation] happened with just that fire in three hours. I was prepared for the embers. I had my hose out and buckets of water and thought I was in a good position to defend. It came so quickly there were no embers, just a great noise. We didn't look back and I think it's good we didn't. Of course it's sad. It's terribly,

terribly sad but as Christians I'd rather think of them as not being dead but as being promoted to glory."

Yvonne: "The loss of life is the most important part of the devastation. My husband misses all his books and notes. He's been evacuated twice now. A lot of us weren't ready for this sort of fire. There has never ever been any fire through Marysville."

**As told to Liam Houlihan,** *Sunday Herald Sun*

# The hardest part is people you were talking to on Friday were no longer with us on Saturday

## Anastasia Scott, 63

Anastasia lost her home in the fires but the hardest part for her is not being able to see some of her neighbours again.

"A bird smashed against the window. Then there was this roar that was increasing. It sounded like a huge locomotive. In the last few minutes, as we were escaping out of Marysville, the visibility was greatly reduced. There were only two cars after us that left Marysville.

"We arrived at a golf course, which we thought was our evacuation point. A policeman waved us on frantically. He was just waving with his hand for us to keep going. The hardest part to accept is that people you were talking to on Friday were no longer with us on Saturday evening. A gardener who had done a lot of work on my property, he was the sort of person every community needs a few of and he was next door on Friday. He wanted some kangaroo paws. They found his body and his wife at their property; they both died. There were people walking their dogs on Friday morning that I haven't seen since. As far as my personal property losses, it was my business, it was my home, it was my life's work. Marysville was wonderful: there were springs, rivers, mountains and rainforests."

**As told to Gemma Jones, *The Daily Telegraph***

# I can't see fire but I can hear it

## John Cintolo, Buxton

John sent his family to safety before he and his brother fought to save the family home. He later tried three times to get to his loved ones before finally making it through at 4.30am the next morning.

"By 7pm a southerly hot wind was blowing at between 130km/h and 150km/h. My brother was hanging on to the veranda post so not to get blown off. A black cloud came down and hovered 2m from the end: it went dark. I could hear fire roaring near me. I screamed out to my brother, Ben: "I can't see the fire but I can hear it."

"Sixty seconds later, 500m north of us, a 1km-wide fireball stretching from east to west exploded and continued north to Taggerty. My first thought was of my family, who were sheltering in Taggerty. At 9pm I tried to go to Taggerty, only to be turned back as the highway was on fire and trees had fallen across the road. At 11pm we tried again and only managed 3km before we were driven back by the heat. We tried again at 1am. As we were driving, trees were falling down behind us and the heat felt like we were in an oven. We came across a couple of cars parked on the side of the road but could not stop for fear of the heat as it was burning all around us. When we got to Cathedral Lane it was ablaze so we drove back to Buxton through the fire, going from one side of the road to the other to avoid the fallen trees. We drove through Buxton to check on our friends. There was a fire in Brian's garden and we put that out. We decided to try one more time to check if my family was safe. It was about 4.30am when we got through. They were OK. We had figured that after the fire passed Buxton, the winds had died down.

"The fire took 10 minutes to travel from Marysville to Buxton, which is 10km away, and 10 hours to get to my friend's property in Taggerty. The fire that missed Taggerty and went east burned into the other fire and went out. There were a dozen CFA fire trucks waiting at Taggerty for a fire that never got to them."

**Via email**

# It was beautiful before so we will make it lovely again

## Gail Dacey, 50, Narbethong

Gail lost her home but is determined to rebuild and create new memories with her partner and children. All she retrieved from the ashes was a precious doll given to her by her grandmother.

"That doll's head is a symbol, a sign. My grandmother passed it on to me, now I have got it back. Life has come full circle. My partner and the boys got out alive. They packed up four dogs and four puppies in the car as flames were coming up the drive. We won't leave, we shouldn't leave. It is our land and we bought it together. It was beautiful before so we will make it lovely again."

**As told to Karen Collier, *Herald Sun***

# A dozen blokes came down today and they built me a bridge

## Terry 'Tex' King, Buxton

When the fires took out a bridge over the Acheron River, Terry was stranded on his property. With no road to his local watering hole, his mates have since rebuilt 'Tex's bridge'.

"We're having a few drinks because we've just replaced the bridge. A dozen blokes came down today and they built me a bridge with timber donated from a nearby mill. The missus isn't happy because now I can get to the pub again. But they reckon they've built it so they can send me home. We cracked a bottle of champagne over it this afternoon. It also means the fireys can get access and get across if anything goes up over that side."

**As told to Liam Houlihan,** *Sunday Herald Sun*

# Tears were there, always close to the surface

## Jacqueline Pascarl, Operation Angel

Jacqueline set up charities for refugees during the Balkans War so when Black Saturday left thousands homeless, she set up Operation Angel to bring much-needed supplies to the victims.

"Have you ever seen a movie where a long fuse is lit and we watch as the flame whooshes along the wick until the explosion? Well, multiply the width of that wick by one million and that will give you an idea of the breadth and speed of the destructive fire's path as it cut a swathe up and down the rolling valleys on the edge of town. Blackened trees denuded of foliage stood to attention on the grey and ash-covered slopes that filled the views from our vehicle windows as we made our way to the distribution point. Destroyed homes, desolate and collapsed, still smoked exhaustedly at the road's edge.

"This pyro destruction is much, much worse than the war zones in which I have worked. Mother Nature has consumed everything that was combustible and the emerging evidence of arson makes the tragic outcome of 7000 homeless and hundreds dead a terrible fact to confront. Our trucks, stuffed to the gunnels with meticulously folded and sorted [pre-loved] clothing ensured that all 20 of our fabulous volunteers felt like Santa Claus on steroids. Driving the lead truck with Tory Oates in the cabin beside me, we had no choice but to stay within the speed limit as my vehicle was so full. Tory and I leaned forward as we climbed hills, accelerator to the floor, but only managing 80km/h or less around the snaking ascent. Forced to take the long route around due to road blocks and enormous fire damage, we drove cross-country and then up the ridge of the once glorious hills overlooking the wine and tourist district of the Yarra Valley – now just blackened shapes covered in a hazy pall.

"Smoke invaded our truck cabins and the visibility was cut to less than 200m along all the mountain ridges that rose above us. The fires were well and truly blazing but held in abeyance by the 1000 volunteer firefighters battling the heat and hellish conditions to protect the townships to which we were aiming.

"Radio was a constant reminder of just how precarious the CFA's situation was, with updates on fire status arriving at quarter-hour intervals. The flames were in a constant state of directional flux due to the high winds that were building and the tinder-dry bush. The winds changed again and the sun was finally visible as we rolled through the gates of the Alexandra High School and onto their sports oval. I got a bit bossy as I used my old aid worker's voice to get our 'shop' up and running, with first customers expected at 2.30pm.

"Trestle tables erected, boxes and boxes off-loaded from pallets. We made quite a sight, truck doors akimbo and organised chaos abounding as we set up individual departments – clothing, toys, underwear, menswear, toiletries and cosmetics, manchester and baby products, a luggage and bag department at the forefront of the set-up.

"At a trickle, the first customers began to arrive to shop. They came, mostly survivors of the tragic Marysville fires that incinerated their town. Most covered in soot, or slightly singed, with a liberal application of burns cream on hands, legs and faces.

"Greed was something we had to foist upon them, some only wanting a single T-shirt or in search of a pair of socks or a jumper, even though they only had the clothes they stood in. 'Oh no, I couldn't. Leave it for someone else who needs it more', was the constant refrain. Tears were there, always close to the surface as our customers faced the reality of replacing all they had lost and the ignominy foisted on them by the ravages of the fires.

"Each of my volunteers will have a separate story, a moment of grief, heartache or destruction confided in them as they supplied and packed and held hands with those we were there to assist.

For me it was the woman who arrived with pallid face, set jaw and clenched fists. Her mission? To find suitable new clothing for her five nephews and nieces to attend the funeral of their mother, who had succumbed to her horrific burns two hours earlier in the Alfred Hospital. She was now responsible for 10 people under her roof as she had opened her doors to anyone who arrived from ruined Marysville. To be able to load her car boot with garments of dignity was one of the

**Dilemma: John Munday made life-and-death decisions**        Picture: Kelly Barnes

biggest privileges I have ever encountered. To give a modicum of peace on just one simple single issue has led me to the belief that Operation Angel must stay active for these people in the months ahead."

**Via email**

# I had this quiet confidence that we could get through it if we did everything right

**John Munday faced the agonising decision to save the crew of his CFA fire truck as residents pleaded with him to save their homes.**

Everyone has a limit. For John, CFA firefighter, the fall-down that always follows the rush hit without warning. It was Saturday morning, a week after he tackled fires that burned the state. He was speaking on the phone with his wife, Amanda. She was at their Eltham home. He had slept at their Acheron property, less than two hours northeast of Melbourne.

As with the previous six nights, he had dropped the night before, exhausted. Sleep is one description for it. Unconsciousness may be a better one. Adrenalin had fuelled his being. Through surviving the inferno of Marysville. Through the 15-hour days since, when he left home in the dark and returned home in the dark, slogged in the CFA incident report room, furnished the media with thoughtful grabs, liaised with CFA brigades about rebuilding and grieved with everyone else for the losses.

This included his son, Angus, 18, who lost his close friend, Stuart O'Gorman, and a former English teacher. The human body will resist extraordinary pressures when pushed. In many cases, this stretches further than the individual would otherwise guess. Yet when those stresses ease and the hormones ebb, the body and mind tend to slip.

This phone call represented the moment when John's brain finally called time. He can't even remember the details of the conversation. Nothing profound was said. There was no direct trigger. But he "lost it". Couldn't speak. Choked up. Then, the moment passed. And John, somehow, felt better for it.

"It was at that point that I determined I needed to try and completely divorce myself from everything for a couple of days," he said. "That was the bottom of the hill for me. I'm just starting to edge up the other side."

The rest of his life, as a father of two grown boys, a CFA regional finance officer, a gardener and a dog owner, could recommence transmission. John, 53, took off his mobile phone and pager. He went outside and tended the garden. It hadn't been watered for seven days, since the morning of the day. But the watermelons, tomatoes and corn had survived. Then he played a round at Alexandra Golf Club as part of a fundraising day. Hit a few clean shots, too. A doctor, he said, couldn't have prescribed a better program of treatment.

Every Australian soldier who served in World War I was a volunteer. Prime Minister Billy Hughes twice tried to introduce conscription, and twice failed. Many who served sought adventure. Instead, they lucked into disease and despair, clods of mud and shards of metal. John, in looking over the bushfire events, describes fears and after-effects that will always dwell within. But others have lived through worse, he said, such as those returned soldiers whose lifelong battles with trauma blur as one of the unspoken social tragedies of 20th-century Australia.

"Everybody says how hard it must be for us but how hard was it for the Diggers, the blokes straight out of school?" he said. "There was no such thing as counselling or any form of peer support, nothing. These guys had to somehow come to terms with it and cope with it the best way they could. Comparing [the fires] to that group of people, there's no comparison in my mind. Or for the guys who went through Changi, the prisoners of war, it's just amazing how much suffering people can endure."

John witnessed sufferings on February 7 far worse than his own. He was stranded on the Marysville football oval, the grass scorched like a checkers board, the town flaming around him, alongside residents who had lost spouses and Marysville CFA crew members who, in every case, had lost their homes.

Among them was Marysville CFA captain Glen Fiske, who awaited information on the whereabouts of his wife, Liz, and son Dalton. "Hard as it was for us, how could you imagine anything worse than that while your township is going up around you?" John said. "If I had been in Glen's position I would have no idea how I would be trying to cope. It's dreadful. And it's not isolated." Glen's wife and son, as the captain was to see for himself the following morning, did not survive. John will quell his own ghosts. He expects time will fade the vision, for example, of a man and two children in a Marysville street, dressed in shorts and thongs, minutes before the blast. God knows what happened to them.

There was also the decision to reject a man's pleas to rescue an elderly couple trapped in their house up a Marysville street. He wanted to help. He just couldn't. John thinks he made the right choice – for the crew to have stayed in the town proper any longer would have killed all of them.

The what-ifs, he genuinely believes, deserve no place in his thinking. He logically feels comfortable – no, proud – of his choices on that strange day. He had prepared the Sunday before. Instead of the scheduled map-reading exercises, John, in a prescient vision of impending hell, had the Acheron crews practise safety exercises that they would repeat – for real – the following weekend. None were injured, he points out, itself an achievement.

Still, John felt helpless as he bunkered down in the walkways of his tanker. Sadness engulfed him when he popped his head up and realised that "everything" in Marysville was on fire. Last week he was buoyed by an email from a woman who was driving out of Marysville as John's tanker drove in. She marvelled that anyone could willingly drive towards what she was driving away from. He says without boast that no one hesitated to go on, even when the destination was obviously doomed. "I didn't feel any fear at all," he said. "It's a bizarre thing to say but I had this quiet confidence that we could get through it if we did everything right."

That morning, John had woken at first light. A weather watcher, he had run his hand over the lawn. No dew. This would be a bad day. Acheron CFA gets called out, in a quiet year, about five to 10 times. House fires or car accidents. Like many CFA towns, it's sleepy.

There can always be fires on hot summer days, of course. Most times, they don't spread far, though there are exceptions. The "campaign fire" of '06-'07, which burned out about a million hectares of northeast Victoria, burned for eight weeks.

Marysville, as John later explained, hosted a conspiracy of ill-intent when the fires hit the town. The lowest humidity of the day. The highest winds. The hottest temperature and the lowest fuel moisture content. He witnessed fires unprecedented for their ferocity.

In this, he is no different to the rookie volunteer on his tanker that day. John Stephens, 47, was on his first major turnout. According to John, he was "absolutely brilliant". Like John, Stephens had never imagined anything like it. Like John, he is unlikely to see anything like it again. John will remain a CFA volunteer. He said he hankers for the camaraderie, when queried. He's been a volunteer for 20 years. Both his sons were junior volunteers from the minimum age, 11, and older son Robbie, now 22, continues to volunteer.

Then a Diamond Creek jeweller, John knew every crew member of the Panton Hill tanker that was destroyed in the Ash Wednesday fires of 1983. He was coaxed to join the Wattle Glen brigade, where he would become captain. After four-and-a-half years of leading, he resigned from the role – "no more petrol in the tank".

At about the same time, he had an epiphany. Despite building a healthy business, he no longer wanted to be a jeweller, in part because he had no time to relish his 0.6ha Acheron property, where he could be a subordinate CFA volunteer – none of the administrative and human resource hassles of leading a bigger station. He took on a temporary CFA role, then accepted the finances position, which had him overseeing the books of those brigades hardest hit by the recent fires – St Andrews, Wandong, Kinglake, Kinglake West and so on.

Everyone knows everyone, or so it seems to John anyway. "One bleeds, everyone bleeds," he said. Not that volunteering is especially glamorous. The recent fires were freakish. Day-to-day, week-to-week can be pretty dull. John mentions this because he suspects there will be a rush on enlistments in coming months. There usually is after a big fire. With the spike, however, follows a steep drop-out rate. "There's very little 'heroism', if you like, it's more about sweeping floors of the station and making sure the truck is clean and doing training," he said. "A lot of it is boring, mundane, basic stuff. The 'glamour' and 'glory', if you can call it that, only comes in very small bursts."

**Patrick Carlyon,** *Herald Sun*

**Trickle: A hose is no match for spot fires near Churchill**   Picture: Stuart McEvoy

# Chapter 7

# Gippsland

- **Origin**

  The Gippsland fire is believed to have been started deliberately about 1.30pm. A southeasterly sends the flames towards Churchill, Koornalla and Traralgon South, hitting Callignee about 6.30pm

- **Destruction**

  In Churchill, as many as 77 homes are razed despite the efforts of 350 firefighters. In Callignee, only four homes are left standing

- **Toll**

  Of a population of 4500, at least 21 people are killed in Callignee

The Gippsland fire has an edge of menace from the beginning. We know, almost immediately, it is deliberately lit. It starts about 1.30pm, when the northerly is still blowing in hot wind off the deserts of Australia. The day is at its most vulnerable. The fire starts leaping along Jeeralang West Rd, south of Churchill, passing a house a few hundred metres away where Alan McLellan, 62, and his partner Dawn Ward, also 62, live. They see the fire and are stunned by its speed. The fire races on, even accelerates.

Around Gippsland people are listening to the radio for news on the fires further north, burning through Bunyip and Kilmore, and are preparing their own fire plans.

These communities that dominate Gippsland are an odd assortment. Treechangers who have made the move from the city, blue-collar workers, farmers. Many men work at the power plant and coal mines of the Latrobe Valley, three hours drive from Melbourne.

Still, they believe they are safe. Despite the black smoke filling the sky all around, the fire is expected to burn through national parks and not pose a direct threat to lives. Which is what happens. Until the southerly blows in about 5pm and turns the fire around.

Peter Evans, 57, arrives home from driving his truck and spends the afternoon watching the fire in the distance from the windows of his home at Traralgon South. The fire is getting thicker and closer. He starts getting concerned, with good reason. The fire has turned with the southerly, which has just started blowing in, and on top of Mt Tassie the communications tower has burned out. Locals can no longer get fire updates from ABC radio. Thankfully for Peter, his wife, Jo, is in Bendigo playing badminton. She calls him shortly after 5pm, telling him he better get out.

Further north, staff at the Healesville Sanctuary feel particularly vulnerable. The sanctuary will not be able to protect itself if the fire turns towards it. And with endangered animals – Tasmanian devils, orange-bellied parrots, brush-tailed rock wallabies, mountain pygmy possums, koalas and eggs and hatchlings – fleeing is not an option either. So they do what they can do, which is sit and hope, at the mercy of the winds.

When the southerly arrives the fire has drifted east from Churchill to Callignee, a town so small it is without pub or school. One in every 10 people here will die soon. Janice Michelsson is home, preparing to ride out the fire. It is 46C and shortly after 6pm. Then a curtain blows aside. It is such small moments that life and death turn on. When the curtain blows aside, Janice sees the fire rolling down the hill, straight for her house.

She runs outside. Yes it is real. A neighbour already in his car yells to her: "Get in." She can't. She has to go back inside and get her cat, Purrball. The photo album is on the bookshelf. She runs inside and grabs her two treasures, then jumps into the car.

The fire takes 57 of the 61 homes in Callignee, including Janice's.

They head north to Traralgon, away from the fire.

Luke Jacobs and Nathan Charles spend the morning keeping cool, swimming in the pool, hosing down the place. Luke is into cars, a member of Valley Drifters Car Club, and with some talent, they say, while Nathan is pretty hot on a BMX bike. In the life of young men, there is more than enough common ground there. They are 21 and best mates and so when Luke tells "Charlsy" his family's Koornalla house, in Traralgon Creek Rd, is under threat, Nathan comes across from Morwell to help out. That is what mates do. Luke's mum and dad, Miros and Alan, are also staying behind to defend their property.

Around the corner, Anthony Sexton spends the afternoon watching the fires around Callignee, a few kilometres to the south. Like so many, he believes the fire might just pass him by. He is in something of a denial, although not totally. Earlier, he sends his brother away on his 1993 Heritage Soft Tail Classic Harley-Davidson, telling him he'll be OK, but, just in case … It is called hedging your bets.

For the most part, though, he really does believe he is going to be OK. So he sits on the hobby farm he has worked for the best part of 30 years, not content to just give it up, and watches the fires. In the garage he has an old Holden Statesman he plans to restore, much like he has been doing with the 130-year-old farmhouse he lives in. Anthony likes to work with his hands. Regardless, he watches the fire – and watches it turn when the southerly comes in some time after 5pm. He is now in its path. Denial turns into panic.

In nearby Red Hill Rd, Mick Flint believes the fire is heading for Mt Tassie. He fails to spot the changing wind. It is not until a policeman tells him the fire is heading straight towards him that Mick changes plans and prepares to fight.

Anthony already knows by now, of course. He realises that he has to get out and goes through his evacuation plan. He grabs a beer from

**Scorched: Shaun Witchell with apples from his orchard**    Picture: Gary Richardson

**With tanks: Frank Gissara (middle) survived by jumping in a water tank with mates Paul Andreou, Tony Fleishcher and Brett Crosby**    Picture: Cameron Richardson

the fridge. Then he heads to his paddock and grabs his horse, Jeune Mark. Jeune Mark is sired by 1994 Melbourne Cup winner Jeune, but is unraced and, as we will find out, a different kind of stayer. Beer in hand, Anthony leads his horse out the gate and quickens to a trot to reach the end of the road before the flames do, as if that might be enough. Then the flames hit.

Tony and Louise Mann dive into a dam to save themselves. The home of their neighbour, Mick, catches alight about 6.30pm. Just a small spot fire, Mick shoots in to put it out. Whump! The wind generated by the fire knocks him off his feet. On the floor of his shed, Mick lies there, wondering if he will survive.

Similar panic is now running through Anthony's head. Facing the firefront, he turns and starts back towards home, wondering if he will make it. The fire races down the hill, quicker than Anthony can run, and probably even Jeune Mark. He is not unraced for a reason. Anthony knows he faces certain death. For some reason – who can explain these things – he takes in the place where he is about to die.

Then Jeune Mark knocks him over a guard rail. Who knows if it is an accident? Who has time to think? Anthony wrestles with his horse before stumbling and once on the ground follows the slope of the land down to Traralgon Creek. The flames reach him and swirl all around but, for two hours, Anthony lies there in the creek.

Hans Vanelmpt is at Callignee where, let's not forget, 57 of the 61 homes will burn down. Hans and his wife Riecky have made the decision, with their daughters Jo, 22, and Stef, 19, to stay and fight. Hans, 49, is in the family shed when the fire hits. It is just 10m from the house but Hans shoots like a startled hare, sprinting for the door. His ears are singed. His shoulder, forearms and thighs get blistered. The fire descends on the home and the Vanelmpt family crouch down inside, hope their only weapon.

At the Jacobs' home, the fire forces Luke and Charlsy, and Alan and Miros, into a garage. Charlie Richardson, 97, on Old Callignee Rd, can't prevent the fire burning down his house. His battle is lost. He leaves his home and heads for a nearby horse trough, wrapped in a blanket, and dives in.

This is the chaos of the fires. Firefighters are doing all that they can. It is not enough. David Tree is fighting the fire near Mirboo North. A koala approaches, tired and weak and burnt. He believes the koala is wanting to be put out of its misery. Tree calls for water and lets the koala drink from his bottle. Another firefighter snaps a photo with David's mobile phone.

At Traralgon South, Eileen Scott has drawn the blinds to stop the 46C sun from shining on her six-month-old daughter Lily. Unable to see outside, she has no idea of the monster descending. Then, she says later, an angel appears. The angel is more commonly known around these parts as Melissa Falzon. She is a Traralgon resident. She obviously keeps her wings well hidden. As Eileen is sitting out the heat, calm and unconcerned, her front door flies open and Melissa runs in, a woman Eileen has never seen before. Melissa grabs the sleeping Lily and runs out with Eileen chasing her. The house erupts in flames before the door shuts behind them.

"She just flew into my house. She saved us," Eileen says.

The people of Callignee die quicker than anybody else on Black Saturday. The combination of a strong southerly and a steep rise to the small community sees the fire front move at unmanageable speed. The CFA says it was uncontrollable from the moment it started.

It is about 8.30pm when the fire finally moves beyond Callignee. Once again it leaves behind small miracles. Somehow, the Vanelmpt family are all alive. Hans walks out and finds every house around him burned down.

Anthony stands up and starts following Traralgon Creek towards his house. He gets home about 10pm to find his house burnt to the ground. The fences are all burned down; the Statesman in the shed is not even good for scrap.

Yet there, standing in the paddock, is Jeune Mark. He has a few burns around his nose and eyes and has certainly looked better, but he is alive. Anthony feels wonderful, however briefly.

The following afternoon, he goes to check on his neighbours, the Jacobs. He has not heard from them. He forces open the door to their garage and inside finds the bodies of Luke and Charlsy, and Alan and Miros. It is believed they died from a lack of oxygen, sucked away by the fire.

This is what the fire does. This is what we see in the grief and sorrow in the days afterwards. It takes small miracles, small joys like finding your horse alive against all expectation, and it makes the devastation complete.

**Paul Kent**

**Saviour: David Tree offers water to Sam the koala. (The photograph doesn't reproduce clearly, as it was taken with a low-resolution camera phone in the middle of the bushfires and under poor light conditions.)** Picture: AAP/AP/Mark Parden

# It was like fireworks going off

## Frank Gissara, 32, Callignee

When fire threatened his home in Callignee, Frank called his mates to give him a hand. The five men sat on the roof and shared a few beers as they waited for the flames. The fireball hit them so quickly the property was already burning when they jumped to safety.

"We only first saw the fire about 30 seconds before it hit. We fought it for about 20 minutes but then the petrol pump caught fire and that was it. We had it pre-planned to hide behind the tank if necessary, but that wasn't an option. We all knew you shouldn't jump into a tank in a fire but there were flames everywhere. We managed to get the manhole open and we jumped in. The water was up to our waists. The concrete started to crack and we took off our shirts, wet them, and used them to block the holes. Gas bottles were exploding against the tank. It sounded like fireworks were going off."

**As told to Jane Metlikovec, *Herald Sun***

# Don't come, Mum, fire has hit us

## Sharyn Conibie, Drouin West, Gippsland

Sharyn first drove her daughter to safety and was on her way home to help her husband and sons fight the flames when they told her not to return as the house was on fire. She was saved by her son who drove to meet her and direct her away from the fires.

"My husband and three of my sons stayed to protect our property at Drouin West in Gippsland. I had left to take my daughter and our dogs to safety. I then planned to return to help. My youngest son phoned me as I was returning to say, 'Don't come, Mum. The fire has hit us'. The reception was not good and I couldn't understand him. As a result he jumped in his car and drove through 3m-high flames for 150m down the road to stop me from turning into our road. He said he couldn't see a thing and the temperature gauge on his car went as high as it possibly could. If he hadn't done this I would have certainly been killed as I would have driven into the full front of the fire.

"We managed to save our house although the veranda caught fire. But most important is the fact that our entire family are all alive. There was a period of 40 minutes when I thought my husband and two of my sons had died as we lost contact as the fire struck the house. I don't ever want or wish for anyone to ever have to go through this again."

*Via email*

# Smoke so thick you couldn't see

## Eric, 78, and Eva, 74, Koegel, Callignee

Eva said her survival and that of husband Eric wasn't a miracle, it was pure determination. On Black Saturday, the pair saved their home of 47 years with the help of their daughter Judy Wallace and teenage granddaughter Monica. The four successfully fought the fire for hours, quickly dousing flames which hit the house three times.

"We had no warning the flames were coming at all but we were ready. We had sprinklers going on the house all day. It looked like a swimming pool on the ground. The fire came so fast we didn't have time to worry about our safety. We had on fireproof clothes, gloves, boots and goggles, and we all had hoses. At one stage the smoke was so thick you could not see. I held my breath as long as I could to stop from breathing it in. After the fire Judy and Monica left. We weren't worried, we knew Judy would come back eventually. We knew there would be no power so we just started the generator and switched on the television. We had plenty of food and water. We were OK."

**As told to Jane Metlikovec, *Herald Sun***

# An angel flew into my house

## Eileen Scott, Traralgon South

Melissa Falzon raced to her parents' home in Traralgon South when she learned of the fire threat to the area. Her mother Zita Szeremeta evacuated, while her father John stayed to defend the house. As Melissa and her mother were about to leave, Melissa noticed a house across the road with blinds drawn. She raced to the house, ran inside and screamed that anyone home should get out. Eileen Scott, 36, was inside with her six-month-old daughter, Lily.

"I had no idea what was happening outside because I had all the curtains closed as it was so hot and I wanted to keep Lily as cool as possible. My husband Andrew was away for the day in Melbourne. All of a sudden Melissa ran into my house. I had no idea who she was, I'd never met her before. She was yelling to get out, that the fire was coming. She grabbed a pile of toys and a pile of Lily's clothes and put them into two bags. It was like an angel had flown into my house. She grabbed Lily and we left and the house erupted. It's gone. We went with Melissa and Zita to Traralgon and spent the night at Melissa's house. She is amazing."

**As told to Jane Metlikovec, *Herald Sun***

# I've never seen a fire like that one

## Ray Holloway, 63, Kongwak

As captain of the Kongwak volunteer fire brigade, farmer Ray Holloway was up at 6am on Black Saturday, joining his crewmates Nigel Braithwaite, Ross Olden and Arthur Grabham for the 100km journey up to the Bunyip State Park. There they fought for 12 hours.

"We've got 23 active members in our brigade. But most come from outside [the town] because Kongwak's only got a population of 30 or 40 people. The majority are dairy farmers. I'm responsible for everyone on the truck. We left Kongwak at 6am. We were in the strike team. The first thought when we saw the fire was, 'It's going to be hard to hold', which proved correct as it turned out. We couldn't hold it, it just spotted out into the paddocks and got bigger and faster and hotter as it went. I've never seen a fire quite like that one."

**As told to Ellen Whinnett, *Sunday Herald Sun***

# The heat inside the cockpit was intense ... well above 50C

## Dennis Corrin, 61, helicopter pilot

A pilot for 40 years, Dennis had been fighting the Bunyip forest blaze and believed it was under control ... until Black Saturday.

"It was the hottest day we'd ever had and it certainly felt like it in the machine. It just got hotter and hotter and the wind got up and of course one little spark and it was away. And then another spark and it just roared. It was the most incredible fire I'd ever seen. You might as well have p.....d on it. It was completely out of control. It was a horrendous sight to see the fire building and building. All you can really do is pull back and watch it go because there's absolutely nothing you can do about it when it's up in the bush burning and roaring forward.

"The wind suddenly changed and within 15 minutes it was Armageddon. The spot fires quickly built up to the point where 10km down the road we could see flames and smoke which were followed by a huge roaring inferno coming out of the bush. The visibility was poor. The smoke was really bad. Normally we can get in close. You can fly into the smoke. If it's too intense you can sort of turn as you go into the smoke and when you see the flames you sort of throw the water as you're turning out. But when this fire really let go, we couldn't get any closer than maybe 100 to 150m away. The heat inside the cockpit was intense, with the temperature well above 50C.

"I have huge respect for the CFA fighters on the ground. We can just turn around and steer away to get out of it. They can't. Sometimes I see them in a position where I wouldn't be. They stand there with their hose ready to protect houses."

**As told to Russell Robinson, *Herald Sun***

# They were stunned by how fast the fire was moving

The people of Gippsland thought they were safe from the Black Saturday fires until someone deliberately started a bushfire.

Everything is relative in the monumental tragedy in Gippsland. For every house that was blasted away in [Black] Saturday's firestorm, another close by was barely touched. People panicked and died fleeing homes that remained standing. Here, the devastated communities are dotted along ridge tops and gullies. They are home to treechangers from the city, earthy farm folk and blue-collar workers who ply their trades in the power plants and coal mines of the Latrobe Valley, three hours drive from Melbourne.

Some of the hardest-hit spots in Gippsland, such as Callignee, perched atop the thickly forested Strzelecki Ranges, are not so much towns as a locality. Callignee doesn't have a pub or a school but the 100 or so people who lived there knew one another and mostly they got on. The survivors have mixed feelings about whether they should rebuild or move down the mountain, where the bushfire danger is less potent. They are deeply angry, too.

The fire that burst upon them just after 6pm, after a day of foreboding with the blistering heat and shifting wind, began by a roadside near Churchill, well over the horizon.

It is believed to have been deliberately lit at about 1.30pm. By 2pm it had roared through properties on Jeeralang West Rd. The flames came within a few hundred metres of the homestead of Alan McLellan, 62, and his partner, Dawn Ward, 62, former publicans who turned to grazing cattle.

Like so many others they were stunned by how fast the fire was moving. At that point, the conflagration was being fanned by a scorching northerly which was pumping hot air from the desert into Victoria. A cool change began blowing across the state by mid-afternoon. Far from bringing relief, it tipped the already red-hot emergency into the nation's worst bushfire disaster.

Peter Evans, a 57-year-old truck driver, was just knocking off work. He and wife Jo have the top block on the Loy Yang housing park near Traralgon South. They built their brick home 23 years ago and raised two children there. As the afternoon wore on, Peter watched with growing alarm the plumes of smoke rising in the distance. He could see them becoming thicker, and closer. Jo, who was away in Bendigo for badminton, phoned and told him to get out. He left at 5.25pm. Their home was ablaze within 30 minutes.

By now the wind change, from the south, had turned the fire on its axis. It ripped through Koornalla, trapping businessman Alan Jacobs, his wife, Miros, 21-year-old son, Luke, and the young man's mate, Nathan Charles, in a makeshift fire bunker beneath their home on Traralgon Creek Rd. They are thought to have suffocated.

On nearby Red Hill Rd, Mick Flint, 45, believed the fire was burning towards Mt Tassie, away from his home, until a policeman told him it was heading straight for him.

His home caught alight and when he tried to put out the spot fire he was blown off his feet by the shrieking wind generated by the approaching inferno. He lay on the floor of his shed, wondering if he would live when the fire hit about 6.30pm. His neighbours, Tony and Louise Mann, were in an equally desperate plight; they jumped in a dam to save themselves.

Scott Frendo had driven up to Callignee from Traralgon to help his father, Alfred, protect the family home on Lyndons Rd. At some point, they decided they couldn't stay. Alfred's body was later pulled out of the wreckage of his car, which collided with another on Old Callignee Rd.

To ask survivors about their plans when the hurt is so raw and all those homes and happy lives have been turned to ash is to invite an empty stare or a snort of derision.

"No one knows," one local man said quietly. "We're all in a daze."

**Jamie Walker, *The Australian***

# We are going to go backwards

## Shaun Witchell, 26, Labertouche

Together with father Brian and farm hand Gary Lowen, Shaun drove six tractors into a dam to save them before escaping. Despite the heartache of having half their orchard ruined, the family will fight and stay on the land.

"It's in our blood and we love it. We don't do it because we think we are going to be rich. We know of many farmers doing it tougher. We are going to go backwards for two years but we'll get through it. The packing shed is gone, the cool storage is gone, nine other tractors are gone. My wife's a teacher and Mum's a retired teacher so she'll pick up some relief work to help us get by. I can't think of anything else I'd rather do than keep working here. You can't take life too serious."

**As told to Karen Collier, *Herald Sun***

# We were just about to renovate the kitchen. It's gone

## Jody Hamilton-Kincaid, 42, Callignee

Jody fled her home three hours before the firestorm descended and had doubts about returning to the area.

"That was my beautiful, four-bedroom cedar home. We were just about to renovate the kitchen. It's gone. My husband's excavator, our small business. Gone."

**As told to Jamie Walker, *The Australian***

# We've got each other and our family and friends are all here

## Natasha Hallas, 23, and Trevor Campbell, 26, Mirboo North

Valentine's Day, a picturesque winery:  Bride-to-be Natasha had her dream wedding all mapped out. But exactly a week before she tied the knot with Trevor, the plans went up in smoke. The nurse spent a hectic shift on Saturday. By Tuesday she knew her wedding venue was off-limits but the couple proved love always triumphs.

"The Boolarra fire came within 2km of our home. We thought about having it [the wedding] later in the year but we really wanted it to go ahead on Valentine's Day. So many people pitched in to help us. Everyone has been so good to us. The offers of help and support have been fantastic. Everyone just wanted it to go ahead and for us to be happy. We've got each other and our family and friends are all here."

**As told to Fiona Hudson, *Herald Sun***

# We touched noses

## David Tree, CFA volunteer

Sam the koala became an international celebrity when she was photographed being given a drink by CFA volunteer David Tree at Mirboo North.

"I could see she had sore feet and was in trouble so I pulled over the fire truck. She just plonked herself down as if to say, 'I'm beat'. I offered her a drink and she drank three bottles. The most amazing part was when she grabbed my hand. I will never forget that."

After being reunited: "Who knows if she recognised me or not but I would like to think so. She was pretty friendly, she gave me a bit of a sniff and we touched noses. I got a bit choked up because it has been such an emotional week. It was just good to see her doing well. You could see where the black soles of her paws had been burnt off and they were pink and looked sore. She's been through a lot. This has been a really tough week so it is good to have one happy ending."

**As told to Megan McNaught,** *Herald Sun*

# Everyone handles it differently

## Joe Gazis, Victoria Police peer support director and clinical psychologist

> Police officers often have to deal with the enormity of a heartbreaking tragedy, but behind closed doors they sometimes suffer from what they have witnessed.

"I think we've come to the stage now where people understand that there's nothing to be ashamed of in talking things over. But having said that, police are proud. They are proud of the people they serve with and proud of what they stand for.

"So some will hold on and then try to access it [the support from the peer system]. If they have seen something upsetting then often their own colleagues will support them and give them that crutch to lean on. They are trained officers and they know what to look out for. Sometimes they will distance themselves with black humour and as long as it is just between themselves, then it can help.

"But if someone withdraws or is affected in some other way, then of course we will offer other support. We have in place a strategy that will ensure that every member who was involved in the fires will be contacted at some time.

"With something of this magnitude it could be two or three months or longer before some people suffer [a delayed reaction]. They might be having a bad week, or acting a little differently at home, they might not even think it is them, they might think others are to blame. Everyone handles things differently. I expect our support groups will be pretty busy."

**As told to Ross Brundett, *Herald Sun***

# From the air the devastation is numbing and the scale of loss is overwhelming

Two days after Black Saturday *Herald Sun* writer John Hamilton took a helicopter flight over the devastated landscape.

Victoria has been bombed into a hideous tangle of blackened paddocks and piles of fused bricks and metal. In places it looks as if it has been torched by a giant flamethrower from the sky. From the air the devastation is numbing and, in places, the scale of lost homes and lost lives is overwhelming.

In just 10 minutes flying over the ridges around Yarra Glen yesterday I counted 57 houses completely destroyed. Along the twisting piece of bitumen that was once Steels Creek Rd, ruined houses stood out like shredded mushrooms in a landscape of lethal black velvet.

Here was a capricious, wilful firestorm that jumped, seared, killed, spared – and moved on. For three hours I flew in helicopter X-ray Delta Zulu with pilot Luc Beaurain at the controls as we covered just one small corner of the catastrophe that has overwhelmed Victoria.

Taking off from Moorabbin Airport we headed east towards Gippsland. Fifteen minutes out we came upon our first huge square of blackened earth, with plumes of grey smoke still rising from burning fence posts, tree stumps and the smouldering ruins of farm outbuildings. To the north there was a huge plume of malevolent brown-grey smoke rising from the Labertouche area as a fire roared back to life.

Setting down briefly at an untouched Traralgon airstrip for fresh directions, we took off again and headed southeast towards rising hills wreathed in blue smoke. Soon we were over forests of scorched pine, standing like packs of black toothpicks. Then we came upon the hamlets of Callignee and Callignee North, hugging two separate ridge tops.

In these places the fire was so fierce the pine trees were flattened as if a black tidal wave had swept to the top of each ridge. Nothing could survive this fire. We circled one ridge and I counted 12 shattered houses and three burnt-out cars. Three people were sitting on the back veranda of one of the few houses that was spared. They did not wave.

A police car, lights flashing, was making its way along the winding road to a point further on over the brow of a hill. Here the road swept down to a creek. But all the way down there were shattered houses, even one right next to the creek with a full dam nearby.

I counted 17 houses gone here, then saw three more heaps of rubble further on. There were dead cattle in a paddock, then four police cars parked along a road. A white van was outside a mound of rubble and twisted iron that had once been a substantial house.

As we circled two men appeared to be carrying a stretcher to a van. Over to the west, perhaps 30km away, the fire had flared again.

A big, evil cloud of thick orange-grey smoke reared upwards from a ridge line. It was being attacked by two water bombers and a huge water-carrying helicopter.

We could hear the radio traffic between the pilots. They referred to the fire as "IT". IT was being attacked as if it were a squadron of enemy aircraft. We flew back to Traralgon to refuel and had to hurry as a yellow and red aerial firebomber had landed and was taxiing to the fuel pump, with another touching down behind it. We were in the way of a war and lifted off quickly.

We tracked northwest to Yarra Glen, back again, free of any signs of fire, over flat brown paddocks and mostly full dams.

Then, as we headed towards the hills again, a massive hammerhead of orange-grey smoke reared. You could see flames ripping upwards through the bush. Lining up to bomb the fire were two more aircraft and two more helicopters, with a spotter chopper hovering high overhead. Again the radio traffic from the men fighting the enemy: "You can see where IT has just jumped the track. We should be able to nail it there with any luck." Then: "Bullseye! Right on target!"

It was almost as if the pilots up here near Mt Benack were fighting the Battle of Britain again. There was the same sense of achievement in the air and they are fighting an enemy just as deadly as any Luftwaffe, an enemy that kills like a World War II firestorm.

The killer called IT, which is still stalking our wide brown land like a demon unleashed from hell.

**John Hamilton, *Herald Sun***

**Inferno: A house is engulfed in Long Gully, Bendigo**

Picture: Rob Durstan

# Chapter 8

# Bendigo

- **Origin**
  Fire starts between 3pm and 5pm. Stong northerly winds up to 50km/h fanned the flames, which spread through Eaglehawk, Long Gully and Maiden Gully

- **Destruction**
  500ha of land and 57 houses

- **Toll**
  By nightfall the city records one death as residents were divided about whether to stay and defend or flee to safety

Let's examine the depth of human stupidity. Fire warnings have been going out for the best part of 24 hours, as we well know. Just the previous evening Premier John Brumby says Saturday could potentially be the worst day in Victoria's history while, that same afternoon, Country Fire Authority boss Russell Rees describes the fire warnings as uncharted territory.

Residents across the state are told to get ready their fire plans. The temperature is above 40C by 11am and by midday it is mid-40s across the state. On top of this Victoria is in drought, a hot wind is howling in at 50km/h, with a stronger southerly due late in the afternoon. So the alarm bells are ringing, right? So try figuring the person driving along Bracewell St, Maiden Gully, a suburb of Bendigo, about 3pm.

They are probably listening to the radio, tapping their fingers to the music that is coming in between fire warnings, when they casually toss their cigarette butt out of the window.

That's how police believe the Bendigo fire was lit. A carelessly dropped cigarette butt.

By now, the Kilmore fire is well underway, control of the Bunyip State Park fire is about to be lost, the Marysville fire is still a whispering death. The state's firefighters are doing all they can do to contain the fires they know about and 5km northwest of Bendigo a new front is about to open.

Nobody knows much about the early parts of the Bendigo fire. If it starts at 3pm, then it sizzles along for several hours before the wind finally picks it up some time after 5pm. Once again, the truth is known only when it is too late. Once again, the fire came too quick. Once again, the description is frightening.

What is difficult for many Australians to comprehend about these fires, in trying to understand how the loss of property and significant tally of fatalities could happen, is the quickness of the fire. Residents at Bendigo and its affected suburbs don't say the fire advanced on them. They don't even say a wall of flame came at them. They say a fireball came at them.

A rolling fireball rips through Eaglehawk and Long Gully. Pauline Keene, 62, is at home in Long Gully, looking in her fridge, realising she needs milk. She grabs $4 and, heading to her car, smells smoke. Luckily for Pauline, police are already right outside. "Run," they say. One word. Pauline flees with only the $4 she has in her pocket.

Everywhere, people start leaving in a hurry. Karen Plant, with her husband Brad and son Kyle, grabs her wedding ring and wedding album and goes. Everything else is gone. Rhonda Swift has just put the vegetables on for dinner.

She gets a whiff of bushfire coming through the airconditioner. Her husband Ron notices embers flying past the window, like a thousand struck matches dancing in the breeze.

"The fire's going to blow through here," Ron yells.

"You'd better get out."

David Fletcher and Steven Hales have decided to stay, to fight to save their properties. They connect three water hoses together, wet down blankets and when the fire starts on a vacant lot across from them, they are ready. They do not have to wait long.

Shortly after 5pm the fire has jumped the street and begun attacking their homes, and they fight. They fight like 10 men and not only do they start winning the battle to save their homes, they start saving their neighbours' homes as well, beating back the flames.

"We put out fires in neighbours' front yards, we stopped it getting under fences and we were able to save one neighbour's pets, including a Shetland pony," David says.

Carol Kane, a cat breeder, prepares to leave. She grabs six of her cats and puts them in the car, hustling her husband Kevin "Mick" Kane to hurry up. Three or four times she tells him to come with her. Mick is 48 and has health problems.

He walks with a stick but is doggedly hosing the house down. Having shifted continually as a kid, he finally gets himself his own home in Daniel St, Long Gully, and for 20 years he and Carol live there. Finally at home.

Here is one of life's survivors. Mick is epileptic. He has seen off two brain haemorrhages and maybe because he has first-hand experience on how fragile life is, Mick knows you make the best of it. This is why, when people try to explain him, they say he really is such a good bloke. "I know it's an overstated thing that people say," David says, "but he really was just a good person. He never said cruel things to people."

Hosing down his roof, Mick is not trying to save just a house. He is safeguarding a life. Protecting everything he has. Then the fire is on them. As quick as that. There is no real warning. Their backyard is alight and trees are exploding.

"Help me," Mick yells. Carol, 47, tries to help her husband to the

**All gone: Carol Kane survived but husband Mick did not**    Picture: Mike Keating

car but he collapses, staggers back up, and then collapses again. His leg is playing up. She tries to carry him, her arm underneath, but can't. He is too heavy. This is awful. This is her life.

The radiant heat from the fire has turned her skin bright red and started to melt part of her car's number plate. At this point Mick's sister Jill arrives with her boyfriend, Michael Ryan. "You go," Michael says, "I'll get him."

Carol leaves knowing her husband is safe. Behind her, she has left her wedding ring, her engagement ring, her eternity ring. But it doesn't matter because Mick will get out and then she will tell him of the $5000 she has secretly saved so they can go on their first overseas holiday. So Mick, who has never been on a 747, can go on his plane ride. Carol heads to Eaglehawk Leisure Centre, one of Bendigo's evacuation points.

Shortly after this point, Jenny Carolan is next door preparing to flee. Her son's friend knocks on Mick's door to see if anybody is home. No answer. It is time to get out. All around, firefighters are doing their best. Soon, the flames, 15m and 20m high, are leaping from treetop to treetop. The heat is as extreme as any of the men have felt.

Bendigo is struggling under the flames. A high-voltage powerline is destroyed by flames. Large parts of the city are without power. The flames are within 2km of the city centre. This is catastrophic.

The fire has moved from Maiden Gully through Eaglehawk and Long Gully and now threatens one of Australia's famous gold towns. Bendigo boomed when gold was discovered in the 1850s, its wealth seeing the city built in the late Victorian colonial style popular in the day. It is the goldmining gullies, though, that are something of a problem. They are proving ideal bushfire fodder. The fire is running terrifically through their low-lying scrub and native grass. Perhaps that is why firefighters are stunned at the fire's purpose.

It seems to be attacking the more densely populated areas of West Bendigo, at the exception of others.

"It was like it came up to something and said, 'No, I don't want you, I'll take you'. It had a mind of its own, like a beast," says Ian Hanley, fighting with the Raywood CFA crew.

When the southerly arrives, the fire changes direction. It heads back towards Eaglehawk Rd, allowing firefighters to set up a perimeter along Caldwell St, Bracewell St, Upper California Gully Rd, the Calder Highway and Eaglehawk Rd, and finally regain some control. Most houses along those streets are empty. At the Eaglehawk Leisure Centre Carol runs into her neighbour Jenny.

"Where's Mick?" Jenny says.

"We can't find him," says Carol. She is relieved she made it and if she can only find Mick now she will be better. Much better.

Back in Daniel St, Mick's home is twisted iron and rubble. The letterbox is charred, the trees are black, lonely sticks coming out of the ground. The clothesline is gone – and the fire has passed.

In the end, Mick Kane has no hope. By the time Michael grabs him the radiant heat is already too severe, Mick is unconscious and Michael can't drag him the 20m or 30m to the car. Not quickly enough anyway.

Travis Fenton is further down Daniel St fighting to save his uncle's property when a neighbour runs past screaming. "The man up the road is on fire."

With neighbour Laurence Clark, Travis and several others race straight to the Kanes' home. The flames beat them back. The difference between surviving the Bendigo fire and the Kinglake and Marysville fires, where the greatest number of fatalities occur, appears to be exit routes.

In Kinglake and Marysville there are few roads out of town. Any halt in traffic soon saw a traffic jam and people caught. At Bendigo people got away, even though the fire destroys 594ha and 45 houses. The city records only one death.

In the days afterwards, Carol keeps busy to stop herself thinking about the horror of her husband's death, trying to prevent those moments that creep up when the mind is still. That is her trauma.

In truth, the ferocity of the fire's attack meant little, if anything, could be done. She is simply another bushfire widow.

**Paul Kent**

**Rebuild: Premier John Brumby surveys the devastation**     Picture: Gary Richardson

# The fire's going to blow through here, you'd better get out

In the days after Black Saturday, *The Australian* writer Corrie Perkin met with locals from the Bendigo area as they attempted to make sense of the horror and started to think about rebuilding their lives.

The Bendigo fire unleashed hell on its local community on Black Saturday. But if the wind had changed direction and caught the CFA off guard, this fire would have sped toward the city's heart, wiping out many more lives.

Touring through the fire-affected northwest suburbs of Eaglehawk, Long Gully and Maiden Gully, you see what might have been. The fire's starting point is two minutes drive from the Calder Highway. Another minute and you're outside the Shamrock Hotel, the city's 1854 gold-rush landmark. More than 92,000 people live in greater Bendigo, 150km north of Melbourne. Mass evacuations would have been near impossible, given the speed fires were travelling that day.

Mayor Kevin Gibbins is still haunted by Black Saturday's potential. A former cop who now owns a newsagency, he says the city is vulnerable.

"What happened on [that] Saturday is a very stark reminder of the place we live in," he said. "We're known as a dry continent, we are a very large city in the middle of the state. There's a lot of open land, it has a very large and growing population and many communities are surrounded by forest. This fire is a huge reminder of all this."

When the clean-up and rebuilding phase begins, areas closer to Melbourne such as Kinglake, St Andrews and Kilmore will grapple with the challenges of the treechange phenomenon. But the discussion is irrelevant to Bendigo. Its fire victims chose Eaglehawk because it's 1.5km from the city's centre. The houses are cheap and the infrastructure, including schools and shops, is strong.

Black Saturday was just terrible, terrible luck in this area. Foul weather conditions and a lit cigarette butt thrown from a moving car or truck window are believed to have started this hell on Earth. It began about 5.30pm on a vacant grassy block in Bracewell St, Eaglehawk. A scorched patch of earth was roped off as a crime scene.

"That's where they reckon the cigarette butt hit the grass and [has] taken off," one CFA firefighter on the scene said. He pointed south. "It's just taken off and whoosh, there was no stopping it."

Luckily, the CFA did stop it. But not before it had ripped through the guts of a well-populated, mostly working-class area. The old goldmining gullies around north Bendigo are ideal bushfire fodder. Native grass and low-lying scrub line these rocky ravines which follow the hills and valleys of Eaglehawk, Long Gully and Maiden Gully.

On a normal weekend these gullies are places to play, to ride horses, go jogging or ride bikes. On Black Saturday it was too hot for much activity. "We did everything we were told to do, we stayed inside and we kept cool," Union St resident Rhonda Swift said.

Some time after 6pm, Rhonda smelt burning grass coming through the airconditioner. She had just started to boil the vegetables for dinner when she and husband Ron noticed burning embers flying past the house. A fireball then raced toward them. "The fire's going to blow through here, you'd better get out," Ron yelled to his wife.

Rhonda only had time to grab her handbag and drive off. Her husband tried for a short time to save their home of 22 years and his aviary of finches, parrots and pigeons but the intense heat forced him off the property. The house, aviary and 40 birds were destroyed.

Like so many other Bendigo fire victims, the Swifts want to rebuild. As they poked through the still-warm ashes looking for jewellery, crockery – anything that reminded them of their life 24 hours earlier – the couple looked grim. How many times over the next few months will their determination waiver? Will they instead move to another Bendigo suburb, away from the grass scrub? And if they do rebuild in Union St, will they ever again feel safe on a hot, lazy summer Saturday?

# We thought we had more time

## Carol Kane, 47, Long Gully, Bendigo

Carol desperately tried to save her husband Kevin "Mick" Kane, 48, who had health complications and relied on a walking stick and a motorised scooter, as fire bore down on their home. She tried to drag him when he collapsed in their yard several metres short of safety. But the intense heat forced her and family members back.

"When I stop and lay down it plays over and over in my head. I told him [Mick] three or four times to come and then the whole back yard and all the trees exploded. Mick staggered up and fell down and I tried to drag him but he was far too heavy for me. The heat was absolutely incredible. It turned me bright red straight away and part of the number plate on the car melted. We just kept wondering whether the tankers would come. We thought we had more time than we did. I think that is what went through our heads; we are in Bendigo, we live in a town. I think that is why we left it so long. We don't understand how it got to the stage it did and there was no one there to help anyone."

**As told to Karen Collier, _Herald Sun_**

# I could hear despair in my voice

As the link between desperate Victorians and firefighters, the call-takers were the first to experience the statewide panic of Black Saturday. For all emergency services there were 10,408 calls in the first 24 hours and another 8000 on Sunday. Some call-takers are believed to have shared final, heartbreaking conversations with those who could not escape the blazes. Yet there was also joy, when they helped save lives and reunited loved ones.

Sophie Kozaris: The 48-year-old clocked on at 5.30pm on Black Saturday. "Just opening the door [at work], I thought, 'Oh dear'. The board was lit up with calls waiting. The initial calls were from people in those houses. [They were saying] 'The fire is here. The fire is here. What do I do? Where do I go?' Taking those [calls] was very tough.

"A lot of calls dropped out and when it's a mobile number, we can't do anything with that because we don't know where they are calling from. People were saying, 'I'm trapped' and 'They are trapped'. Neighbours were looking out for one another. It was all about the people [not property]. I heard, 'There are people in number 55. Eight people are trapped'. It was really horrible.

"Every time you keyed in an address, it wasn't a house here and there [destroyed]. It was a whole street. As the night progressed, the whole situation changed. We were taking calls from relatives looking for their loved ones."

Sophie has since played back some of her calls from that day.

"That wasn't a bright idea. Just listening back to my own voice, the despair in my own voice. That was echoed because I could hear that in my colleagues [too]."

**Erika Bachmann:** For Erika, 41, the first glimpse of the tragedy to follow came late in the morning of February 7. "Eleven am. I will always remember that. That's when it all went off. There were people in their houses, surrounded by fire. People saying, 'My husband is out there, we need help, we need help, the fire is coming'. But one call I distinctly remember was [from] a lady who was cool and calm, that was extraordinary. It really got to me. She told me their names … three young men who were left on the property to defend their farm and they couldn't get out. And I don't know what happened to them. That's the really hard part."

**Neil Foster:** The ESTA chief executive is extremely proud of his staff. "They deal with this sort of emotion every day and that's why they are so carefully selected and trained. Black Saturday was a true test of their professionalism and they served the people of Victoria very well."

**As told to Evonne Barry, *Sunday Herald Sun***

# It can be quite emotional listening to such traumatic experiences

## Tim Clancy, paramedic and peer assistant

"We have a peer support program which operates 24 hours a day so that we can respond any time our members find themselves at critical incidents. But this was something different. We have so far contacted 350 officers involved. I've been up there [in the fire areas] twice and we have some paramedics who live in the area or have relatives in the area and with some of them there is a sense of survivor guilt. Some are more affected than others. We call them first and we also have face-to-face meetings. It's a well-organised procedure, which we first developed more than 20 years ago, after the Russell St bombing. We work in pairs and we can keep an eye out for each other.

"It can be quite emotional listening to such traumatic experiences. They've had to treat people with shocking burns, administer fluids, monitor pain relief and travel with them for long periods, and a lot of these paramedics are quite young so, yeah, you do feel what they are going through.

"They often tell you that it's the little things that catch them unawares. They will get through the tough moments and then someone will say something about their kid and that's what will floor them."

**As told to Ross Brundett, *Herald Sun***

# Help is at hand. We all grieve, but we will rebuild our communities

## Victorian Premier John Brumby

John Brumby spent Black Saturday night in Bendigo, where flames licked houses just a kilometre from the centre of town. Earlier in the day he had prepared his own rural property at nearby Harcourt for the onslaught of high temperatures, as did his parents who live at Coleraine in the state's west. Throughout Saturday an increasingly anxious Brumby was unable to contact his elderly parents, Malcolm and Alison, as the fire bore down on the town's 1000 residents. Firefighters stopped the flames 500m from their home.

"It's been, like for everybody, a week of intense emotion, intense loss, devastation and unbelievable sorrow and heaviness, and that's I think what every Victorian and every Australian has felt and that's what I've felt. The human cost of these terrible fires has been horrific. Amid our devastation, Victoria's volunteers have risen heroically to meet the crisis. Victorians always rise to the challenge in times of adversity and this tragedy has brought out the very best in our community. I thank all of our emergency service workers for their tireless work. I know you are physically and emotionally exhausted. I know that these fires can seem overwhelming. But please know that you have the prayers and gratitude of so many Australians behind you.

"Our volunteers and career firefighters are heroes in the truest sense and I want to acknowledge each and every one of them and to thank them all for their amazing efforts. In addition to our frontline workers there are also tens of thousands of people whose voluntary work over the past few days has been just as vital to the firefighting effort.

"These people have been providing emergency accommodation, handing out blankets, making sandwiches and drinks and, in many cases, just helping their neighbours out in whatever way they can. If you have been a part of this effort, you have shown the true meaning of selflessness and courage and you are an inspiration to us all. On behalf of all Victorians, I thank you and I ask you to continue your heroic efforts.

"But we will get on top of these fires. Together, we will rebuild the property and possessions lost. We will put communities back together and Victoria will recover. Help is at hand. We all grieve but we will rebuild our communities."

**Life-saver:** Amelia Coombes and Paul Mercieca were saved by Eurobin CFA captain Barry Mapley, as they sheltered in their ute

Picture: David Caird

# Chapter 9

# Beechworth & Mudgegonga

- **Origin**
  Blaze starts 3km south of town at 7pm. It heads to Yackandandah, Dederang, Gundowring, Kergunyah South and Mudgegonga

- **Destruction**
  In total an estimated 30,000ha of state forest and private properties are destroyed

- **Toll**
  Two lives are lost in the small rural town of Mudgegonga, proving even the smallest of townships can't escape the fire's wrath

Craige Ingram is 26 and all energy. "What other boxes?" he says. "We can get more on. What about that one there?" It is days after the fire and Australia is responding. Tens of millions of dollars have already been raised. Inside the hall across from Whittlesea Community Centre thousands of bags of clothing are arriving and being sorted. Women's and men's clothing first, then shirts and pants, and finally sizes.

Craige has driven in from Hoppers Crossing, an hour away, in his truck. He comes because he thinks they could do with the help. "It's starting to flow," he says. He is stacking boxes on the back of his truck, and working beautifully at that. "Now that we're starting to get some stuff ..."

The police have opened the roadblocks to the affected towns. Relief trucks with food and clean water, with can openers and generators and toiletries, are finally being allowed up the mountain. If they can get it on the truck, it's going.

"Twenty-five minutes ago they told me I had 24 minutes to get the truck out," Craige says. He is working like he is born to do this job. He is organising trucks so every last space is being filled. He has a team of four or five men helping him load his flatbed truck and a refrigerated truck next to him. He is ordering one box to get on in front of another box, telling the men to hurry, keeping them focused and in tune. By the time he is finished you could not squeeze a pencil on to the truck.

Born to it. "I'm a sales rep," he says. He is not of this work at all. He works in sales and sometimes he drifts across and helps in co-ordinating the logistics at his company, which is all the experience he needs when he arrives at Whittlesea.

The relief effort is one small part of the massive job that needs to be done in the days after the fire. The big one, of course, is the royal commission. That is the one everybody needs because it is the one with the answers.

The lessons to hopefully prevent it happening again.

Victorian Premier John Brumby has done his bit. He has already promised the royal commission will have the "broadest possible" terms of reference. "Everything, absolutely everything, is on the table," he says. "We want to leave no stone unturned so that every Victorian that wants to have their say about these bushfires should have that opportunity."

Brumby has appointed former Supreme Court judge Bernard Teague QC as royal commissioner. Under the terms of reference Teague will look at the preparation and response to the fire, which is so general it means nothing. Thankfully, Brumby has also empowered Teague to look at "any other matter" he deems appropriate. He will need to look at everything from early permanent firebreaks to increased fuel-reduction burning, early warning systems to green planning codes, to fire bunkers and every other idea or solution that is raised.

People died most often because when they decided to flee it was too late. The fire was too quick for them. What can fix that? Teague has until August for an interim report. His final report is due by July 2010. His work has already begun.

Meanwhile, here at Whittlesea, the best of mankind is going about their business. People are working coalminer's hours to get the work done. They sit down only long enough to eat and do whatever is asked, no matter the chore.

The victims of the bushfires, who call themselves survivors, are appreciative and respectful of their work. In turn, Australia is behind them. And as the week stretches out these survivors stand up and go back to their lives, with so little fuss it is not until they are all gone that it becomes apparent.

They stand up from the ash and they rebuild their homes. They stand up because that is all they can do. They rebuild their homes and by doing that they rebuild their communities, and in their communities they find their strength.

There is tragedy in these bushfires. It is in every corner you look. But there is greatness, too, and it is the spirit of the people.

**Paul Kent**

**Aftermath: Grace Wilson, who lost parents John and Sue** Picture: Renee Nowytarger

**Meltdown: Dwayne Ward with what is left of his aluminium boat** Picture: John Smith

# My hair was on fire, then I realised I was hanging on to a gas bottle

## Amelia Coombes, 24, Mudgegonga and Barry Mapley, 67, CFA captain

With their home on fire and gas bottles from the welding shed exploding, Amelia and her boyfriend Paul Mercieca were sure they were going to die. They decided to flee in their Land Rover and were only saved by the bravery of CFA captain Barry and his crew.

Amelia: "I didn't want to stand up. My hair was on fire, then I realised I was hanging on to a gas bottle. Ash was falling on the connector hose and I tried to put it out with my finger. I didn't want the hose burning. Then someone threw me a blanket. I didn't know what to do but someone [CFA firefighters] yelled out to stay down so I did. Fire was coming over the top of me and then I felt all this cool water fall on top of me."

Barry: "I'm not a bloody hero, it's just the Aussie way. I did a recce. I didn't want to be there. That fire was unstoppable. A gas bottle took the roof off the house and then there was another big one [explosion]. My son-in-law said, 'Get out of here, we are going to die'. Then I saw this truck. We nearly hit them. Yep, it was howling. It was sparking and fireballing, coming over the top of them. They wouldn't have survived. All the protection that girl had was the board on the back of the ute. I threw her two blankets, the first one blew away. I don't know how she stayed there. If she had stood up her head would have been blown off."

**As told to Georgie Pilcher, *Herald Sun***

# One more minute, we wouldn't have made it

## Karen and Dwayne Ward, Mudgegonga

Karen says she and husband Dwayne owe their lives to a brave policeman who, despite the imminent danger, drove to their property and warned them of the deadly blaze approaching.

"It was the tone of his voice. He said, 'You should go and you should go now'. We jumped in the cars and drove to the top of the hill and watched our house burn. It was glowing red with flames 12m in the air. If we had have done what they tell you and stay inside and wait for the fire to pass we would have exploded. That copper saved our lives. He is the bravest man I've ever met. Even a couple of minutes later, one more minute, we wouldn't have made it."

**As told to Georgie Pilcher, *Herald Sun***

# There is nothing at all, it's all gone

## Grace Wilson, 22, Mudgegonga

Standing alone among the ruins of her childhood home, holding one of the last remaining keepsakes of her loving parents – a charred tin sunflower garden ornament – Grace struggled to comprehend the reality of Black Saturday's bushfire.

"There is nothing at all, it's all gone. Mum had a big chest full of all the baby albums and wedding albums. We don't have hardly any photos of them." The twisted corrugated iron, rubble and ash in no way resembled the home her handyman father, John, and green-thumb mother, Sue, built 18 years ago to nurture their family. Grace was metres from where her mother's body was found in a front room of the house after fire ripped through the Mudgegonga property. Her sense of shock was palpable.

Her father's body was found by police in the backyard about 9am on Sunday. Standing in the driveway after walking through the property, her sister Samantha, 19, clutched a ceramic model of the Disney character Pluto, a present from her grandmother, which was one of the only things the fire left intact.

"It doesn't have a single crack or anything," she whispered.

A cubby house built for the girls just metres from the house was left untouched by the fire. Even its cotton curtains survived.

A Toyota Camry was still parked in the now-collapsed garage and a Mazda Bravo, with a trailer attachment in the driveway, was also facing away from the exit, suggesting the couple was taken by surprise. Neighbours described the blaze as a firestorm that charged properties with little warning. Many had the decision of whether to stay or go made for them when seemingly distant flames arrived in minutes and surrounded their properties.

Grace said her parents were well known and well loved. Her fiance, Blair, said John and Sue had welcomed him into their family and had been thrilled to hear of their engagement. "[They were] very friendly, very loving," he said. "They loved to live life."

He had spoken to Sue on Saturday before the fire struck. "She just wanted to know how everyone was and the fire was coming but [she said] it was no real danger," he said.

**Angus Hohenboken,** *The Australian*

# People don't like to confront the fact they aren't coping

## Sandy McFarlane, professor of psychiatry at the University of Adelaide

Having closely studied the impact of the Ash Wednesday bushfires on its victims, Professor McFarlane said most of those who lost everything in fires manage their survival extraordinarily well. It may be a year or more before victims realise they need counselling.

"One of the great misconceptions is that people want counselling. They have a remarkable capacity to survive. Most don't come in for any counselling until well into the second year. They generally present to their GP feeling physically crook. People don't like to confront the fact they aren't coping so they go to enormous lengths to minimise their suffering."

**As told to Stephen Lunn, *The Australian***

# We were working alongside CFA volunteers. All of them exhausted

## Peter Evans, 48, NSW fireman

Peter is a strike team leader from Sutherland Rural Fire Service and has 30 volunteers under his control. Peter's team came under threat from the Beechworth fire while protecting the town of Dederang.

"We're stationed at the northern end of the Beechworth fire protecting Dederang, working alongside Country Fire Authority volunteers.

They're all absolutely exhausted. The conditions here are extremely dry and the fire behaves quite erratically once there's any wind around. I'm standing about 500m to 600m from the firefront at the moment but we're getting spot fires 3km to 4km in front of the fire, which is affecting Dederang. We're faced here with a large area of uncontained firefronts with very-hard-to-establish containment lines.

"I was called about midnight on Sunday and was asked if I could go to Victoria. It took about an hour to ring around and organise crews and vehicles and we then headed off for Albury at 6am. I've been a volunteer for about 29 years and married for 28 years.

"Your wife is never happy to see you going to things like this, particularly because they don't know what we can expect to find. But my wife has always been supportive.

"Her only advice was to be safe and to come home."

**As told to _The Daily Telegraph_**

# Sometimes we just sit there with them, just share some silence

## Rob Vun, Defence Force fire taskforce chaplain

Rob said that in his role silence can be just as useful as talking. "We talk to them if they feel like it or just provide a presence so they can approach us when they want to. Sometimes we just sit there with them, just share some silence. I think they are happy just knowing you are there and with them. A lot of them [in the taskforce] are very young, I'm talking 20, and if we are told about someone who has seen something or experienced something, or if we see someone who is emotional, we will try to offer some support and maybe refer them to one of the counsellors. Basically we are providing first aid, assessing people and seeing whether they need to get more assistance."

Rob, one of five chaplains in the taskforce, was full of praise for the professionalism of his colleagues. "I think the one thing my team have all said is how well the force has stood up to it all. They have done themselves proud. As for me, I will be debriefed along with the other chaplains and counsellors. It has shown me how life's priorities can change so quickly. A person's life is worth much more than mere possessions ... so precious."

**Ross Brundett,** *Herald Sun*

# A long road to renewal

Milanda Rout lost her home in the Victorian bushfires of 1997.
Covering the Black Saturday fires as a journalist for *The Australian*
brought back memories of trying to rebuild a new life from the ashes.

Standing in the charred remains of so many houses destroyed by the Black Saturday fires, watching the devastated survivors try to hide their desolation as they sifted through the ashes of their homes, I feel I have to say something, do something.

"If it is any consolation," I say, almost cringing at the sound of my own voice, at my feeble attempt to console them, "You will be OK." The only response I get from residents in Kinglake or Flowerdale is a raised eyebrow or a look of disgust that says, how dare you contemplate such a remark, let alone say it.

"No really, it's horrible now but you will be OK," I say, trying again. "Trust me, I have been through it. I have lost my house in a bushfire and eventually you will be OK." But deep down I know nothing I will say – or anyone else for that matter – will help these survivors in that moment. It is just such a devastating, isolating, numb feeling to comb through the ashes that were your home, the centre of the universe, of your identity. Such sentiments did not help my family when we picked through the ruins of our home in the Dandenong Ranges in 1997. And they were from close friends and loved ones, not some journalist met a few minutes before.

My family was fortunate enough to escape with our lives when a deliberately lit fire ripped through the hills east of Melbourne on January 21, 1997. Unlike those hundreds of people grieving the loss of their relatives who were killed in Black Saturday, a pain I could not begin to imagine, we only lost our home.

I remember the day as being particularly windy and hot during the school holidays. I was at home with my two younger brothers enjoying my last break before starting university. As recounted in many stories during the 12 days, the fire just came up too fast. One minute there was a small plume of smoke on the horizon; the next, there was a wall of flame in the back garden of our Ferny Creek home.

My mother, my brothers and I panicked. All our fire plans were out the window in the face of the terrifying 10m flames that seemed to roar down at us. We grabbed our dog, a few possessions and fled to the nearest fire refuge. We were lucky; we were alive. Some residents a few streets away were not so fortunate. The fire claimed three lives that day and destroyed more than 40 homes.

The next day it rained. That was the first thing that made me angry instead of just being in a disconnected state of shock. A day after nature had so devastatingly interrupted my rather idyllic childhood with a raging inferno, the only thing that could have stopped it arrived 24 hours too late. I remember freezing in T-shirts and shorts, the only possessions I had left, and wearing an over-sized jumper that did not belong to me. I remember sifting through the ashes as the rain fell on the ground and the mist hid the charred black trees. But my strongest memory is the desperate feeling of just wanting to go home. I wanted out of this nightmare. I wanted to throw away this crappy jumper that did not fit, tell everyone to go away, and go back to my room. Sit on my bed, dressed in my own carefully chosen clothes, stare at photos of my friends and my family, even dig up a favourite old teddy bear or doll. But I knew my once relatively easy teenage existence of friends, family and fun was gone. My life, my identity was changed forever.

"We underestimate how losing our homes can then unravel our sense of identity," says trauma expert and University of Adelaide psychiatry professor Sandy McFarlane, who studied the survivors of the Ash Wednesday bushfires in 1983. "People who have lost their homes say to me they never realised the relevance material possessions have on their lives. There is a terrible sense of discontinuity. One woman told me the fire had drawn a line in her life and the one before the fire had ended when it was reduced to ashes."

That was exactly how I felt after the bushfire claimed our home. As a distraught young adult, I felt as if someone had come along and struck me off the register of people living on this planet. After 18 years, there was nothing on this world to prove I even existed. I had no birth certificate, no driver's licence, no library card, no baby pictures, no silly drawings from primary school, no report cards, no ticket stubs collected from favourite films, no nothing.

Once the shock of just surviving the bushfire wore off, I began to resent everyone around me for having all this. I hated everyone. I know it is completely irrational and ungrateful, but that is how I felt then. I even hated the close family and friends who came to our aid and housed and clothed us. I hated them because they had a home to go to and their life was normal.

I remember sitting in the living room of a family friend with my two shell-shocked brothers, watching friends of a similar age fight over a tennis racquet. They kept arguing over who it belonged to, while our parents looked on in another room. At that moment I felt like screaming at them, saying they had nothing to complain about because they had a tennis racquet to fight over, a house, a life.

I also was furious at the people on the periphery of our lives trying to help us. As we traipsed around relief centres set up by the incredibly generous and supportive Salvation Army and Red Cross, I could not believe the rubbish that people donated, however well intentioned. Why would we want to wear crappy unwashed used clothes or get toys that did not really work? My mother has never forgotten the comment made by one local resident trying to organise accommodation for us, which turned out to be a completely unliveable dump. "All you need to be is warm and dry," the local condescendingly quipped.

Chairwoman of the national mental health disaster response committee, Beverley Raphael, says one of the most traumatic experiences about losing your home comes from this crushing loss of self-respect.

People go from having their own homes and lives to having to rely on other people for the basics: shelter, clothes, food and water.

"You feel like you have lost your dignity," Beverley said. "You have lost the basic things that make you feel independent, have confidence and give you dignity in your lives. The last thing you want is second-hand goods."

But at the same time as bushfires bring out the worst in humanity – a neighbour of ours who lost their house, too, spotted tourists picnicking in the ruins of ours – it also brings out the best. We were able to use the money donated to the Red Cross by thousands of strangers to begin to reconstruct our lives.

Beverley believes giving survivors access to resources, from both the government and the generous community, is the key to starting the rebuilding process. The sooner the survivors get out of the homes of their friends and family and into their own, the better, even if it is just temporary accommodation. That is why giving people access to money is critical, as opposed to second-hand goods.

"It allows them to make their own choices," Beverley said. "Because [for these people] it's new steps and new decisions in a totally new world." Trauma experts describe the time immediately after a disaster as the "honeymoon period". It is when the tragedy is on the front page of newspapers, it captures the attention of the whole world, scores of people are donating money and the devastation is being acknowledged. But, soon enough, the public moves on with their lives and expect survivors to do the same. "The community withdraws and goes back to their lives and people are left with this terrible loneliness," Sandy McFarlane says. "With the loss of your home, you are really out there on your own."

And this is when the most difficult part begins for survivors; at least that is what my family found. Not only are you dealing with ridiculous bureaucracy, trying to get your identification back and fighting with insurance companies, you also have to cope with the feeling that you are abandoned. I remember one local telling a mutual friend of our family, "Shouldn't they be over it?" four months after it happened. Sandy says the best message to get across to bushfire survivors is that losing your house is a monumental trauma that does take a while to come to terms with, sometimes five to 10 years, and it is OK to grieve. "Don't underestimate the journey ahead of you but don't think you are alone in this either," he says. "Don't try [to] make your life what it was … or you will become trapped in the past. This is an opportunity to try [to] change things for the better."

I could not agree more and that is what I was trying to get across to the people I met. It is normal to feel desolate, displaced and angry at the world over what has happened. Yet there is a light at the end of the tunnel. It is a long road to recovery, but with the incredible support of key family and close friends who stick by you beyond the honeymoon period of the disaster, you do move on.

My family decided not to rebuild our home in Ferny Creek. We could not face the blackened trees, the constant reminder of our loss and the everlasting fear that would hang over us every summer of it happening again. We did not want the threat of potential arsonists, of 40C days with hot northerly winds, to become our annual obsession.

Instead we spent several years living in different cities and states, creating new experiences and new memories. We are now all happily living in our apartments and homes in Melbourne and Sydney. I have a room full of treasures – or junk, as my husband likes to call it – some of which really should be put in the next rubbish collection. I still do not like going up to the Dandenongs, to the road where our house stood and another stands today. I prefer to remember the good times of Ferny Creek and not the bad.

This January, for the first time, I completely forgot about the anniversary of the bushfires. It was only when my husband and I were trying to get our wriggling new puppies to ingest heartworm tablets that I remembered. Following the instructions to mark the date I had given the tablets to them, I got my calendar out and worked out the day: January 21. I could not believe I had forgotten. So this date now has a new, better meaning, however trivial. January 21 is no longer just the day I lost my childhood home; it is when I give heartworm tablets to our two gorgeous pugs.

**Carnage: Burnt-out crashed cars litter the road out of Kinglake** Picture: Mark Smith

# The Lost

Black Saturday is Australia's biggest natural disaster, with 210 people believed dead and others perhaps still missing. At the time of publication, authorities are yet to release an official list of the missing and the dead. Among those named by their families as missing are:

## ● Kilmore East & Wandong

### Steve Lackas, 37
Heathcote Junction
Described by his friends as "a top bloke", the loving husband and father was a well-known speedboat racer and veteran of the V8 Superboat Championships.

### David Stokes
Upper Plenty
The devoted father of four and grandfather of four was a retired religious education teacher who continued to support local youth organisations.

## ● Strathewen & Kinglake West

### Peter Avola, 67
Strathewen
The mechanic was a true gentleman and friends remember him as a generous, wonderful and loving family man. He leaves behind his wife of 43 years, Mary, and his children, Andrew and Suzie.

### Sue Evans, 46
Strathewen
The bright and bubbly animal lover was well-known as one of the owners of Diamond Creek Pet And Aquarium Supplies and was the loving mother of Jon Le Gassick. She was the proud owner of dogs Spike and Chewy.

### Carol Holcombe
Whittlesea
The teacher was a keen gardener who also loved music. She is remembered as a kind lady by many whom she taught English and maths.

### David Holcombe
Whittlesea
The recently retired teacher was a much-loved father who loved music. He was a member of the Melbourne Welsh Male Choir.

### Aldo Inzitari Jr, 5
Kinglake West
Affectionately known as AJ, Aldo Jr was the baby of the family, much adored and loved by his parents and two older brothers.

### Jesse Inzitari, 11
Kinglake West
A caring older brother to Aldo and great friend to Jonathan, Jesse will be remembered by many for his infectious smile.

### George Jackson, 74
Strathewen
The friendly delivery man and true gentleman was described by family

as a bit of a larrikin who enjoyed the occasional skydive and who lived alone on his farm.

### Jon Le Gassick, 18
Strathewen

The popular Year 12 Eltham College student loved life and enjoyed the company of his many mates.

### Daniela Marulli, 41
Kinglake West

A loving wife and mother, Daniela is sadly missed by her husband Aldo Inzitari and her son Jonathan, 14.

### Greg McIver, 59
Strathewen

The Vietnam War veteran and loving husband of Judy was described by family as a passionate man who would do anything for his family and friends. He was loud, gregarious, enthusiastic and committed to all things he undertook in life.

### Judy McIver, 59
Strathewen

The devoted wife of Greg and mother of one was a respected theatre nurse by all staff throughout her 14 years at Warringal Private Hospital and at Ballarat Base Hospital.

### May McIver, 84
Strathewen

The proud mother of four was remembered fondly by friends for her different thoughts and philosophies on life, including that whipping up a batch of scones can fix almost anything.

### Haydn McMahon, 17
Strathewen

The active and caring teenager lived life to the full and, according to friends, was a cheeky and down-to-earth bloke who enjoyed CanTeen camps.

### Kaya Mehmedoff, 18
Strathewen

Described by his friends as having the "best laugh and the best attitude", Kaya had just finished high school and was looking forward to a promising future.

### Brian Naylor, 78
Kinglake West

The loving father of five graced TV screens for decades as a popular newsreader, most notably on Channel 9. Friends remember him as an active man as well as a consummate professional with a mischievous side.

### Moiree Naylor
Kinglake West

A devoted mother of five and grandmother, Moiree often watched in the studio while her husband read the news until his retirement in 1998.

### Bob O'Sullivan, 48
Strathewen

The former CFA volunteer was well-known as one of the owners of Diamond Creek Pet And Aquarium Supplies, along with his partner Sue Evans. He was described by family as a rock, a beautiful man and a loving step-father to Jon Le Gassick.

### Donna Paulka
Strathewen

The mother of three had recently realised a lifelong dream, opening her own homewares and gift shop.

### Terry Paulka
Strathewen

The father of three and carpenter,

who loved motorbikes, was a keen worker for the community, recently heading a team to renovate an old school hall.

## Damien Spooner
Strathewen

Described by his father as not just a loving son but his best friend and a wonderful brother who enjoyed flying model aircraft. He was a former Strathewen cricketer.

## Marilyn Spooner
Strathewen

Described by her husband as a "wonderful wife and friend" during their 37 years of marriage, Marilyn was well-liked and respected at the cleaning products firm where she had worked for two decades.

# ● St Andrews & Steels Creek

## Charmian Ahern
Steels Creek

The loving wife of Leigh will be remembered by friends as a kind, warm and beautiful person who was always willing to help. She was a unique and beautiful soul who worked with special needs kids for the past 11 years at Birralee Primary School.

## Leigh Ahern
Steels Creek

The loving husband of Charmian was described by friends as a cheery, warm-hearted man who showed limitless kindness. His lasting legacy to the community included recording and transcribing the oral histories of the local senior citizens.

## Jenny Barnett
Steels Creek

The loving wife of John was a Victorian National Parks Association researcher who was passionate about protecting animals.

## John Barnett
Steels Creek

The respected Melbourne University associate professor, who cared for the environment and the welfare of animals, was a devoted husband to Jenny.

## Erryn Bartlett, 5
St Andrews

Beloved daughter of Gary and Jacinta, Erryn was a much-loved younger sister who loved to draw and swim.

## Gary Bartlett
St Andrews

A loving husband and father, Gary loved playing basketball, football and cricket and is remembered for his warm smile.

## Jacinta Bartlett
St Andrews

The mother of two was a loved and respected member of the Moreland City Council staff where she was unit manager contract support.

## Angela Brunton, 48
St Andrews

The loving partner of Reg Evans and award-winning artist held exhibitions throughout Victoria and ran a gallery in St Andrews where she was also actively involved in the community.

## Raye Carter, 68
St Andrews

This great-grandmother had been helping CFA volunteers when she returned to her home to protect her pet goats.

### Reg Evans, 81
St Andrews

A legend of Australian film and TV, Reg is remembered for many great character roles such as the station master in *Mad Max*, Keith Purvis in *Blue Heelers* and Jack Kelly in *The Man From Snowy River*. One of his most recent performances was in the movie, *Dying Breed*.

### Jaeson Hermocilla, 21
Yarra Glen

The keen sportsman loved tennis, basketball and hockey and was completing an arts/ commerce degree at the University of Melbourne.

### Melanee Hermocilla, 23
Yarra Glen

The caring youngster was in her final year of a commerce/law degree at Monash University and was an active breast cancer fundraiser.

### Gareth Jones-Roberts, 48
Yarra Glen

The dedicated family man was a keen inventor who developed a method of hanging paintings that had been adopted by galleries across Victoria and loved motorbike riding.

### Gail Leonard
Steels Creek

The grandmother of nine was highly involved in the Steels Creek Community Centre with her husband Greg and, according to friends, enjoyed old movies and croquet.

### Greg Leonard
Steels Creek

The loving husband of Gail was described by friends as an intelligent, hard-working man who was scaling back his workload as a wine business proprietor to dedicate more time to his cattle and vineyard. He was fondly remembered for wearing "a very Aussie hat" and always smiling.

### Greg Lloyd, 22
Yarra Glen

The dedicated Christian and long-standing member of the Suburban Baptist Church was a talented musician who had just started his dream job as an accountant.

### Lloyd Martin, 85
Humevale

The popular tenor worked as an interstate truck driver before setting up the highly regarded Pine Ridge Stud, breeding and racing horses alongside his wife, Mary.

### Mary Martin
Humevale

Mary met her husband when she was just 17 and worked as an usherette in the theatre where he was performing. She was respected in horse breeding circles and was a founder of the Wakeful Club for women in the thoroughbred industry. She kept her age a closely-guarded secret.

### Allan O'Gorman, 55
Humevale

The partner in real estate agency franchises at Wallan and Whittlesea was described by his friends as a happy, easy-going gentleman always willing to help out a friend when they were in need.

### Carolyn O'Gorman, 50
Humevale

The mother of three was a respected dietician who made a lasting contribution to the health and wellbeing of the Plenty Valley community and was highly regarded by her colleagues.

### Stuart O'Gorman, 18
Humevale
The natural entertainer had a charisma and wit which always stole the show.

### Dr Rob Pierce, 62
St Andrews
The loving husband to Jan was a gentleman and a pioneer of sleep apnea research. Professor Pierce was the director of respiratory and sleep medicine at the Austin Hospital as well as director of the Institute For Breathing And Sleep.

### Graeme Savage, 58
St Andrews
The "warm and kind" husband of Elizabeth and father of three was a construction manager at Ace Contractors Group in Eltham and had a strong interest in music.

### Marcel Smits, 56
St Andrews
The courier company owner had a passion for motorbikes and wife Dr Carole Webb said he died with their beloved six cats and two dogs.

### Dr Chris Towie, 53
Reedy Creek
Despite battling his own hearing problems, the popular GP was an outspoken advocate for the underdog and keen animal lover.

## ● Kinglake

### Crystal Breeze, 15
Kinglake
The Whittlesea Secondary College student was a happy and fun-loving big sister to her siblings, Nathan and Teagan.

### Nathan Breeze, 13
Kinglake
The Whittlesea Secondary College student was described as a wonderful teenager who was "full of heart".

### Adrian Brown, 33
Kinglake
The adoring dad and loving husband was the editor of the magazine, *Squares Around Victoria*.

### Brielle Brown, 3
Kinglake
The fiercely independent girl had a wonderful knack of getting her own way and had her older brothers wrapped around her finger. She enjoyed watching *Maisy* DVDs.

### Eric Brown, 8
Kinglake
The Middle Kinglake Primary School student was an "ardent Essendon supporter", maths whiz and loving big brother to his two siblings, Matthew and Brielle.

### Matthew Brown, 7
Kinglake
The fun-loving little man shared his brother's passion for the AFL and had big dreams of becoming a train driver.

### Mirrabelle Brown, 33
Kinglake
Adrian and Mirrabelle were teenage sweethearts who first met at a creche while their parents were square dancing, a passion they carried on into their adult years. Mirrabelle has been described as a generous and cheerful mother.

### Mackenzie "Macca" Buchanan, 15
Kinglake

The kind and caring "skater dude" had a fantastic sense of humour and, according to friends, enjoyed playing basketball.

### Neeve Buchanan, 9
Kinglake

The beautiful Kinglake West Primary School student was a bubbly and chatty young girl who had a dazzling smile.

### Melanie Chambers, 23
Kinglake

The vet nurse was a bubbly person with a kind nature who had devoted her life to helping sick animals.

### Penelope Chambers, 21
Kinglake

The former Plenty Valley Christian School student was a kind-hearted horse lover who had a vivacious personality.

### Danny Clark, 37
Kinglake

The hardcore blues fan has been called one of the world's true gentlemen. He was a devoted brother and uncle who died alongside his niece and nephew, Neeve and Mackenzie.

### Alexis Davey, 8 months
Kinglake

The beautiful baby girl was described by friends and family as having big blue eyes and a heart-warming smile.

### Jorja Davey, 3
Kinglake

The girly youngster with a gorgeous smile was lively and enjoyed playing with her little sister, Alexis.

### Natasha Davey
Kinglake

The kind and caring mother of two shared a passion for Alaskan Malamutes with her childhood sweetheart, Rob.

### Rob Davey
Kinglake

The wine merchant was a loving husband and father of two with a heart of gold. The mad keen St Kilda fan's spirit and enthusiasm meant he was constantly the life of the party.

### Arthur Enver, 57
Kinglake

The fun-loving train driver was a devoted partner of 35 years to survivor Petra. He was a keen skier, enjoyed playing tennis and had a passion for fast cars.

### Teagan Haymes, 6
Kinglake

The youngster was a "beautiful little girl with the world at her feet" who adored her older siblings, Crystal and Nathan.

### Geoff Hyde
Kinglake

The loving husband of Suzanne was a practical, community-minded man who had started a small business making timber frames.

### Suzanne Hyde
Kinglake

The adoring wife of Geoff and constant community volunteer was involved in many organisations including the Kinglake Ranges Neighbourhood House and the Bollygum Park group. She also worked on the local community journal *Mountain Monthly*.

### Barry Johnston, 58
Kinglake

The former primary school teacher was an active member of the Australian Education Union and was a passionate environmentalist who enjoyed his rural lifestyle.

### Debbie O'Shea, 37
Kinglake

The caring mother of two and dedicated wife of Graham was described by friends as having had a wonderful sense of humour.

### Graham O'Shea
Kinglake

The devoted father of two and adoring husband of Debbie was described by friends as a kind man with an interest in judo.

### Lyric O'Shea, 8
Kinglake

The beautiful, caring young lady was an enthusiastic dancer and lively soul who loved her brother Trey to bits.

### Trey O'Shea, 10
Kinglake

The cheeky young lad enjoyed playing Star Wars and Indiana Jones and was an adoring older brother to little sister, Lyric.

### Caitlin Rolands, 14
Kinglake

The popular girl was a sports enthusiast who excelled at tennis at her local club.

### Karen Rolands
Kinglake

The adoring wife and mother of two was a caring childcare worker who often looked after other people's children on her property.

### Nicola Rolands, 12
Kinglake

The blossoming socialite had a passion for art and was a typical girly child who loved jewellery and fashion.

### Paul Rolands
Kinglake

The maintenance fitter was a true family man who will be remembered by friends as the man who would do anything for anyone.

### Danny Shepherd, 32
Kinglake

The loving husband of Bree was a kind and generous man who worked at Leisurelink in Geelong as an exercise instructor.

### Dimitrios Tsimiklis, 35
Kinglake

The truck driver and mechanic was an adoring husband to childhood sweetheart Tanja and, according to friends, loved life and the country.

### Tanja Tsimiklis, 39
Kinglake

The dog groomer loved the simple life and was happiest living in the country with her husband, Dimitrios.

### Tina Wilson, 36
Kinglake

The "tough and resourceful" New Zealander was the loving mother of three beautiful children and dedicated partner to survivor Sam Gents.

### Eileen Zann, 62
Kinglake

The loving wife of Richard and keen artist was described by friends as a gentle soul. The former New Zealand Ballet Company dancer worked as a dance teacher and devoted herself to voluntary work.

### Eva Zann, 25
Kinglake

The adventurous young woman was described by friends as having a cheeky spirit. She was embarking on a promising career in public relations and was a much-loved team member at Cancer Council Victoria.

### Dr Richard Zann, 64
Kinglake

The father of two was a world-renowned zoologist and a global leader in the study of zebra finches and bird behaviour and communication. He was held in high esteem by generations of undergraduate students at Melbourne's La Trobe University.

## ● Flowerdale

### Gavin Russell Dunn, 39
Flowerdale

At home in the bush, the keen pet owner had an affinity with animals. He always made time to help his neighbours care for their animals, particularly their horses.

### Robert Harrop, 83
Flowerdale

A "bushie" at heart, the popular local Mr Fixit worked repairing boats and was never too busy to help out family members and friends by working on their cars.

## ● Marysville

### Kate Ansett, 43
Toolangi

A classical ballet dancer, Kate had developed a love of gardening and worked at local nurseries.

### David Balfour, 47
Marysville

The professional firefighter worked as a volunteer fireman before taking on the role fulltime in 2007. The much-loved father of three died while trying to help others.

### Jamie Bowker
Marysville

Nicknamed the "Blue Fox" by his friends, he was looking forward to becoming a dad and husband.

### Steve Fisher, 44
Toolangi

Described as a "typical country boy", the father of two, who had been in the navy, had only recently bought his dream bush home.

### Dalton Fiske, 12
Marysville

The Alexandra Secondary College student was a loving brother and friend who enjoyed playing golf, cricket and riding his bike.

### Liz Fiske, 45
Marysville

The devoted mother of three, loving sister and aunt has been described as one of life's beautiful people.

### Geoff Grady
Marysville

One of two managers of the Fruit Salad Farm Country Cottages, the well-known local identity was fondly remembered by those who visited the area for his caring nature.

### Nicole Jefferson, 29
Marysville

Remembered by many as a fun-loving friend, she was looking forward to the birth of her first child and marrying her sweetheart, Jamie.

## Patrick Jennings
Marysville

The co-manager of the Fruit Salad Farm Country Cottages; remembered by friends as a warm, generous host.

## Dean Lesmana, 20
Marysville

The Indonesian student had been studying commercial cooking in Melbourne and wanted to see some of the countryside.

## Laurel Lewis, 81
Marysville

The untiring worker for the community volunteered her time and skills to many organisations, including hospitals to support those in need and the Australian Institute of Genealogical Studies.

## Elizabeth Liesfield, 44
Marysville

The British-born guest house operator touched the lives of many locals and visitors with her generous and kind-hearted personality.

## James Liesfield, 14
Marysville

The happy teenager was remembered by friends as a cheeky lad who always had a smile on his face. He was described as a great friend and a loving big brother.

## Matthew Liesfield, 13
Marysville

The keen student was a promising piano player who was loved by his many mates and family.

## Errol Morgan
Marysville

Beloved wife of Harley, Errol loved the outdoor life but her passion was family history research.

## Harley Morgan, 70
Marysville

The chainsaw artist loved to take visitors on guided tours of the dozens of sculptures in his garden. He also helped teach others the craft via the internet and was a volunteer firefighter.

## Isak Nilsson
Marysville

The art distributor has been described by colleagues as a remarkable man, despite the father of three's penchant for occasionally teaming super-short shorts with odd socks.

## Kirstie Nilsson, 39
Marysville

The mother of three is remembered for turning Marysville into a magical place with her Christmas shop.

## Len Postlethwaite, 82
Marysville

Marysville's oldest male resident was a champion axeman and had been a wood merchant. He enjoyed playing football, golf, tennis and later bowls.

## Dr Ken Rowe, 63
Marysville

The outstanding leader in education was a passionate researcher who chaired a national inquiry into the teaching of literacy and who continued to work after his retirement.

## Rudi Rudi, 28
Marysville

The Indonesian was studying commercial cooking in Melbourne and was an enthusiastic photographer, keen to capture the rural landscape on film.

### David Sebald, 62
Marysville

The semi-retiree ran the local real estate agency with his wife and was well respected and loved in the local community.

### Marlene Sebald
Marysville

The well-known member of the community and loving mother of three ran a real estate agency with her husband, David.

### Bill Walker
Narbethong

The builder who was in his 80s was also a talented green thumb who gave back to the community as a flower show judge.

### Fay Walker
Narbethong

The mother of four who was in her 80s was a gifted gardener who, along with her husband, had transformed their property into a showpiece that had been entered in numerous competitions.

### Geoffrey Walker, 53
Narbethong

Described by his friends as intelligent, kind and friendly, the avid collector of postcards and other memorabilia spent hours on his latest passion, 3D photography.

## • Gippsland

### Nathan Charles, 21
Koornalla

The well-liked BMX bike rider and keen drift driver was a great friend, testimony to which is that he died trying to help his mate Luke Jacobs.

### Alan Jacobs
Koornalla

The earth-moving machinery distributor shared his love of car racing with his son Luke.

### Luke Jacobs, 21
Koornalla

The popular but fiercely-competitive racing car driver was nicknamed the "baby-faced assassin" by his rivals and was an up-and-coming star of drifting, an extreme form of car racing.

### Miros Jacobs
Koornalla

The devoted wife and mother was a softly spoken lady who supported her family on and off the track.

## • Bendigo

### Kevin Kane, 48
Bendigo

The loving husband is remembered for his beaming smile and great laugh. His wife Carol was about to surprise him with his first trip overseas.

## • Beechworth

### John Wilson
Mudgegonga

A keen cricketer and one of the region's greatest batsmen and an enthusiastic golfer, the builder provided jobs for many young locals.

### Sue Wilson
Mudgegonga

The former nurse was a loving mother and wife who was heavily involved in the local netball community.

**Compiled by Michelle Collins and Jorja Orreal, Sunday Mail**

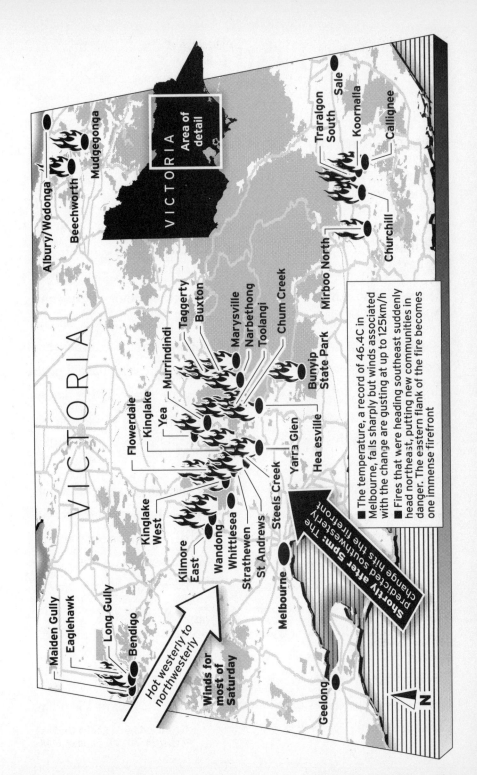

Maiden Gully
Eaglehawk
Long Gully
Bendigo

Albury/Wodonga
Beechworth
Mudgegonga

VICTORIA

Flowerdale
Kinglake
Yea
Murrindindi
Taggerty
Buxton
Marysville
Narbethong
Toolangi
Chum Creek

Kinglake
West
Kilmore
East
Wandong
Whittlesea
Strathewen
St Andrews
Steels Creek
Yarra Glen
Hea esville
Bunyip
State Park
Mirboo North

Melbourne

Geelong

Traralgon
South
Koornalla
Sale
Callignee
Churchill

VICTORIA
Area of
detail
VICTORIA

Hot westerly to
northwesterly

Winds for
most of
Saturday

**Shortly after 5pm:** The
predicted southwesterly
change hits the firefront

■ The temperature, a record of 46.4C in
Melbourne, fa ls sharply but winds associated
with the change are gusting at up to 125km/h
■ Fires that were heading southeast suddenly
head northeast, putting new communities in
danger. The eastern flank of the fire becomes
one immense firefront

N

## News Limited's acknowledgements

This book is a collection of individual stories from the Victorian bushfires, featuring deeply personal contributions from people directly affected by the bushfires, and their friends and relatives, along with the people who came to their aid — fire fighters, doctors, nurses and wildlife rescuers. It also contains accounts from journalists on the ground and those who were involved in co-ordinating the response.

News Limited would like to acknowledge those who contacted us to tell their stories in their own words — the heroes fighting the flames and those who miraculously escaped. These stories from those most affected have been reproduced throughout this book with minimal editing.

News would also like to acknowledge the immense contribution of its journalists and photographers, who all demonstrated discretion and professionalism in a time of great personal and professional strain. Special mention to Paul Kent *The Daily Telegraph* who reported from the towns ravaged by Black Saturday and who returned to the area in the weeks since to write the opening narrative for each chapter.

The book will act as a tribute and a fundraiser with all proceeds from the sale of the book (excluding GST) to be donated to The Salvation Army's Victorian Bushfire Appeal. ($1 million has also been donated by News Limited to the Australian Red Cross Victorian Bushfire Appeal.)

There are some people without which this book would not have been possible. We would like to pay a special thanks to Alice Marshall of News Limited for her help in making this book happen; Jill Baker *Herald Sun* and Peter Flaherty *Herald Sun* for their dedication in helping compile the survivors' first-person accounts; and a special thank you to all the journalists and photographers who gave their work and time freely.

## Journalists

We would like to thank the following News Limited journalists who contributed to the book: Piers Ackerman *The Daily Telegraph*, Evonne Barry *Sunday Herald Sun*, Jill Baker *Herald Sun*, Terry Brown *Herald Sun*, Ross Brundrett *Herald Sun*, Mark Butler *Herald Sun*, Patrick Carlyon *Herald Sun*, Karen Collier *Herald Sun*, Cheryl Critchley *Herald Sun*, Clementine Cuneo *The Daily Telegraph*, Julie-Anne Davies *The Australian*, Shannon Deery *Herald Sun*, Anthony Dowsley *Herald Sun*, Stephen Drill *Herald Sun*, Mike Edmonds *Herald Sun*, John Ferguson *Herald Sun*, Peter Flaherty *Herald Sun*, Ashley Gardiner *Herald Sun*, Tim Habel *Herald Sun*, Ewin Hannan *The Australian*, John Hamilton *Herald Sun*, Angus Hohenboken *The Australian*, Liam Houlihan *Sunday Herald Sun*, Fiona Hudson*Herald Sun*, Gary Hughes *The Australian*, Matt Johnston *Herald Sun*, Gemma Jones *The Daily Telegraph*, Kate Jones *Herald Sun*, Holly Ife *Herald Sun*, Matt Johnston *Herald Sun*, Paul Kent *The Daily Telegraph*, Aaron Langmaid *Herald Sun*, Paul Leigh *The Daily Telegraph*, Stephen Lunn *The Australian*, John Masanauskas *Herald Sun*, Grant McArthur *Herald Sun*, Stuart McEvoy *The Australian*, Megan McNaught *Herald Sun*, Geraldine Mitchell *Herald Sun*, Al Mival *The Sunday Mail*, Jane Metlikovec *Herald Sun*, Caroline Overington *The Australian*, Georgie Pilcher *Herald Sun*, Corrie Perkin *The Australian*, Michelle Pountney

*Herald Sun*, Emily Power *Herald Sun*, Stuart Rintoul *The Australian*, Russell Robinson *Herald Sun*, Norrie Ross *Herald Sun*, Milanda Rout *The Australian*, Natalie Sikora *Herald Sun*, Marion Taffe *mX Melbourne*, Nui Te Koha *Herald Sun*, Gareth Trickey *Herald Sun*, Shaun Turton *Leader Newspapers*, Jamie Walker *The Australian*, Ellen Whinnett *Herald Sun*, Geoff Wilkinson *Herald Sun*, Lauren Wilson *The Australian*, Anne Wright *Herald Sun*.

## Photographers

We would like to thank the following photographers who contributed to this book: Kelly Barnes *The Australian*, Craig Borrow *Herald Sun*, David Caird *Herald Sun*, Nicki Connolly *Leader Newspapers*, Alex Coppel *Herald Sun*, Mark Cranitch *The Courier-Mail*, David Crosling *The Australian*, Ian Currie *Herald Sun*, Aaron Francis *The Australian*, Nicole Garmston *Herald Sun*, John Grainger *The Daily Telegraph*, David Geraghty *The Australian*, Darryl Gregory *Herald Sun*, Jon Hargest *Herald Sun*, Mike Keating *Herald Sun*, Rebecca Michael *Herald Sun*, Stuart McEvoy *The Australian*, Renee Nowytarger *The Australian*, Norm Oorloff *Herald Sun*, Trevor Pinder *Herald Sun*, Cameron Richardson *The Daily Telegraph*, Gary Richardson *Herald Sun*, Chris Scott *Herald Sun*, Mark Smith *Leader Newspapers*, Matthew Turner *The Advertiser*, Nationwide News Imaging Department.

Special mention to Tanya Cadman for her picture of Peter Thorneycroft, Rob Durstan for his picture of a house in Long Gully, and AAP/ AP/ Mark Parden for the picture of Sam the Koala.

## Design & production

We would like to acknowledge the design work in this book undertaken by Vinnie Taylor *The Daily Telegraph*, assisted by Franc Conn *The Daily Telegraph* and Dave Matthews *The Daily Telegraph*. Thanks also to Paul Leigh *The Daily Telegraph*, who worked on the fire map graphic.

We would also like to thank the following who donated their time to copy editing the book's text: Grant Jones *The Daily Telegraph*, Cecily Ryan *The Daily Telegraph*, and Simon Wheeler *The Daily Telegraph*.

## Paul Kent's acknowledgements

The copy for the chapter introductions in this book were written over the course of a week at the end of February. For that reason, sourcing of the material came from my own notes taken during the week after the fires, interviews done during that week, and also from researching other stories written by other journalists during this same period. I have not credited them individually during the writing because, frankly, I did not want the copy to read like a reference book. However I want to thank those journalists whose strong reporting told many of the stories that shape this book. They include: John Ferguson, Patrick Carlyon, Cameron Stewart, Milanda Rout, Stuart Rintoul, Cheryl Critchley, Julie-Anne Davies, Justin Vallejo, Holly Ife, Justine Ferrari, Stephen Lunn, Alice Coster, Matthew Clayfield, Lauren Wilson, Lex Hall, Stephen Drill, Sue Hewitt and Eleni Hale.

# HarperCollins Publishers' acknowledgements

It has been a great privilege for HarperCollins Publishers Australia to publish *Black Saturday: Stories of Love, Loss and Courage from the Victorian Bushfires* as a tribute to those touched by the fires that ravaged Victoria in February 2009. We have all been deeply affected by what we have read and what those who were involved endured. This book is a lasting legacy to the indomitable human spirit and the courage displayed by so many. The stories emerging from the bushfires have emphasised, once again, the strength of the written word. As publishers we firmly believe that it is important to collect such first person stories as an ongoing testament for the future.

As a company, we would like to recognise the work of our dedicated staff at both HarperCollins and our sister company News Limited.

This book would not be possible without the generous donations of time, resources and specialist advice from the following companies and individuals. We thank you:

Norske Skog has kindly donated the paper this book is printed on, Stora Enso has provided the board on which the cover is printed, Graphic Print Group has printed the cover, Protectaprint has provided the finish on the cover and Griffin Press has printed the internal pages of this book and bound it.

Toll IPEC has travelled this book to booksellers around Australia; Activair has freighted the book across the Tasman to New Zealand; and Castle Parcels is distributing the book within New Zealand.

Richard Potter has provided expert legal advice.

The booksellers of Australia and New Zealand have given it a home upon their shelves.

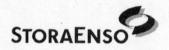

Griffin Press